With Best Wi... ...5
and Good ...
Frank C.

Charles E. Nicholson, O.B.E., R.D.I., M.R.I.N.A.   *Frontispiece*

JOHN NICHOLSON

Great Years
in Yachting

NAUTICAL PUBLISHING COMPANY
ADLARD COLES · COMMANDER ERROLL BRUCE · RICHARD CREAGH-OSBORNE
Nautical House · Lymington · Hampshire

in association with
GEORGE G. HARRAP & COMPANY LIMITED
London · Toronto · Wellington · Sydney

© *1970 John Nicholson*
SBN 245 50304 8

First published in Great Britain in 1970 by
NAUTICAL PUBLISHING COMPANY
Nautical House, Lymington, SO4 9BA, Hampshire

Composed in 11 on 13 pt Baskerville (169)
and made and printed in Great Britain by
THE CAMELOT PRESS LIMITED
LONDON AND SOUTHAMPTON

" *Ships and barges, brigs, topsail schooners, and sailing-drifters have gone for ever; and now our fleets of sailing-trawlers and spritsail barges are dwindling fast. When they also have vanished, the hideous triumph of progress will be complete. Of all our splendid sailing-craft and sailormen no trace will remain, save a few museum models and the vague tradition of an art called seamanship.*

I say no trace will remain, but trust that it may be true of commerce only. Surely the sailing-yacht must survive, for in her alone will men find satisfaction of an instinct which drives them, regardless of progress and reason, to venture out to sea."

Extract from *Sailorman*
by Lieut.-Commander E. G. Martin, O.B.E., R.N.V.R.
Late Admiral of the Royal Ocean Racing Club

Contents

	Foreword	11
1.	My Grandfather	13
2.	My Father	16
3.	Some of the cast	28
4.	Family craft	41
5.	The great schooners	71
6.	Ketches and yawls	83
7.	One Designs	88
8.	Captains and skippers	97
9.	Hired assassins	125
10.	Unusual craft	129
11.	Summer-house	143
12.	*Nyria*	147
13.	23-metre cutter *Brynhild*	152
14.	*Shamrock IV*	155
15.	*Astra*	164
16.	*Candida*	168
17.	23-metres in general	171
18.	*Shamrock V* and J class in general	175
19.	*Velsheda*	188
20.	*Endeavour*	191
21.	*Endeavour II*	197
22.	Thoughts and jottings	201
23.	Power yachts	209
24.	Sound in the shipyard	223
	Appendix Camper & Nicholson's, 1780–1968	227
	Index	231

List of Plates

Charles E. Nicholson   *frontispiece*

                                                        facing page
2. 'Uncle' Malden as a 'Dictator'   14
3. Benjamin Nicholson on his yawl *Rose of Devon*   14
4. FAMILY CRAFT. *Tammie* running with a fair tide, bound for
   the West Country   15
5. FAMILY CRAFT. *Sagitta* with the author and his wife racing in
   the Solent   15
6. FAMILY CRAFT. *Flame* with cutter rig racing at Cowes   64
7. FAMILY CRAFT. *Deb*, with the author and his sister, Mary 64
8. *Norada* reaching off the Peel Bank   65
9. *Bloodhound*, Charles E. Nicholson's most successful ocean
   racing design   65
10. *Czarina*, 564 tons. Benjamin Nicholson's largest steam
    auxiliary topsail schooner   80
11. *Margherita*, probably Charles E. Nicholson's fastest
    schooner   81
12. *Creole* with her original sail plan, when owned by Sir
    Connup Guthry   96
13. *Fortuna*. The late Mrs Collins sailing her old class Redwing 97
14. *Toucan*, Mr and Mrs Bee MacKinnon's new class Redwing 97
15. *Gareth* and *Carolla*. Two very successful small racing yachts 112
16. Mr Macomber and Captain John Evans fishing in
    Scotland   113
17. Skipper Williams and *Mouette* crew   113
18. UNUSUAL CRAFT. *Oma*, powered by a 450 h.p. Napier Lion
    engine driving an aerial propeller   144

facing page

19. UNUSUAL CRAFT. The Royal barge *Nore*   144
20. *Nyria*, after being converted to Bermudian rig for Mrs Workman   145
21. *Istria* off Cowes Green travelling fast   145
22. *Brynhild*, 23 metre, reaching past Osborne Bay   160
23. Mr and Mrs J. Stuart Blackton presenting a 'tea' rose model to Sir Thomas Lipton   161
24. *Shamrock IV*, the 'ugly duckling'   161
25. Charles E. Nicholson sailing *Candida* in a two-reef breeze   176
26. *Astra* leading *Endeavour*   177
27. *Candida* running with the mainsail well reefed   177
28. *Britannia* after conversion to Bermudian rig   192
29. *Shamrock V*. Here she is racing close-hauled   192
30. Deck view of *Enterprise* showing ten-sided alloy mast   193
31. *Velsheda* running before the introduction of track to raise the spinnaker boom   193
32. *Endeavour*, showing double clewed jib and using a temporary boom   208
33. *Endeavour II* with white painted steel mast and Park Avenue boom   208
34. S.Y. *Marynthea*. The last steam yacht designed by the firm   209
35. M.Y. *Pioneer*, the first large diesel yacht ever built   209
36. M.Y. *Ara*, showing sloop-like profile and cruiser stern   224
37. The second *M.Y. Crusader*, 926 tons, the last flush-decked motor yacht   224
38. The Norwegian Royal Yacht K.V. *Norge* off Torquay   225
39. SOUND IN THE SHIPYARD.   225

Foreword

I have allowed myself to be persuaded by numerous friends to write of my father and his designs and work, and indirectly of the family business of Camper & Nicholsons. I set on record some of the events that occurred in my youth and during those years I spent with my firm, and in this story I tell of the great yachts and yachtsmen and the great characters among the professional yacht skippers in the days of which I write.

My wife, to whom I owe so much, is critical of this action and wonders, perhaps rightly, whether many would wish to read it. Much of my story covers the between-the-wars period. The fact that the timing of my birth admitted me to an era that will never return was my good fortune and, in referring to those more spacious days, trust no reader will think that I have a chip on my shoulder.

The present world-wide sailing scene embraces an expansion in the sport that was never envisaged even a few years ago; little did we ever contemplate this virile and vast increase in the number of medium and small craft or, indeed, the trends that were started in America by the adoption of mass production nor, till later, the necessity for marina development. As in the car world, utter congestion is with us in our more popular waterways where we are not so fortunately provided for as in America or Scandinavia.

Peace, as the world knew it, has never come again but the more fortunate ones in these islands, or wherever they may be, can seek refuge and relaxation in the delightful pastime of 'messing about in boats'. I should have liked to have spent twice as long in writing this book; it is one of hasty impressions and, I fear, lack of chronological order aggravated by the serious loss of records.

I should like to set on record my appreciation to my wife for correcting my unusual spelling, to my friend John Henderson for verifying dates, tonnages and other details to the extent, as he puts it, of 'making my day'. I am also grateful to Gerry McMullen for helping me in writing the book, to Frank Murdoch, to Keith Beken for his kind assistance with his beautiful photographs and finally to Adlard Coles true sailor that he is, and his partners in the Nautical Publishing Company for implying that these jottings are worthy of modest presentation.

ACKNOWLEDGEMENTS

I am also indebted to Oxford University Press for permission to publish the extract from *Sailorman* and to Mr Wm. McC. Meek for Plate 2, the *Evening Standard* for Plate 19, Mr Monty Spry for Plate 25, Mr Edwin Levick for Plate 30 and Mr E. J. Edmonds for Plate 39.

J. N.

1 My Grandfather

Benjamin Nicholson, J.P., my grandfather, was born in 1828 and died at the age of seventy-eight in 1906 when I was seven years old. His father was John Henry Nicholson, for many years Commander of H.M. prison ship *York*.

I have an interesting oil painting of that ship lying off Gosport viewed from Haslar Creek with Royal Marines exercising the prisoners on the beach by Blockhouse Point and with much harbour activity in those days of pure sail. Behind the ship is Ratsey & Lapthorn's original sail loft which stood intact, exactly as then, until bombed in the last war.

My grandfather, many of whose activities I learned of through my parents, was head of Camper & Nicholson's, the well-known firm of yacht designers and builders, and was an eminent and respected figure in Gosport.

He was for many years actively associated with the public life of the town and, during a long spell on the Bench as J.P., was noted for his inclination toward leniency rather than severity, his aim being to reform rather than to punish.

He married in May 1852 Sarah Ann, daughter of the late William Brideaux Watson, and had three sons and five daughters whom I mention later.

Grandfather's home was Stanley House next to Trinity Church on the south side of the little town of Gosport. This house together with the large rectory, the church with its separate belfry, some terraced houses and a nice old inn completed that corner of Gosport. Stanley House was a fair example of Queen Anne architecture and to me as a youngster it was vast with its four storeys, basements and fine great room at the top with a huge octagonal window arrangement giving views over the town and out to the south over Spithead. It had good stabling and a fair sized garden; the second storey was flanked on the south with splendid wrought iron balconies and the spiral staircase in the middle of the building was a joy to us children and a nightmare to our parents.

I was born in a quiet little crescent known as Linden Grove but can only remember our next and much larger house, Leventhorpe, in which we lived until moving out to Lee-on-the-Solent in 1912.

When at Leventhorpe I used to venture down to Stanley House with a basket of eggs for Grandfather and was scared lest he might be at home. As a rule my Aunt Bessie was there to greet me and I was always given Turkish Delight and then taken to the bowels of the establishment to quench my thirst from a great stone jar with tap which I imagine was some special water for Grandpa. This expedition was not too hazardous as my route was across 'The Bunny', which was an area of grassland, and by the model pond which exists today and where international model yacht racing still takes place.

Grandfather's last yacht was the 151-ton yawl *Rose of Devon* and it must have been 1905 when my mother and I joined him for a brief part of his last completed cruise to the West Country. I remember well when we were anchored at Swanage and how on the Sunday he and my mother went off in the four-oared gig to church, Grandfather with the yoke and white cotton rope tiller lines. In their absence a member of the crew took me out in the dinghy so that I could sail a perfect little model cutter in the tradition of the yacht of the day—black topsides, copper-coloured bottom and vast bowsprit. It had a little lump of lead at the trailing end of the rudder and went to wind'ard so well that this deckhand had to row hard to catch it.

I remember the return from church with Grandpa commanding 'way enough' coming in to the gangway and the oars with blades raised smartly aloft as the gig crept nicely alongside. Captain Routh was on the platform to help Mother aboard.

After tea we had a drive in a Victoria carriage and I enjoyed the box-seat. We went winding up to the Foreland and on the way the coachman and I had to walk while Mother and our host reclined in their seats. We looked down on Old Harry, the isolated chalk

3. Benjamin Nicholson on his yawl *Rose of Devon*.

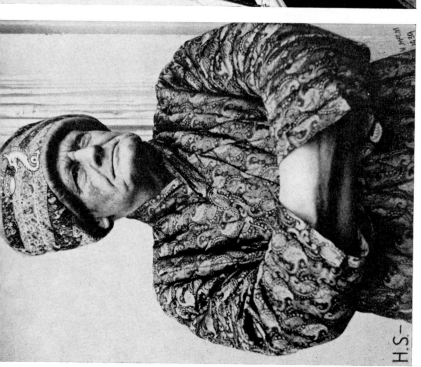

2. Uncle Malden as a 'Dictator'

5. FAMILY CRAFT. *Sagitta* with the author and his wife racing in the Solent.

4. FAMILY CRAFT. *Tammie* running with a fair tide, bound for the West Country.

pinnacle that had stood so long and which I grew to love in later years. It was soon after we returned to Gosport, I think, that the old gentleman set off on his last cruise to the West with his eldest son, my Uncle Ben, among his guests. During this cruise he was taken ill and Uncle Ben instructed the captain to return to Gosport. I never saw him again.

His family were the three sons Benjamin, Charles and Arthur, and five daughters. The eldest, Rhoda, married Alfred Starling Blake who became Lord Mayor of Portsmouth. Regrettably he died in his prime and Aunt Rhoda had a great struggle to educate their four sons who were such a tribute to her. Leonard, the eldest, later became a Lord Mayor of the City and, in turn, his younger son Alfred held the same office and has recently relieved Sir John Hunt as Director of The Duke of Edinburgh's Award Scheme, the great movement for youth.

Jessie married Tom Lapthorn, a most able solicitor who guided the family finances for many years and whose old established business is still operating; Louie married Edwin Lapthorn, J.P., a member of the sail-making business, whilst Nell and Bess remained spinsters.

My Aunt Nell was a very gifted artist and after studying at the Slade and in Paris enjoyed the hobby throughout her life and had several pictures hung in the Academy. She was our favourite on my father's side and, having seven aunts and uncles on my mother's side, we children were never short of Christmas and birthday presents.

I remember very little of my grandmother Nicholson who was bedridden in her later life, but I do remember going upstairs to see her in her crocheted cap and heavy shawl and being so disappointed that she enjoyed the skin off the top of her glass of milk. Granny Edmonds, on my mother's side, lived longer and always had a sixpence on hand when I called on her; she always aired the view that one son was worth fifty daughters, which I hoped was only in my presence. Today my son Christopher's little Benjamin is the great-great-grandson of that fine old shipwright and gentleman.

2 My Father

These two words alone cause me to think very deeply and, indeed, to realize that what I shall record is a most inadequate tribute to a very wonderful genius and gentleman.

I know full well how fortunate I was to be the son of Charles Nicholson, but perhaps, before enlarging upon him, it would be better to touch upon the family. On June 11th, 1895, he married Lucy Ella Edmonds, one of the family of five daughters and three sons of William Edmonds, solicitor, of Portsmouth.

My father's first house in Gosport was in Linden Grove where I and my brother Harry before me and my sister Mary were born. Later we moved to the large house named Leventhorpe, which I have mentioned, where we had a most happy life, particularly I with my elder sister Mary. There my dear brother Harry died after an accident on ice on one of the frozen moats at Stokes Bay. I was old enough to remember how we used to play together and to appreciate what a great little chap he was when he returned in the evenings from his kindergarten school in Southsea to which I went later.

Leventhorpe saw many changes and events of joy and tribulation. The disastrous fire at the Gosport office in 1910 was the most bitter blow to Firm and family in their long history and, since I appear to be the only member so far attempting to record their history, that calamity is indeed serious at this moment. Many celebrated yachts were designed in that house and I remember the routine of assisting Father to set up his drawing-board on trestles and the collection of weights and battens from a cupboard in the evening peace of his quiet home (usually my bedtime). He was a genius at transferring his thoughts on form quickly to paper. Unlike so many who treat the body plan or sections as their draft basis his first thoughts were always to get in the waterlines. He did this at wonderful speed and, if pleased, invariably gave a pretty poor exhibition of whistling a tune. He was not at all musical, as was my mother, but his attempts always denoted satisfaction.

I think nearly all his draft designs emanated from his home; for many years he had no drawing-board in his office and when he had it was merely for laying out plans. I think that what impressed me most was that so many of his designs were 'first-shotters' and required the minimum of re-fairing by his Chief Draughtsman.

Before enlarging on this wide subject of design I shall touch on some of his recreational activities. As a young man he was quite keen on tennis and golf and later enjoyed many years of trout fishing. His golf was utterly unorthodox with everything wrong; his swing was very limited as he played with his thumbs pointing down the shaft; he always wore boots, thus preventing any flexibility of the ankles, usually a starched collar and, in the earlier days, a Norfolk suit with belt. Thus, general movement was somewhat restricted but his play was dead straight. When I was young he gave me a stroke a hole, and later half a stroke; then as the pendulum of time swung in my direction, trout fishing ultimately became his only relaxation apart from sailing. He was not a deft dry-fly man but enjoyed towing a large March Brown on which the fish, after seeing so much of it, surely hooked themselves in desperation.

I would say that Father was among the best helmsmen of his day and, having so often designed the craft he steered, he knew exactly what they liked. He was kind and tolerant to a degree in so many things and ways but in his private sailing he was, perhaps, a trifle selfish as he so loved sailing. Though we younger members of his family often implored him to stay a little longer in some of our lovely British estuaries we used virtually to crash from port to port and, being a racing man at heart, we had to work really hard if anything of a rival was on the scene. It is, perhaps, not unnatural that this characteristic has prevailed among us all! Only in his later life did he really enjoy relaxation afloat and it was in 1939 when lying off Sandbanks, Poole, with the lovely Purbeck backcloth that he pronounced to me, "What a charming place it is." I, of course, remembered the many times we were chivvied out at dawn in the years that had passed.

Father made the mistake of taking Mother to sea in bad weather too soon and the result was that she saw little of him in summer when he attended all the regattas round the coast. They were a very devoted couple but I suppose the only time my mother accompanied Father afloat was for Cowes Week and that was an annual institution. Occasionally also she would enjoy a run in the family launch, usually with a friend or friends who did not often get afloat except for the invariable trips to Lepe in the blackberry seasons of the past.

Father was the most alarming driver of motor-cars we ever knew but he had wonderful hands that got him out of trouble on many occasions. Whether we lived at Gosport or Lee he had a habit, usually on a Saturday, of arriving at lunchtime with a Royal Marine and with a broken bicycle in the back of the car. He favoured a little right of centre on the road and on several occasions as a Marine was sweeping out of the Forton Barracks gate for his week-end leave he might have the misfortune in timing to meet Father. Luckily no physical damage occurred. The unfortunate victim was given a good lunch, a cigar and a new bicycle on the following Monday. Lee's was the cycle shop and they must have done well out of Father.

I shall recount only one of his many car-driving incidents and this was a miracle. We used to pick up an uncle of mine on Sunday mornings in winter and run over to Hayling Island for golf. On one occasion there was a motor-cycle and its basket-work sidecar on the crown of the road in front of us when, suddenly, it stopped dead in its tracks. There was a road to the left and a raised path on the left of our main road; Father tried to go sharp left but was about to hit the hedge in the side road so he quickly steered the car to the right and, with a tremendous bump, we mounted the steep curb (I was thrown out of the back seat on to the folded hood) and pulled to a standstill having missed a corner lamp-post on the right and a steep bank to the left. It was a remarkable feat of driving and snap reflex action. When Father walked over to the wretched motor-cycle driver the man merely smiled; when he came back to the car I asked him why he had smiled and he quietly replied, "The man was frightened."

It must have been round about 1912 that we moved to our first house at Lee-on-the-Solent; it was called Beechcroft and is now the residence of the Captain of the Royal Naval Air Base, H.M.S. *Daedalus*. We had a wonderful life here with our own dinghy and a permanent winch on the beach where, in those good days, we left all gear aboard and nothing was ever stolen. We four children used to go whiting fishing in this excellent little boat and this always worried my mother who forced herself to engage in some domestic duty to take her mind off us. I had some difficulty in persuading my younger brother, Richard, not to stand up to reel in a fish which he so often did in his excitement.

It was here that we had a large meadow and during the review of the Fleet we were asked to put down a white sheet so that Paul Verrier, the French pilot, could land between trips over the Fleet. This, it will be remembered, was known as Winston's Regatta and was a strategic prelude to the First World War, Churchill then being First Lord to the Admiralty.

In 1913 Father acquired a piece of land opposite Beechcroft and built a fine house named Stanley House after my grandfather's house in Gosport. This was the year he started on the design of *Shamrock IV* for Sir Thomas Lipton and, as my mother said at the time, a fatal time to build a new house. Indeed, I remember the architect slipped up on several things. The larder was over the stokehold, the windows hinged from a third of their width and were hopeless in a place where it blew so hard, and so much space was overlooked in the roof that a large playroom and an additional bathroom were added.

This house stood almost at the edge of a low cliff and we had a path giving direct access to the beach. We also had a hard tennis court and a spacious lawn on which bicycle polo was a popular pastime.

It was about this time that my father's great friend Major Malden Heckstall-Smith was living at Kingsworthy near Winchester. Known by a wide circle of friends as 'Uncle' Malden, he thought nothing of cycling over for lunch and back in the evening. I believe he was one of the strongest men I knew and we all adored him. He became Father's greatest friend and admirer after the death of Herbert Reiach. (I refer to both these gentlemen elsewhere.)

Later we moved to a very charming house, Dormers, where we lived for some years and after my mother's death Father and my sister Mary, who lived with him, moved to a near-by house at Hill

Head. Dormers was purchased by Admiral Bell Davies, V.C., and his widow only left there recently. Stanley House was pulled down to improve the runway to Lee aerodrome.

I remember when I married in 1928 and bought a house some four miles inland the family were shocked that I should make such a move, but, due to its exposed position, Lee is an almost impossible place to grow flowers or trees and I knew I was doing the right thing.

It is odd to think that from my preparatory school at Lee, when we lived at Gosport, I used to train home at half term on a funny little railway that was removed many years ago and later, when I joined the Firm, I would make the same journey by car sometimes as often as four times a day!

At this point I must mention two activities in which my father and the Firm were involved during the First World War which I think are of particular interest. Father was wonderfully versatile and always ready to try something new if he felt that its initiation was sound. During the First World War he developed a small design office in London and, in partnership with his great friend Herbert Reiach, founded Laminated Wood Ships Limited.

At that time there was an alarming shortage of steel and he felt that small vessels could well be constructed of comparatively unseasoned timber with laminated planking as well as beams, framing, and much of the remaining construction. In its day it was a most functional development and almost the adoption of the then well-known Isherwood system of steel construction. At least two sizes of small cargo vessels were designed but only a few of either size were ever laid down—one at Gosport named *Lignum,* and two of 182 ft at Lymington. I do not believe the latter were ever launched but I do remember, when I was working in the drawing office at Gosport, that some exploration party was interested in *Lignum* and I was planning the arrangement of dog kennels and chicken houses on deck with fine high sea-going coamings.

The trouble was that ship owners were far too conservative to invest in what they felt was an experiment, although it was a technique that was applied to racing yachts as far back as 1913 with such boats as *Shamrock IV,* the 15-metre *Istria* and others. (In the last war we tried to persuade the Admiralty to adopt laminated construction for the single skin planked M.F.V.s, some of which were shipped to warm climates where their planking shrank and they sank as they were lifted overboard.)

Around 1916, in the knowledge that their respective sons were keen on aircraft, Father teamed up with Sir Charles Allom (for whom we had built the successful *Istria* just before the war), and founded the Gosport Aircraft Company. M. Herman Volk was appointed Manager and as soon as the little factory was organized we received an order for a number of F.B.A. flying-boats. These were two seaters with side by side seating and were used for training as well as for submarine reconnaissance. We rented a waterside timber yard at Southampton for the fitting of the wings to the hulls and were soon getting into quite good production. The finished article was lifted into the Itchen and our test pilot, David Carnegie, with whom later I flew quite a lot, did his stuff.

Apparently the Ministry thought well of us and we went on to the construction of the larger F3 type flying-boats and finally F5s which carried a crew of five. It was while we were on the construction of the latter, for which we had an order for fifty, that Father was invited by the Ministry to design a larger experimental flying-boat hull, known as N4. This wonderful conception was completed to his design and structure and, in my view, was amongst the most artistic and functional exhibits of his great genius. After N4's hull was completed it was towed on a special trailer to the Phoenix Dynamo works at Bradford for the installation of the superstructure and ultimately to Felixstowe for test flying where, I believe, it was crashed but I was never allowed to learn the true facts.

The war ended and our last contract of fifty F5s was cut down to ten. Things looked black indeed and we obtained permission from the Ministry to use one of these ten boats for demonstration purposes in an attempt to interest the Dutch Government in the purchase of flying-boats. Our liaison officer was Colonel the Hon. Ralph Hope Vere and with David Carnegie, Herman Volk, an engineer and myself we tried to lift off at Netley in a flat calm with full tanks and, perhaps, too much gear aboard. Father was seeing us off in the 20-knot family launch and, by steaming past us at speed, created sufficient wash to allow us to come unstuck and creep dangerously low over Netley Hospital. I feel the rest of those two months in

Holland is not for this book. After a struggle to keep going Father
returned to his yachts and Allom, whose son Cedric was killed in the
war, returned to his great business in Hanover Square.

I had one very pleasant trip to Italy with Father after the war
in connection with the charter of the 1,822-ton steam yacht *Iolanda*
which at that time was owned by my firm; I believe it was in 1926 or
1927. We planned to meet a Mr Moses Taylor and his family at
Naples when the charter was to start and, fortunately for us, their
arrival was delayed for some ten days. It was Christmas time and I
remember sipping orange juice on my bedroom balcony in gorgeous
weather. I also remember that at dinner on the train from Paris to
Naples we talked of Mussolini and an elderly lady, who happened to
be at the same table, quietly rose and slipped away. We had, of
course, said nothing derogatory and we presumed that it must have
been out of order to mention the name in conversation.

We saw Capri, Sorrento, Vesuvius and other places and I remember taking a spool of film on Vesuvius, each exposure at a different
speed and aperture, as it was four o'clock in the afternoon; when
developed they were all equally good as at that altitude the atmosphere is so remarkably clear.

The noise, looking down on the formation of a new cone, reminded me of being in the shaft tunnel of an Atlantic liner with a
following sea; as the stern lifts so cavitation occurs and a sound like
that of Vesuvius is created.

We went to Rome for a few days and I found it quite difficult to
photograph all that I wished to as Father was rushing round with his
Baedeker, keen to miss nothing.

I should mention that in those days my firm handled a good deal
of yacht speculation and having been most successful in the sale of
another well-known steam yacht my father persuaded my somewhat
more restrained Uncle Arthur to agree to the purchase of *Iolanda*.
She was a most expensive vessel to maintain and was for several years
a complete white elephant. I remember the sense of deep relief that
was felt when she was ultimately sold. Like so many fine American-
owned power yachts she was transferred to the Admiralty for 7s. 6d.,
the cost of a certificate of transfer, and served in the last war under
the name of *White Bear*.

Apart from our stays in America in 1920 with *Shamrock IV* and in 1930 with *Shamrock V* I was never again abroad with Father except when we were in Switzerland one year. We were at Wengen but it was too high for my mother who went down to stay at Interlaken whence Father came up daily. He became remarkably keen on ski-ing and, in spite of his age at the time, he was quite proficient but got so dry in the mouth with excitement that I had to keep him plied with orange quarters. Oddly enough this condition also prevailed at the start of a yacht race but quickly disappeared after the starting gun.

I was a keen follower of motor racing and I remember one occasion when Father joined us at Brooklands for the Junior Car Club's 200 mile race. The 1,100 c.c. cars raced in the morning, the 1,500 c.c.s after lunch and he came up for the latter.

I remember seeing all those races from their inception and the joy of Brooklands was the unlimited freedom of the place. One could gaze at the 'innards' of the A.C., Alvis, Aston Martin, Bugatti, Fraser Nash, Sunbeam Talbot, or Darracq. The latter three were all designed by Louis Coatalen and raced under alternate names annually.

The morning race for 1,100 c.c. cars was usually a small affair embracing Morgans, Amilcars, and Salmsons and after E.B. Ware had a fatal crash due to a burst back tyre these Morgan three-wheelers were barred. One year a team of wonderful little Fiats came over from Italy. They were outstandingly fast and the three drivers, Nuvolari, Campari, and Ramponi fortunately all raced amongst themselves as one after the other blew up.

The year that Father joined us there was an A.C. driven by Joyce of Pass & Joyce, the agents at that time. It was fitted with a crab track, the rear wheels being closer together than the front, and since we had these excellent little cars in the family, off and on, Father elected to back this car, placing his bet with the regular bookmaker to Brooklands, Long Tom who, needless to say, was all of six feet six tall.

Kenelm Lee Guinness was there but not driving and, bumping into Father, they disappeared just before the start. This was a most impressive affair with the exhausts echoing back from the Vickers sheds. Later, when we found Father, his comment was that once you've seen the start you've seen everything!

It was Guinness, of course, who took a team of Sunbeams to race at Barcelona in his trawler-like yacht *Ocean Rover* and he and Sir Henry Segrave had an alarming time when their cargo of cars came adrift. This yacht was later owned by Sir Alfred Goodson.

The motor racing fraternity of that time were a wonderful bunch of sportsmen and many were yachtsmen too, including such names as Lord Howe (a great Bugatti driver), George Eyston, Whitney Straight, K. Lee Guinness, Sir Malcolm Campbell, Sir Henry Segrave, 'Babe' Barnarto, Billy Cotton, Hector Dobbs and the pioneer 'veteran' Napier for whom we built a large motor yacht. George Duller, of course, was the great hurdling horseman of his day and a Brooklands favourite.

I never recaptured the Brooklands atmosphere elsewhere in England.

Father's motto in life was 'a little of everything' and I suspect that Gerald Lambert's farewell cocktail party on his schooner *Atlantic* at Torquay in 1935 was among the few times that this was exceeded. This party is so well recalled in Lambert's delightful book *Yankee in England*. Father told me later that Lambert had filled one of the several trophies he had won with a special mint julep and, as the evening wore on, he and Bill Stephenson topped up this cup with anything that was handy; that, indeed, was a little of everything.

I suppose that great pre-war year was among the happiest in yachting history and the advent of Lambert's visit, with his J class yacht *Yankee* and the lovely three-masted schooner *Atlantic*, brought a wonderfully friendly international flavour to the racing scene. We serviced these fine yachts at our Gosport yard and, naturally, as the season wore on we and many yachtsmen got to know Lambert and found him a fine sportsman with much charm and immense humour.

Frank Payne of Boston, designer of *Yankee*, whom Father and I had met previously in 1930 in America came over with him; I know not why, but he always reminded me of Alfred Mylne and I'm sure he would not take exception to this. I've referred to this Lambert 'invasion' elsewhere and can safely say that 1935 was for me a wonderful year afloat.

In 1939 we had our *Tammie* afloat at Poole with the children ashore at Canford Cliffs. Father was there in *Flame* (I have mentioned the occasion earlier) and it was while visiting my aunt and Uncle Arthur in the Branksome Towers Hotel that I heard Chamberlain declare war on Germany.

We returned to *Flame* to tell the sad news to Father and after lunch he sailed home to Gosport. I preferred to lay up my boat at Sandbanks as I felt she might be safer there. It turned out to be a wise move, as during the two major raids in the Portsmouth area a large number of yachts and stores housing gear for over a hundred craft were lost.

It was during the war that age began to make its mark on Father and, although as enthusiastic as ever, it was inevitable that I should take over.

After the war he sold his beloved *Flame* and his post-war sailing is described later.

Turning to other events in his great life, it was in 1934 that he became the first Freeman of the Borough of Gosport in recognition of his wide achievements in bringing to the town trade in variety over so many years, and in particular as recognition of his inspired master-piece, the America's Cup challenger *Endeavour*.

In 1936 he was honoured by the Royal Society of Arts with the Diploma of a Royal Designer for Industry; that honour, the first to a yacht designer, brought him considerable pleasure including that derived from his frequent meetings with members of that Faculty.

By a happy coincidence he became the recipient of the Order of the British Empire on his eighty-first birthday. He was an honorary member of the Council of the Royal Yachting Association, a member of the Royal Institution of Naval Architects and a Liveryman of the Worshipful Company of Shipwrights. He was also a member of a large number of yacht clubs of which I know the old Royal Thames in Piccadilly, was his favourite. When the club moved west to larger premises, and found it necessary to bring in a large number of non-sailing members, he most definitely reserved his views on the issue.

Like his father, he was Commodore of the Royal Albert Yacht Club, a privilege which I too enjoyed for a number of years and I suspect that seldom, if ever, have three generations of any other family held this office.

There was no shadow of doubt that Father was happiest afloat, but I'm sure his next choice would be his old yard at Gosport which he had built up to produce the finest craftsmanship in the world. His staff and everyone in the Firm held him in great respect, in fact many of them almost worshipped him. One could sense, the moment he entered a building shed, that the men were pleased to see him and even more so if he conversed with one or two. Like his father before him, he knew his job inside out, but whereas grandfather would invariably castigate a man if he had no grease near the handle of his saw, or criticize a fellow for discarding a plank of witch-elm due to sap (which is the best part in that material) Father seldom had reason to be unkindly critical. On one occasion, however, when preparing to launch Madame Heriot's *Ailée* we were together and he spotted the size of the bolts attaching the wood launching ribbon to the steel hull and which supported the hull on the launching cradle. Dear old George Moth was foreman at that time and was very distressed when Father advised him that these bolts could have been about half the size.

He had a habit of borrowing a foreman's foot-rule and putting it back in his own pocket; these all accumulated in a drawer at home and one of my jobs was their redistribution.

His capacity for every aspect of the work he loved was immense; he did not drive his fellow creatures but they, in their admiration for him, drove themselves.

In international yachting he was in the forefront of the formulation of racing rules during the whole of his active life. He was also something of a diplomat and often deplored the casual reception given to foreign yachtsmen, including our American cousins. In those earlier days the Y.R.A. as a body lacked the faculty for hospitality we so much enjoyed when abroad. On one occasion his friend Clifford D. Mallory was over from the States for a conference and they dined together. Mallory quietly asked him to sign his menu 'as it was the only entertainment he had received' on that little visit. Next day I remember well his criticism of the Y.R.A. Council and indeed of its Chairman.

These conditions fortunately no longer prevail and I know of at least one journalistic friend who throughout his sailing life (and he is still sailing) has, with full enjoyment, gone out of his way to see that our foreign visitors feel at home.

We all have our traits and one of Father's was 'cutting things fine'. I remember that at the annual Christmas family visit to the pantomime we had to precede him with my mother and when he arrived he usually had to sit on the steps of the dress circle until the end of the first act. If travelling to Town by train from Portsmouth the skippers of the ferries might see him running from his office in front of the building sheds and would remain at the pontoon until he was aboard, to their financial benefit.

My earlier recollections of Father go back to Leventhorpe at Gosport. He would take me to the greenhouse before breakfast and select a good ripe tomato beaded with condensation. One late summer I remember us picking the pears and placing them all in a barouche, a four-wheeled wicker-work reclining vehicle that was acquired when one of the family had back trouble.

On Sundays we youngsters were given our 'Bino' (tonic) by him in the manner of a ritual; we were lifted on to a large chest of drawers on an upstairs landing and each in turn had his tot.

I remember my first sail with him in Bembridge harbour in the family One Design *Limpet* and marvelled that we didn't capsize and finally I remember him taking me in his arms in the morning room when he wished to tell me of my brother Harry's death, and his grief.

The last time I heard him lament was on a Sunday morning after a major air raid when we were climbing over the rubble. I took his arm and tried to cheer him up by explaining that reconstruction would provide a more efficient yard. He agreed, bless him.

I refer throughout these notes to many of his exploits and to incidents I had with him and I know of no man who ever had a more devoted son.

To conclude this unworthy tribute to a wonderful man we must look for a lighter note. At an R.N.V.R. dinner he and Sir Phillip Hunloke were among the guests and Father was not too well. His host, Commander Harry Vandervell told him not to worry but to try to make them laugh. Hunloke's was a breezy speech and when Father rose he told the assembled company that he would let them into the secret of being a successful yacht designer; you could have heard a pin drop as he pronounced, "GET THE RIGHT MAN TO SAIL YOUR BOAT."

3 Some of the cast

My father had a wide circle of friends but, as with most of us, only a few are specially rated favourites and in his case the number was three. As the pattern of friendship might be likened to a shooting target, I will deal with the three in the bullseye first and later with a few who were in the inner.

I hardly remember Mr Hill who was best man at Father's wedding. I believe he often wore a black morning coat and maybe this sombre clothing made its impression on a very young person. I saw him in family photographs and heard much of him in my youth. He was responsible for the design of Portland breakwater, but whether he was a marine civil engineer or an all-rounder I cannot say, but I always remember his emphatic assertion that the best climate in England was to be found between the Seven Sisters and Portland Bill, a pronouncement with which I am inclined to agree.

Herbert L. Reiach was, I am sure, the greatest of all my father's friends. For some years he was employed in our Gosport office, many years before I joined the Firm, but I do vaguely remember when he left us to found *The Yachting Monthly* which I think must have been around 1906 or thereabouts. He was one of the kindest and most generous men we ever knew, quiet in manner with a deep sense of humour and great understanding of human nature. As children we all adored him and as he stayed with us so often we felt he was almost one of the family.

I remember when I was taken to Town to have my tonsils cut, as happened in those days, my nurse cut my bread and butter into fingers and dipped them into my boiled egg to assist in the painful business of swallowing and Mr Reiach, as we always knew him, sent me a little circular clockwork train that just fitted my bed-table. How I blessed him for that lovely toy.

Reiach introduced great humour and good English into his *Yachting Monthly*. His *nom-de-plume* was M.I.N.A. and I and many of my friends still enjoy reading my father's bound volumes. The paper was most artistic with work by Donald Maxwell, Briscoe and others and Briscoe's amusing cartoons 'Things we have all met' were both humorous and beautifully executed. It also had a most useful little article every month named 'Our Portrait Study' depicting the yachting history of prominent people which I often used for reference. Reiach was a superb draughtsman whose magnificent pen sketches frequently appeared in the magazine.

Both he and my father did morning exercises, and I remember one Clyde Week when we were staying at Dunoon and Reiach had the next room to me that, when the maid entered with his morning tea, he was on the floor. Next morning I heard a knock and the maid saying, "Will yer be doin' yer antics this morning, sir?" My neighbour on my port side was a Scottish journalist who amazed me by ordering a large whisky at that early hour.

When I was old enough to join up in the First War I hoped to join the R.N.A.S. but knowing my father's wish that I should stay on the water rather than in the air, Reiach who was living in London saw their mutual friend, Commander Harry Vandervell, who arranged my Admiralty interview. In no time I was being asked "Why is the sky blue?", "What are methylated spirits made of?" and "Are the walnut trees still on the ramparts at Gosport?" I also had to box the compass with pen and ink as the interviewer said it was harder that way. Soon after I joined H.M.S. *Hermione* at Southampton for a potted course of seamanship and navigation.

My father had promised me £25 if I did not smoke until I was twenty-one, and, to this day, I remember that fatal Sunday on which I reported for duty. After signing on, the officer of the watch on the bridge a Lieut. Bestick, said that the captain wished to see me and took me down to the wardroom where Captain Boothby was playing bridge. He looked up, asked me to take a cigarette, and said he would be with me in a minute. I sat smokeless and, after a chat during which he kindly enquired after Father, I was directed to the gunroom and was again offered a cigarette. It was at that moment that I met Gerald Paterson who, after crashing in the R.N.A.S. joined the R.N.V.R. We spent the rest of the war together in the Irish Sea and both he and his wife are now amongst our oldest friends.

To revert to smoking, I noticed at navigation classes that Lieut.-Commander Lenthall permitted smoking and my neighbours kindly and continually offered me their case or packet. The days went by and when ashore one afternoon I walked into a tobacconist's and bought a small packet of a brand that is still for sale today and which at that time were reputed to be the mildest. For some reason or another I preferred Egyptian and smoked them freely for a time. The first time I went on leave I admitted my relapse and, perhaps flushed with my appearance in His Majesty's uniform, my dear parent promptly gave me the cheque.

Before I joined the service Herbert Reiach, knowing my preference for flying, wrote the following in my autograph album; it was 'off the cuff' and discloses his humour and brilliant mind.

A FLIGHT OF FANCY

Knowing well your predilection for to fly,
All a-ratting and a-crackling in the sky,
   Making exhibition flights
   At extremely dizzy heights,
I'd suggest it's somewhat risky—
   Particularly risky—
Quite immoderately risky, Master John.

Yet in spite of what I'm saying, you may soar,
Counting me and all my preaching quite a bore;
on a dinky new two-seater
Something infinitely neater
Than my metre that may peter
Out before I've really warned you—
Really adequately warned you,
Yes before I've warned you fully, Master John.

Now the good Lord made the land for to stand on,
So before it's solid surface you abandon,
Do not treat the matter light,
For perchance you may alight

In a way you don't expect—
Nothing led you to expect,
In a way you never thought of, Master John.

If you've time—the which you won't have, I'm afraid—
Remember the prophetic words I've said,
And if I'm in the crowd,
Just holler long and loud,
And I'll do my best to catch you,
My very best to save you, Master John.

But it's possible I mayn't be there or then,
Not knowing your arrangements where and when,
So note well from aloft,
Someone equally—'m—soft,
And drop into his waistcoat,
His Aldermanic waistcoat;
For you that is the best plan, Master John.

And doing as I have carefully directed,
Don't let the waistcoat's owner feel dejected,
But tactfully remind him
To take things as they find him
In this world of ups and downings,
Particularly downings
Unpremeditated downings, Master John.

It was Herbert Reiach who assisted Ewing McGruer in founding his hollow spar company which started around 1923 near our Gosport premises by our large lower slipway. The McGruer patent was successful for small spars but a topmast they made for the racing cutter *Terpsichore* whipped like a trout rod and broke one day when heeling and toeing in a jumpy sea off Cowes after a race. It made the Twickenham rugby goal-posts which are the best I ever saw.

After his retirement Herbert Reiach lived with his sister on his barge-yacht *Velsa* on the East Coast and, with the passage of time, we saw less of this dear man and finally heard that he had died on board.

This sad vacuum for us all, and particularly for my father, was only later filled by Malden Heckstall-Smith whom in fact we knew and loved for some years before Reiach's untimely death. My first

vivid recollection of Uncle Malden, as he was known by a wide circle
of friends, was when he was living at Kings Worthy and used to
cycle over on his sturdy B.S.A. bicycle for lunch and return afterwards, a remarkable achievement which I have mentioned earlier.
He always wore a Norfolk suit in those days, belted and full of
pockets. Children adored him; he could waggle his ears, was full of
novel ideas for their entertainment, and always made them feel he
was as young as they were—a priceless asset. He had a brilliant
mathematical brain which in his later life was eclipsed by the greater
brilliance of his son Hugh to whom he would pass on his theories for
master analysis.

In 1914 Malden founded the Boat Racing Association. I have a
copy of the original little red book of rules from which I see that
Sir Charles Allom was president, T. D. McMeekin was Vice-
President and F. A. Richards was Hon. Treasurer. The permanent
Technical Committee included Captain R. T. Dixon, J. M. Soper,
F. G. Morgan Giles, Linton Hope, my father, a Lieut. Craven and
G. U. Laws. I cannot remember the last two but the latter might
have been a Dr Laws connected with Lloyd's Register. Since all
were friends of Father's and some of myself I feel I should say a little
more about them.

Sir Charles Allom, who later owned the celebrated 23-metre class
cutter *White Heather*, was Commodore of the Royal London Yacht
Club for some years. I remember at one Cowes Week, when the Alton
Salvation Army band regularly came over to play, they were
grinding out a tuneless hymn one evening when Sir Charles was on
the balcony. Resplendent in his cloak over his mess-kit he leant down
and addressed the band leader, suggesting that if he played a better
tune he would give them a fiver. I don't remember the tune but the
result was refreshing.

That night a full moon was emerging from behind Norris Castle
and Sir Charles asked me if I could see the girl on the right with
her head bent back being kissed by a man. I could not, so he sketched
it for me and on looking again, there they were. I have often drawn
the attention of friends to this which is, I think, a quite delicate and
unusual phenomenon.

T. D. McMeekin used to live at Hill Head, the village next to
Lee-on-the-Solent, and was a great small-boat helmsman. He owned
one of our little 16-ft One Design boats run by the Lee Sailing Club

and was a trifle free with his language so that my sister and I knew him for years as 'the swear bird'. Later he was Commodore of the Ranelagh Sailing Club and he and I corresponded for a great many years.

Captain Dixon was without any doubt among the finest helmsmen in the south. He hailed from Falmouth, and was for many years on the Council of the Y.R.A. (as the Royal Yachting Association was then known). He owned 6-metres, the celebrated cutter *Lady Maud* and, in 1930 and for a few seasons after, he successfully raced the 8-metre *Cutty* that we had built for Captain Dowman of Falmouth. The latter gentleman repurchased the celebrated tea and wool clipper *Cutty Sark*, now docked at Greenwich, and owned at various times *Lady of Avenil*, *Lamorna*, and the larger schooner *Mermerus* ex-*Gina*. After his death it fell to me to value his various vessels for probate, a sideline in our business that someone had to do, and I valued *Cutty Sark* as a very good sheer hulk but took into account her rotten 'tween decks and little and poor canvas. Her hull was in wonderful condition.

I only met G. M. Soper once. He designed some fine vessels of which I think the 278-ton ketch *Xarifa*, built to his design at our Gosport yard in 1912, was among his best. She was built in excess of Lloyd's rules and is in commission to this day. Soper, I remember as a rather dour person in a bowler hat.

Linton Hope was a brilliant small-boat designer who regrettably died in his young prime and who, had he lived longer, would I am sure have made a great name in the limited designing circle of larger yachts. I used to play golf occasionally with his son who was self-taught and played for the R.A.F. and who was also a Schneider Trophy pilot.

Morgan Giles was another clever small-boat designer and a pioneer dinghy sailor and I often thought that, in dinghies, Uffa Fox started where Morgan Giles ended. I often fell in with Morgan Giles at R.N.V.R. reunion dinners and enjoyed his bright and amusing charm.

Reference to these gentlemen in some measure of variety goes to show the great number of senior yachtsmen who regarded Malden Heckstall-Smith both as a friend and a great benefactor to the technical side of yachting. Unfortunately there was a twist to all this

c

and to the virile development of the Boat Racing Association over the adoption of one or two good One-Design classes and the development of a splendid formula for an 18-ft waterline racing boat to which four were built.

The then Y.R.A. was a comparatively small association in those days, governing racing in 6-metres and over but with no interest whatsoever in the smaller classes due to the antagonism of a small minority. Friction developed between these two bodies and the little B.R.A. was banished from the yachting scene until as late as 1949 when my father and Malden evolved the present 5·5-metre rule. For a measurement rule to be revived after thirty-six years must be a record in the technical annals of yacht racing.

During the last war Father and Malden corresponded freely on the details of modernizing this rule. Amazing exhibits passed between them and one I remember, from Malden, was a Spratt's puppy-biscuit bag folded so as to demonstrate his proposed method for spinnaker measurement.

When all was finally completed the rule met a small sector of opposition among the Technical Committee of the Royal Yachting Association but was finally adopted. A few good-looking yachts were built before certain trends in hull form were conceived by clever designers and, as time went on, changes took place. We built a prototype named *Deb* and, with no competition, she was raced in the Solent Q class before others formed a small class the next season. Designed to produce a fast boat with far less displacement than a 6-metre (which some described as a 'half-tide rock'), they were never really popular in British waters but were immensely so in a few other countries.

Uncle Malden was a very popular guest in the large racing classes and we had many fine sails in *Nyria* and her later 23-metre sisters and in the J class. He was not fussy about his attire and never wore socks in summer but usually a white linen hat. As Official Measurer to the Y.R.A. we all felt that his love of the science of his work appealed to him far more than the remuneration and we felt he often overlooked the payment of his fees.

It was Malden again who devised the first measurement rule for the Royal Ocean Racing Club, perhaps the best rule of its day formulating, as it did, the fair handicapping of a menagerie class that started chiefly among a handful of sea-going cruising yachts in 1925.

Malden often came to stay, and his general topic was boats and more boats but, with him, it was never boring for a moment. He was simple in his descriptive power and once when discussing the merits of particular types of hull form for fast Admiralty craft he quietly stated that 'water does not like surprises'.

My last few memories of dear Malden were, in sequence, firstly at a dinner given at the Royal Thames Yacht Club with Lord Queenborough in the chair. Malden was opposite to me and I had the misfortune to be placed next to a pretty distressing fellow who was not only drunk but insisted on telling numerous crude stories. Malden, seeing my discomfort, leant over to me and in a clear voice said with some emphasis, "I don't think we wish to listen to that fellow do we, John?" The result was quite extraordinary and an example of Malden's penetrative powers; the annoying fellow simmered and ate his dinner.

Once and once only Father and Malden attended a point-to-point race meeting, the H.H. at Bentworth, now transferred to Hackwood Park. I had just given Robin Steele a list of horses which I thought were worth a modest flutter when I met my daughter who promptly told me that Brian Butler's horse didn't stay, so off I went in search of Steele. I never found him but just before the start of the next race, after the horses had gone down, I saw a large elderly gentleman in a white linen hat strolling in the middle of the course. I rushed over to Malden and led him to safety. I've no doubt he was meditating on some factor to the benefit of yachting.

We used to find him accommodation at Cowes during the Week and I remember on his last visit going ashore to see how he was making out. We found that he had met a little girl and, by mutual consent, they accompanied each other to and from the Island Sailing Club balcony. They were utterly complementary, he explaining all the craft to her whilst she fetched him from and delivered him to his lodgings. The great old man must have been so happy to spend his last Cowes with a sweet young child and how I wish that she could read this.

To touch on some of my father's friends in the 'inner' as I put it at the beginning of this chapter; his affection for our Chief Draughtsman at the Gosport yard, Louis Jacobs, was as deep as my own.

For some years after his retirement Father used to come to the office
to enjoy the atmosphere he had lived in for so long. The first thing
he liked to do was to take a peep at Jacobs, sometimes hardly saying
a word but usually producing an apple or a bar of chocolate for
him and, if the room was empty, leaving it on his drawing-board.

Another great friend since his boyhood was a really unusual
character who became Commanding Officer of the C.M.B. Base in
Haslar Creek during the First War after serving in the Mediterranean; I dare not in this book expose all I knew of that gallant band of
officers but I may say that many of them were good yachtsmen and
the Mess had an atmosphere of its own. Joe F. C. Hannen was that
C.O. He was reputed to be the first baby to be born at Lee-on-
the-Solent where his father had a rather nice hotel. He was a founder
member of the Lee-on-the-Solent Sailing Club and throughout his
life this little club was among his chief interests; he was in the top
flight of Solent helmsmen and raced in America in the first of the
British-American 6-metre team races.

A good all-round sportsman he was games master at Stubbington
House Preparatory School, well over six feet tall and endowed with
a splendid sense of humour. On one occasion when playing village
cricket against a local side on a ground near the road descending
steeply into Bursledon on the Hamble River, he thought that if he
could lob a ball on to the road he could get a lot of runs; there were
no boundaries as the ground was rather small. Eventually his chance
came and we were told that the batsmen ran sixteen runs before
collapsing with exhaustion.

For a time he was secretary and sailing companion to Sir Thomas
Glenn-Coates and eventually he leased a good hotel at Lee where he
spent the rest of his life sailing, and often winning in his Club One
Design boat that he loved so much.

One of my last and most happy sails was on a Sunday with Joe
Hannen, a Captain Joe Brunton who also had an abundance of
humour, one John Bradstock and my wife, in our little 10-ton sloop
Tar Baby. We called at the Island Sailing Club at Cowes before
lunch, going ashore in a little seven foot six inch pram dinghy with
the two Joes, both large people, and someone on the Club balcony
shouted "I wish I had my camera." This was in mid-October;
the moorings had all been lifted and we anchored just clear of the

fairway. After taking their quota of gin ashore the ship's company went off on board for lobsters and hock in the cockpit.

I often thought that yachts could remain in commission until the frosts arrive, as it is then that internal condensation occurs, but today, with G.R.P. hulls, they can remain afloat indefinitely provided they are well ventilated.

Joe often accompanied us in our family yachts and was a regular starter in my father's *Flame* in the races in the Channel such as the Morgan Cup sponsored by the Royal Ocean Racing Club.

On the occasion of celebrating my father's eightieth birthday we had a small luncheon at a Southampton hotel, limited to family and directors, at which we presented him with a splendid oil painting of *Endeavour* by Frank Mason. The only 'outsider' at this luncheon was Joe Hannen which confirms my point about his friendship with our family.

Ian McDonald, our Southampton yard Manager, and Father hit it off very well; not only had they tremendous respect for each other but Father always found Mac's splendid humour and cheerfulness refreshing on his many visits to that yard. Looking back, it seems odd that one had to go through two toll gates in those days, one at Bursledon Bridge and the other at Northam Bridge and this was a country drive on a dusty gravel road. Today the tolls have gone, the road is splendid but nearly all through built-up areas and, with the threat of a 'Solent City' ahead of us, it may be wise in the not too distant future to commute by boat from yard to yard to save time.

We had a yard bo'sun at Southampton for a great many years named Jimmy Lay who kept a large number of cats to keep down the rats in the yachts' stores. He fed them after the yard was closed every evening and our milk bill—as my wife once spotted when glancing at the firm's accounts—was as much as £50 a year. I suspect that the passing of cotton canvas has eased the rat problem nowadays. It was an accepted fact that, at Christmas time, Jimmy would fall into the Itchen river in order to tap his boss, Mac, for a tot of Scotch.

Although they did not often meet, both Father and my father-in-law much enjoyed each other's company, both being great sailors in different spheres. The latter, James Sherren, C.B.E., was born at Weymouth and had a remarkable life. He went to sea in sail, starting first as a boy, from Liverpool, and, when mate in *Falls of*

Halladale, a fine old carrier of the nineties, he sat for his master's
ticket but unfortunately his eyes let him down. He then became a
student at the London Hospital and, with his young wife who was
also a Weymouth girl, lived in digs at Whitechapel.

Having little education but a wonderful brain he soon qualified
and became a fellow of the Royal College of Surgeons, specializing
in abdominal surgery; later he became Vice-President of the Royal
College of Surgeons. In the First War he was in charge of officers'
hospitals and, with the rank of colonel in the R.A.M.C., his friends
were amused to see him as a soldier with his seaman's roll. He also
revised the Board of Trade medical requirements for ships and in his
spare time was a good violinist. At the height of his surgical fame,
when only in his early fifties, he retired and returned to his old love
—the sea—as a ship's surgeon.

When he finally retired both he and my delightful mother-in-
law used to visit us a great deal. She would invariably wake the
grandson of the moment and he and I used to 'quarter deck' on the
lawn before lunch. Whenever I took him to the yard he insisted on a
visit to the warehouse where he would draw off a fathom of lightly-
tarred Italian hemp and hold it to his nose with his eyes shut. I'm
sure it took him back to his sailing days.

As my wife's family lived at Broadstone, Dorset, we were married
in Wimborne Minster and at the reception the toast was proposed
by our oldest friend present—Mr Tom Ratsey. I have never before
seen the old fashioned small-brimmed yachting cap nor a corn-
flower blue shirt and collar worn with morning dress, but the great
old gentleman, with his 'goatee' beard, made a charming speech.

Not only was he among my father's great friends, but he had met
Mr Sherren by chance when he was surgeon on one of the Cunard 'A'
boats running from Liverpool to Canada, the way Tom Ratsey
preferred to travel to the States. Apparently they had talked far
into the night on the merits of *Thermopolae* and *Cutty Sark* and both
were great authorities on sail.

Mr Tom was a great autocrat in his heyday but, like so many,
he mellowed in time. On the last occasion that I called on him he
asked me what I was doing at Cowes and when I replied that I was
calling on 'Bekken's' he criticized my pronunciation of the word
Beken, since when I've always used the long E.

On calling again on Mr Tom, whose age was affecting his memory, I noticed that he was standing with feet apart and hands behind his back in front of the fireplace with a large slate hearth; he looked down and then looked up at me asking "And how is Mr Sherren?" The name of my father-in-law was written in chalk on that slate hearth.

In *Britannia*'s day Sir Philip Hunloke warned Tom Ratsey that H.M. King George V wished to see his celebrated old yacht *Dolly Varden* and that they would call after a race one day in Cowes Week. Tom gave his crew special white duck trousers for this occasion and when, one afternoon, his son Chris spotted the Royal Barge approaching Tom's immediate command to his crew was, "Put your trousers on quick" and, to Chris, "Give me my teeth." Chris was always rather sensitive and dived into hiding but when His Majesty inquired of him he had to be presented.

Being a rather younger contemporary of Chris's I naturally saw more of him than did my father but he often joined us when racing in *Flame*.

Although Father had a wonderful circle of American yachting friends including both Harold and William Vanderbilt, George Cormack, Paul Hammond, Clinto Crane—whose designs he so much admired—and a host of others, I believe his greatest friend from 'over the pond' in his younger days was Mr William P. Stephens and I have the copy of his splendid book *Traditions and Memories of American Yachting* that he gave to him. The inscription within reads:

> Charles E. Nicholson
> with regards of W. P. Stephens
> the last of the Cutter-Cranks
> and affirmative Jib-headed Crank
>
> Bogside, Long Island. June 9th, 1942

The other great friend was that enchanting fellow Alf Loomis. I have always put him top of all marine writers and in spite of Alfred being half a generation younger I rather felt that he filled the vacuum for some years after Mr Stephen's death. Another great sailor, Alf contrived to put things over in a unique and refreshing manner and his humour was of a delightful kind of its very own.

He came over purposely to get Father's 'profile', as he put it,

for the American paper *Yachting* and stayed a couple of nights
with us. It was at the time of the last series of British-American
6-metre team races which I personally thought were among the best
events in the history of international yachting and more akin to polo.
On the second afternoon of his stay we ran over to Cowes in the
launch to see a few Sixes tuning up and had tea at the Royal
Corinthian. As we left Alf looked astern saying "We've got nothing
like that in America", referring, of course, to the five clubs all so
close to each other.

On both mornings he and Father were closeted in the office and
after landing from the launch at the end of the second day Alf
turned to me and said, "I've got nothing out of your dad." This
was no surprise to me as I knew that he could never talk well of
himself and perhaps I too have inherited some of his art of digression.
I promised to send my own little 'profile' to Alf and, with those notes
and his flair for interpretation, it read uncommonly well and I still
have a copy.

So much for my father's friends. With the sad passage of time there
can, I fear, be few remaining who really knew and enjoyed his
company and charm.

I intended to conclude this chapter with a short list but found,
happily, that it was far too long to attempt—a discovery from which
I derive a great sense of comfort and satisfaction.

4 Family craft

In a saga of this kind the subject is so wide that the sequence of events inevitably becomes somewhat disrupted and it is best to give one's memory its head and carry on. I hope my readers will accept this view and forgive what may be a rather disjointed story.

History relates that my father's first boat was a sailing punt and this may be so as I have a faded photograph of this craft in operation with ladies in floral hats heavily veiled. His next boat was the celebrated *Blue Boat*, also before my time, which was equipped with such an ambitious sail plan that he was known by his friends as 'old forty-ropes'.

When we were all young children we often stayed at a small hotel in Botley which in those days was right in the country. Father and my Uncle Ernest (on my mother's side) often sailed together at night usually preceded by a 'standard' supper of chicken and angels on horseback at the old Café Royal in Southsea. Each would phone up his respective wife stating that Ernest was staying with Charlie, and vice versa, and it worked out well until they overlooked the fact that both wives were staying with their children at this hotel!

One night when they were sailing round the Isle of Wight Father took a rest with Ernest at the helm. They were roaring down towards the Needles on a strong ebb and with no wind and Ernest, seeing a large buoy ahead, shouted down to his companion to come up. This was the Warden Ledge and, fearing the worst, both were greatly relieved when the build-up of tidal pressure around the base of the buoy served as a 'fend off' and swept them clear.

On one occasion—it must have been about 1891—after building a cutter for Comte G. de Polignac, Father decided as she was leaving the yard to accompany her with his little boat towing astern. After going well out to sea the Count felt it was time that Father returned and urged him to set sail for home. Before casting off he was handed a bottle of champagne and as the day was warm he soon pulled the cork and after a time fell soundly asleep; on waking up he found the little *Blue Boat* had sailed him almost back to harbour.

Later Father acquired a rather well-known Itchen Ferry type yacht named *Tammie* designed by a publican with an eye for a boat and, in fact, pretty for her type. He bought her from a Mr Lapthorn of the sail-making firm who in turn had bought her from her designer, a Mr Balne.

Plate 4 shows *Tammie*'s sail plan, though the working headsails are not set as she is carrying a spinnaker. *Tammie* was a good example of a cruising yacht of her day. She had a gaff cutter rig with the usual lengthy bowsprit of those days and her boom end was some seven or eight feet abaft her transom stern; she set a working topsail and the usual staysail, jib and jib topsail; she had poor head-room but was well built and is still going strong as I write this. The panelling of her little saloon was edged with gilt finish and she had gimballed oil lights—so much more cosy than electric—sofa beds in the saloon and two folding cots with their accompanying 'donkey's breakfast' mattresses.

My Uncle Ernest was often a guest and the ensuing stories point to his unique character. One Saturday after we had raced our Lee One Design he was coming to join us afterwards in *Tammie* for a sail over to Fishbourne. We went on board and having waited for him as long as patience allowed we sailed over to Wootton Creek and after the usual pleasant cockpit evening gossip we turned in. Round about midnight someone shouted "Is that you, Charlie?" It was Ernest who had been detained ashore; he had hired a rowing skiff from Southsea beach and rowed all the way to Fishbourne and our first duty next day was the return of the skiff.

We returned to our mooring in Haslar Creek that evening and on entering harbour Ernest confided in me that "In a few moments the owner will shout 'down topsail, down jib, down staysail, down main' and we shall be on the mud." He was right. Somehow Father had a knack of leaving things too late and that too was how we hit the bridge at Yarmouth on one occasion.

Next week-end we planned to sail round the Island and Ernest told us that he would bring the lunch. It was to be a stag party— Ernest and his son my cousin Bill, Father and I—and, as *Tammie* had been scrubbed that week, she was on a mooring in Coldharbour to the north of the yard.

As usual Ernest was late and, with next to no wind and the tide ebbing fast, we began setting sail at moorings to save time. Just as I was rowing our guests from the quay I saw a well-known tide mark just showing out of water and my heart sank. As we drew alongside *Tammie* was well aground and remained so for the rest of the day.

Being September Ernest had kindly brought grouse and a very good Madeira for lunch and as we enjoyed this, sitting in the somewhat sloping cockpit, he amused us with a running commentary on the beauties of the scene as we did an imaginary sail round the island.

We had many happy seasons in *Tammie* cruising to the West Country and on one of these passages I had the longest row of my life. It was evening and we were bound for Weymouth with a falling wind. Father had decided to pop into Lulworth Cove and as we came out the wind died right away.

Tammie had a Buffalo petrol engine in her large fishing cockpit, encased in a mahogany box with an elaborate filigree brass top; this outfit never worked but the casing made a good table. There was only one thing for it so I took to the dinghy and towed *Tammie* all the way to Weymouth. I remember it was a gorgeous summer evening and we must have had a fair tide; the sun sinking behind Portland Bill was beautiful. I also remember our arrival alongside the quay at Weymouth and how I took a line to a bollard, tying a bowline round it with an audience of disappointed fishermen who, I rather unkindly suspected, were resentful at missing a tip.

Our return from that cruise saw us all in a nasty position in Portland Race. As I have already mentioned, *Tammie* at that time had a large fishing cockpit and as we approached the Bill the wind dropped and, with the spring ebb building up, the over-falls were alarming. We lengthened the dinghy painter in hopes that it would not strike us and, having no steerage way, we tossed about in a sickening fashion. Father, with three of his children in that much too large cockpit was, I could see, really worried but after about half an hour when we were near the tail of the race a little easterly breeze sprang up and we gratefully trimmed our sheets and made for Portland.

As a youngster I enjoyed anchoring in that harbour and always admired the smart handling of destroyer flotillas coming in at speed and mooring up alongside jetties with great precision. Years later when I owned *Tammie* we spent a particularly unpleasant night at anchor off Wyke Regis at the north-west end of the harbour. There was a steady and annoying scend, and rolling continuously on the shallow anchorage with gear dropping all over the place made us vow never to anchor there again.

Under Father's ownership *Tammie* brought the family a deal of fun and my sister Mary and I loved seeing all the fresh places. Dartmouth, I think, was our favourite harbour and it was here one evening after supper while we were washing up in the cockpit that Father, seeing the wash-up bowl, kindly decided to empty it over the side. That was the last of our cutlery! With the limited headroom Mary used to comb her hair standing under the open forehatch.

Tammie was purchased by Mrs George Ratsey of Cowes for her son, Colin, to learn cruising.

Father's next yacht was *Bryony* the ex-8-metre class that we had built to Dr Froude's design and, although not much good in the class, she made a fast cruiser. He owned her for no more than a couple of seasons or so and I can only remember one little incident off Yarmouth on the occasion of peace anniversary celebrations, I believe. The little township was a picture that evening; decorations by day called for bunting but that night the old walls and many window sills had candles lit in glass jars and the reflections in the water (we were lying in the Roads) were quite charming. There was a fine firework display and, not to be outdone, I put a large distress rocket in a bottle on our stern and proudly set it skywards. Next morning our beautifully snaped and tapered yellow-pine deck was badly charred.

On another occasion many years later in 1935, when Gerry Lambert came over with *Yankee* and *Atlantic*, we were off Yarmouth in my father's 33-ton yawl *Flame*. We had no race that day and I went off in the outboard-driven dinghy to the mark-boat to see the J class fleet go round. It was about slack high water with just a nice light sailing breeze; *Astra* was ahead followed closely by *Yankee*. As *Astra* rounded bedlam reigned; orders were being shouted, canvas was lashing and winch ratchets were whirring and clacking as she trimmed her sheets for the broad reach. As *Yankee* rounded nothing was heard apart from the thrash of canvas and the odd spoken word from Gerry to Frank Payne. I would not have missed that moment for words and, as on many other occasions when sailing with or against Americans, I was always impressed by their slick drill and quiet efficiency. I believe many of our crack offshore racers of today are handled like this, some, maybe, even better.

Turning from Yarmouth to the near-by town of Lymington on the mainland, the regattas there were often held in boisterous weather which, in our family, we always referred to as 'Lymington form'. The saying is that if you can see Yarmouth from Lymington it is going to rain and if you cannot, it is raining.

I remember my anxiety when racing our 8-metre *Sagitta* at Lymington; we usually started off Jack-in-the-Basket and finished up the river in front of the Club. Inevitably the tide would be out, the channel was very narrow and invariably too, the Yarmouth steamer would be approaching us. Our skipper always advised keeping to leeward of her and I always feared running aground as she took our wind, thus momentarily increasing our draught; it was a case of neck or nothing and far too close a shave for my liking.

On one occasion Father and I were racing Sir Ernest Roney's 8-metre *Emily* in a very hard breeze indeed. We were sleeping aboard *Flame* and our family launch had come over too. Soon after the start, whilst running up to that usually invisible 'mark-boat off Sowley', our spinnaker halliard parted and it took a great deal of time to retrieve the sail from the water in quite a sea and while moving pretty fast. As there was no prospect of catching the others we hauled down our flag and returned to the river.

Instead of lowering the main off the entrance and blowing up under our foresail Father elected to get well up the river before taking down the main. When we headed up to do so the hanks got jammed on the track and we were soon aground on the east bank of the river. We then noticed that *Flame* too had dragged and was aground on our bank and when the launch *Gelyce* came to our assistance she got our kedge rope round her propeller and all three of us were well and truly on the mud!

Being a regatta day the Royal Lymington Yacht Club soon

spotted our plight and the Commodore himself, Major Potter, very kindly came to our aid in a splendid husky Club boat and towed us, one after the other, safely into deep water. I must say it was blowing true to 'Lymington form' and as we all returned to the Club the Commodore jokingly told Father that he would claim the design for a new 8-metre as salvage.

My father's next boat after *Bryony* was the ex-12-metre *Margit IV*, designed by Sir Thomas Glenn-Coates and built by Robertson's of Sandbanks, and he named her *Lucella* as my mother's names were Lucy Ella. He did not own her for long and sold her, I believe, to a Norwegian.

He then acquired another 12-metre, *Cyra*, which had also been built by Robertson's and designed by his good friend Alfred Mylne. She was 27 tons and the smallest twelve ever built. He gave her a yawl rig and we had many happy seasons with her. Oddly enough, when recently in our kitchen, I spotted in a cupboard a cup which may have been used for mixing mint-sauce or for something even more humble; anyway, I removed it with a sense of deep nostalgia and it is now in a bookcase in this room. It is of good china, white with a blue and gilt rim and the old family racing flag, blue and red vertical, blue to the hoist. I believe my sister and I gave this service to Father.

I remember well a cruise we had to the West Country in *Cyra* when we were weather-bound at Poole for three days, lying off Brownsea Island (then owned by the van Raalte family). Anxious as ever to press on, Father decided to bend the dinghy's lug to the mizzen mast, set a staysail abaft the mast, and storm jib. Under this rig we fairly shot along to Portland but it rather displeased me as well as my sister Mary—a splendid and natural sailor—as we had on board my younger sister Ruth who was never happy in hard weather. I sat her up to wind'ard in the cockpit so that she looked at the sea disappearing rather than coming at us and plied her with green apples which, it may not generally be known, is quite a good antidote for *mal de mer*.

It was said that Father quickly distressed my mother by sailing with her, to start with, in far too boisterous conditions and she was soon put right off sailing. She had a deep love for the country—a love that I too inherited—and so in this respect my dear parents went their different ways and Father attended all the British regattas alone when we were young.

My younger sister Ruth took after her mother and while she enjoyed sailing in normal weather she hated hard winds and had my full sympathy. For my part, all through a long and varied sailing life, I have loved every moment of fine sailing breezes in good summer weather, but openly confess that I get no pleasure whatsoever in sailing or racing in anything more than a one-reef breeze. I am referring, of course, to those days of large mainsails—in these days reefing the modern small mainsail hardly ever occurs. I have always felt that racing in the lighter conditions and in up to a good whole-sail breeze required more skill to win than hanging on to a tiller with two reefs and a cold sky.

In the same vein I used secretly to think that 'Fiddler' Payne was quite sensible, with his various 12 metres named *Vanity*, to stay at moorings when it blew hard.

A more appetising purchase loomed up and *Cyra* was sold to Colonel Hollway who had a place at Seaview. The Colonel also owned a nice little twin-screw motor cruiser named *Sigrid*, built by us in 1925 for Mr Fred Blake who was Commodore of the Lee-on-the-Solent Sailing Club and, having a game hip, hunted the local beagle pack on horse-back.

After this slight digression I must leave *Cyra* and revert to Father's later acquisition.

In 1900 we built a 33-ton cutter, *Flame*, for a Mr Cundell. It is often the case when a design is successful that the basic features are embodied in contemporary craft. In this case the 20-ton cutter *Ilex* built in 1899 was the prototype for *Flame* and the 47-ton cutter *Westwind* built in 1906 for a client in Buenos Aires, was a rather beamier third sister. All were lovely sea-boats and *Ilex* had a great many successful seasons in the hands of the Royal Engineer Yacht Club.

Flame had found her way to France before the First War and her keel had been used for bullets. I cannot remember how Father heard of her but I know he did not bother to see her or even ask someone else to do so; she was teak planked on oak frames and I presume he had enough faith in his craftsmen to risk a purchase blind.

I remember when she arrived and was hauled up in a building

shed how good she looked. He gave her a modern lead keel, removed all the cement and punchings from her bilge, and rigged her as a yawl with, in my view, far too large a mainsail. Her fittings below were of Sussex oak, a variety of that wonderful and most ornamental species that has the appearance of a shoal of whitebait in the grain.

Flame brought more fun to Father and his family than any of his previous yachts and, as his racing mate for many years, I remember we seemed always to be reefing which was a tedious job with a rectangular box-sectioned boom and eyelets and lacings as opposed to reef points or a roller boom.

One of her features was a fore-and-aft skylight seat over the ladies', or aft, cabin with its back-rest fore-and-aft and the skylight sashes opening underneath the seat. I believe I could write a little 'curtain raiser' around this particular object. It was frequented on race days by senior guests who may have had to hang on a little but who were never in the way.

I remember one particular episode connected with this seat; it was during Cowes Week of 1927, the year I became engaged. H.M.S. *Ramilles* was the guardship and my fiancée, her sister with her husband, and I went on board for the dance. I also noticed my friend C. A. Kershaw—then a lieutenant and, poor chap, officer of the watch that evening. To digress for a moment, it may be remembered how he, partnered by the great W. J. A. Davies, played the finest rugby one ever saw for the Navy and for England year after year; never were there two better halves in the game.

The dance was a good one and long after the liberty boats had ceased returning guests to shore we could not find my future wife's brother-in-law who eventually was unearthed from the gunroom. Our loyal deckhand was not to be found at the appointed place and as it was very late we expected that he had given us up. I climbed over the wall of the Custom's House and borrowed a dinghy from the Island Sailing Club to return to *Flame*.

The girls retired to the aft cabin while I slipped down to the saloon sideboard before joining my companion on that skylight seat. We yarned until the sun was coming up over Norris Castle and then turned in on our sofa-beds in the saloon. I doubt if we had more than three hours' sleep but we awoke as fresh as larks. When the girls

joined us for breakfast they complained how we had kept them
awake, adding "But we did enjoy your stories."

Flame had a good layout for her size with a comfortable forecastle
for four hands (we carried three). Just forward of the saloon were the
galley to port and Father's cabin to starboard; the saloon had two
good sofa-berths and at the aft end there was a companion to deck
which terminated below at a steerage berth to port and, to starboard,
a spacious toilet with door to vestibule and another to aft cabin;
Father's cabin also was 'completely plumbed'.

Apart from her rather excessive sail area my only other criticism
was her magnificent bronze tiller which, I believe, was Father's
delight and which Jim Taw, our splendid deckhand, spent hours in
cleaning. This thing swept the entire cockpit area and, with tiller
lines in use in a blow, the comfort of sitting in it was ruined. She
eventually had a wheel fitted, but not in our time, and what joy it
was to scheme out the working of that wheel.

Many interesting guests came on *Flame* both for racing and
cruising and I suspect that 'Uncle' Malden was there more often
than most. The other yachting 'uncle', Harry Vandervell, usually
had a sail in Cowes Week and I dare say many of his beautiful
coloured cine films were shot from *Flame*. One could ramble on about
those interesting guests, particularly those at the round the coast
regattas.

I remember during one Cowes Week that great naturalized
American yachtsman, Ducky Endt, giving my wife a recipe for a
nice bowl of roses on Christmas Day, which my readers might be
amused to try. The roses are cut in bud and, with sealing wax applied
to the end of the stems, are laid in a biscuit tin on layers of tissue
paper. The lid is taped round carefully to make it airtight and the
tin is then placed in a hole in the ground some two feet deep and
covered over with soil. On Christmas Eve, with any luck, your blooms
should be ready. Only about half of ours were as we did not seal the
tin sufficiently.

We won the first Morgan Cup race in *Flame*, starting and finishing
from the Royal Thames Yacht Club signal station on Ryde pier.
Our crew were a rather mixed lot, but I remember we had my
cousin Roy Lapthorn who was a very good amateur sailor and owned
a pretty little Fife cutter, William McC. Meek of Lloyds who was a

D

fine heavyweight and splendid on the mainsheet, Rex Curtis of
Hill Head, next door to Lee-on-the-Solent, who was a splendid
dinghy sailor, and one or two more whom I fear I've forgotten.

I believe that the entry was the greatest in tonnage in the history
of this race sponsored by the Royal Ocean Racing Club, as one sizeable yacht was the equal of ten or so of those of today. The fleet
included the schooners *Lamorna* and *Suzanne*, the ketches *Sylvia*,
Kathleen, and *Dawn Star*, the latter owned by Mr J. J. Morgan, the
donor, and several others. Our private rival was the little bald-
headed cutter *Neith* owned by Sidney Houghton who, with his quite
small son, had crossed the Atlantic the year before.

On the whole the wind was light all the way out, but we had a
nice breeze on the way back next morning. As we passed the Needles
outward bound Rex Curtis told me he had never been out of the
Solent before and was so elated that he had to lie down on deck to
calm down. Many of the larger craft were out ahead, our little rival
was nicely astern and *Suzanne* was well out on our weather bow.

We all went below to tea leaving our skipper, Jack Grist, at the
helm with our deckhand Nobby Connor. It seemed that the wind
was, if anything, dropping and we discussed tactics over tea. It was
Father's wise decision at that moment that virtually gave us the race,
but before I describe our strategy I should mention that Grist
suddenly yelled, "On deck gentlemen—quick."

We scrambled up the companion and out ahead was quite a
phenomenon. A sharply defined straight white line with a heavy
black covering over it—obviously a thundery squall—was approaching. Father ordered us to let all sheets fly and within seconds it
struck us, fortunately dead ahead. The wind was gale force, the sea
was flat, and the thunder was right over us; it left us as fast as it had
come, lasting only ten minutes or so, and we all tumbled down to
finish our tea after a good look round. *Suzanne* appeared on our beam
to leeward of us having been wiped off her course and we sailed by
some of her deck gear, lifebuoys, cushions, etc. Looking astern we
couldn't see *Neith* in the haze.

Apparently the Sunday papers next day described this freak squall
as striking the coast along a sector from Dungeness to Portland Bill.
Many mothers and nannies had to fly to their charges but fortunately no casualties were reported.

By now the wind had almost gone so we decided to embark upon our little gamble in the knowledge that the ebb tide would set in some three hours later. We hauled up on our course well to the east and, as it proved, it was the right decision. We were surprised that none of the others made this move, but I put it down to the fact that many had professional skippers aboard who love their compass course to a destination regardless of the elements.

We lay up to Barfleur and by midnight there was just a whisper of wind and I was beginning to feel a trifle elated. At dawn we just managed to edge round the east of the Cherbourg breakwater and by the time we reached the west end there were our rivals all kedged and lifeless. It was amusing to converse with several of them including Sir Howard Frank in *Lamorna* wearing a resplendent dressing gown. Some, in fact, were very surprised to see us, the more so as we squared up on our course for Dunnose! I remember I turned in, suggesting they should wake me at noon but, always a good sleeper, they left me until I awoke at 4 p.m. with very little of the race left.

We crossed the line, lowered sail and found a berth for the night and were dining at the Signal Station before we heard the next finishing gun. As the meal progressed so the guns continued which made it all the more pleasant!

As we returned to Gosport next morning and passed the yachts moored up in the tier off the yard, Alf Jones, our Devonian shipwright chargehand, had mustered the chaps to give the Guv'nor a rousing cheer, a thing I doubt would ever happen in these days. Then, it was the foremen who ran the yards and not the shop stewards.

The Royal Thames had its first Signal Station on Stokes Bay pier and the racing from there was probably the best in the Solent but service requirements drove them over to Ryde. When Commodore Rostrum of the Cunard suggested the use of Stokes Bay pier and tenders to clip some two hours off the time from Southampton to London, it seemed a good idea.

Many, I remember, preferred racing from Ryde rather than Cowes but I believe the courses from the Royal Albert at Southsea are the best in the Solent and for smaller craft I prefer Bembridge every time.

For a few years we enjoyed the revival of the Anglo-Swiss races from Southsea, with the respective teams racing in Swallow class boats and I am sure we were all very surprised at the first-class handling shown by our guests, particularly as the conditions were so completely different to those on their Lake Thun—they all seemed to hail from the Thunersee Yachtklub. When at a dinner before the races I explained that Portsmouth was an island and that where the sailing took place the conditions were very different to their lake, their spokesman in his reply referred to Switzerland as 'an island, but surrounded by mountains'. I also remember at that dinner we were discussing the advent of the 5·5-metre class and one fellow was not too good with his English; his friend turned to him translating 'funf comma funf' and I thought that had I owned one it would have made a good name for her.

Father entered *Flame* for the Fastnet race in 1933, mainly because the entry list was very small and at least three American boats had entered. It was a light-weather race and we were fortunate enough to have Bobby Somerset as navigator. He and I took a watch each.

We started from Ryde in very light conditions which prevailed for two days. As we were shaping up for Portland from the Needles the brothers Olin and Rod Stephens were a few cables ahead of us and as we were overhauling them we tried to keep to leeward; every time we did so they politely bore away so eventually we passed on their weather and Father shouted through a megaphone that theirs was 'a very clever boat' which they acknowledged with a wave. This, of course, was *Dorade* in which they had won the trans-atlantic race that year and which was the forerunner of a great fleet of offshore racers to follow. Without doubt Olin is the world's most accomplished sailing yacht designer today and Rod is 'out on his own' as a great assistant to any designer and as an offshore sailing man.

On this occasion they were setting a rig in the fore triangle that I had never seen before and once only since on Freddy Last's old 12-metre *Noreen* which was designed by Anker and built in Norway in 1917. The rig consisted of three overlapping headsails and, as we were on a very close reach, they were all standing well.

We were first boat at the Bill and a little later the flood started and the wind dropped, so we bent on rope after rope and kedged. Later we heard that *Dorade* and others had not kedged so soon and had drifted back a little.

It was a perfect summer's night and, while lying some six miles SW. of the Bill, I remember seeing the glow of the lights of Exeter and smelling new-mown hay. Dawn came and although we had taken in the kedge as the tide turned there was hardly any wind for most of the day. In the early morning, with a mirror-like sea and simply wonderful visibility over miles of beautiful coastline, we were passed by Major Jack Blake motoring back to the east in his auxiliary cutter *Hilbre* with his splendid paid hand. They told us that we were the first boat they had seen since leaving Dartmouth.

It took us all day to round Start Point and then we collected a nice true breeze that took us well round the Lizard and softened again as we were in Penzance Bay, I will not describe all the details of the rest of this race but will give a short account of it and of an unfortunate occurrence which led to our downfall.

As the old girl leaked a little in the tuck we used to pump out after tea each day and most unfortunately, after rounding the Longships, someone stowed the galvanized iron pump handle in the sail locker hard under the compass. This was a disaster that we did not know of until we sighted the Irish coastline next day.

During my watch below I heard Bobby saying, "Check a little more," several times and thought "Good, the wind is freeing us" and after our 'usual' which was Bovril with a dash of Scotch (and so like real mulligatawny soup) I took over from Bobby.

At dawn we could not recognize the distant land and after a great deal of checking Bobby pronounced that we were heading for Galley Head. This was a great disappointment and meant that we spent all day in pretty light wind reaching off the Baltimore coast, largely assisted by a fine balloon foresail that we had carried since the start. We rounded the Rock about 6 p.m. and converged with little *Dorade* on her course some two hours later. We knew then that that pump handle had lost us the race.

That night was uneventful except that I wished Bobby would not wear rope soled shoes and that he would not stump around on the balls of his feet. Next day the wind went round to the east and we had the best wind of the whole sail; at times it was really fresh and *Flame* was reaching at her fastest, but unfortunately it was getting thick and Bobby was worried that he might not see the white Coastguard building on the high land approaching Cape Cornwall. He went aloft several times and, sure enough, there was his marker looming through the haze.

Bobby was a fine navigator, a first-rate sailor, and there was no one nicer to sail with. He brought his own cook too, a splendid fellow who never turned his hand to anything else but his galley and THAT, I thought, was as it should be. One of his great variety of dishes was known as 'race-food' but I cannot give a recipe beyond mentioning that it was 'laced' with mushrooms, sultanas and an ever-changing variety of chopped meat.

We used to keep all our vegetables in the dinghy right aft but when the supply of green stuffs was exhausted we stowed the dinghy in its rightful position and Bobby made himself a skipping rope, taking much exercise abaft the mainsheet buffer. When I asked him what it was all in aid of he replied that he was going up to Balmoral the following week.

I should have mentioned at the outset that we had left the mizzen-mast ashore and, in the expectation of usual 'Fastnet weather' we had also eliminated the jib topsails to improve rating. This of course was a pity as things turned out.

We had a deal of fun and it was a very jolly party. I remember catching a garfish on a mackerel spinner and dangling it through the skylight over Stuart Clark's nose when he was well asleep. There were always amusing discussions between owner and navigator as to standing in to a headland or standing out to sea, particularly at eventide.

Coming back off the Cornish coast we had light wind and much haze and, in fact, fog off the Gribbin; here we stood in so close to check the tide that while listening for surf we saw it and went about.

Roy Lapthorn, a cousin and referred to earlier, was jolly good company in my watch and we spent many happy hours discussing this and that. Somehow at sea, with none of these wretched shore-going interruptions, the mind is clearer and people get to know more of one another.

There is little further to report on this rather pleasant race apart from one final incident. As we rounded the Nab Tower we pinned in the mainsheet two-blocks under its lee and as we filled hard on the freshening wind to shape for the finishing line at Ryde, the foot of the mainsail suddenly tore off the boom and started frapping and flogging; no one had moused the shackle of the out-haul slide and it must have been 'creeping' all the time during the race.

How we live and learn. It took us some twenty minutes to get the main off her and flake it down through the fore-hatch—I remember how that good cook watched us from his bunk—and another ten minutes to set the trysail; by that time we were uncomfortably near the Bullock Patch. Anyway, we felt it had been a splendid sail and *Flame* had played her part in boosting a poor British entry.

It was that year that we sailed up the Lynher river at the end of Plymouth regatta to dine with Bobby Somerset at Ince. He showed us his new store with much enthusiasm as he was about to purchase the American-built schooner *Nina* and bring her over next season.

This proved a bitter disappointment to him after owning the well-known deep-water cutter *Jolie Brise* with her easy sea-going action. He found *Nina*'s action so bad that he never brought her home. She was in fact a very clever design by Francis Herreshoff, built purely for offshore racing with no pretensions for sea-kindly habits; she had a remarkably flexible rig and was a fine powerful little ship, but she had hollow ends to a rather full mid-body resulting in a measure of 'hobby-horsing' under certain conditions of sea.

I last met Bobby when he came over to our Gosport yard in his yawl *Trenchemer* from Portugal to search for any useful items that might be available—winches, old sails, etc., that sometimes can be found. A year or so later he had that tragedy on the island of Rhodes and a gallant and charming fellow was taken from us.

We had a great many races in *Flame*, both round the buoys and passage racing, particularly down West as well as various Channel races. I remember one of the latter with a good party of guests including Chris Ratsey to whom I had become very attached. I liked his rather autocratic manner; he was a deep thinker and had a rare sense of humour.

We had for this race borrowed a specially large spinnaker—one from a 12-metre I believe—and when running towards Le Havre at night the halliard broke and the sail unfortunately became caught in our offset auxiliary engine propeller. It took ages to get it aboard and, being first boat at the time, it was distressing to see those astern coming up on us and some sail steadily past.

It was a lovely summer's night with a good moon and occasionally we heard the sound of the hunting horn coming from Mr Leigh Newton's yawl *Old Fox*. Somehow, to me, it was extremely satisfying although miles from its natural setting. Riding and sailing are pretty complementary and some of our best helmsmen and sportsmen, for example Isaac Bell—perhaps the greatest of all—Herman Andreae, Donald Muirhead, Sir Philip Hunloke and others have been masters of hounds.

We had, of course, our fill of races round the Island in all of my father's yachts except *Tammie* but in those days it was not the cavalcade of today.

In the earlier days at Cowes my sister and I used to implore Father to drop the hook as near to the Royal Yacht as would be polite. Loyalty in my family has been almost like a fever and I can never forget the thrill we had at seeing the then Prince of Wales and Princess Mary skipping on deck before breakfast or Their Majesties coming ashore in the superbly maintained steam barge with perfect enamel, perfect bright brass and with perfect precision. Her Majesty in her usual toque with umbrella or sunshade always sat aft to port so we knew exactly where to look.

In those days we always went over the side before breakfast, my sister in one complete dash from her cabin while my approach was more leisurely for many reasons, but as the years wore on our swimming took place elsewhere, usually in Osborne Bay.

Sometimes if we had a yacht on our hands for sale we would use it for Cowes and I think that of these the yawl *Namara* was the largest, being 102 tons. At that time I was quite a youngster and remember that Claude Graham-White had one of the earliest seaplanes he was to use in a race round Britain. He kept it on the Green beyond the Squadron where it was roped off and I never saw it flying. I think it was a 'marinized' Maurice Farman Shorthorn and it had 'Wake up England' painted on the nacelle. I remember straddling the sailcoat over *Namara*'s large boom and imagining that I was Graham-White.

Another yacht we used at Cowes was a steel-built 59-ton motor yacht named *Lou Pitchoun* built at Wivenhoe in 1910; this must have been in 1911 as I know that was the year we built the 19-metre *Norada* for Fred Milburn. *Lou Pitchoun*'s main vice was her tendency when lying at anchor to roll when anything went by and another is apparent from the following episode.

We left Cowes on the Sunday afternoon for Gosport for some reason or another and slept aboard that evening. On the Monday morning we were going over to Ryde for the start of Ryde Week and had breakfast en route. Father was to race aboard *Norada* that day and seeing her blowing along through Osborne Bay under her foresail from Cowes he told our skipper Bill Baker to go towards her and, as we closed, he took over the helm from Baker.

This yacht had a single screw Fay & Bowen American petrol engine and Father must have thought her propeller rotation was left handed as he came alongside at an acute angle, rang full astern and hit his latest creation almost bow on. Fred Milburn rushed up in his pyjamas exclaiming, "What the hell are you doing Charlie?" Father jumped aboard and the damage was examined; luckily *Norada* had only a 'greenstick fracture' of the sheer-strake and was slipped that evening, after the race, for quick repairs.

Norada had four owners up to 1948. After her brief life (1911–14) in the 19-metre class, which was limited to four yachts, and her return to the class during a short post-war revival when she was owned and raced by Sir Howard Frank, she was bought by Sir Victor Warrender, Bart. who installed an auxiliary motor and used her for cruising for some ten years. In 1949 she appeared in the Register under the port of Andros and thus she went the way of so many others. I think those four lovely 100 tonners *Corona*, *Mariquita*, *Norada*, and *Octavia* were among the nicest racing yachts of their size.

I seem to be going astern rather than ahead with my father's yachts but I must mention that in 1906–7 he owned a little 16-ton steam yacht named *Zouave* built by Hayes of Stony Stratford in 1898. She must have been Bill Baker's first little command. We used to visit Wootton Creek when the river was almost empty and one could drop the hook where ever one wished. It was gloriously quiet but was spoiled, I thought, by too many wasps.

Beaulieu River was another favourite haunt. It also was almost void of yachts and there were probably far more swans. I remember one birthday of mine in September when my mother produced a splendid cake and, cutting a good slice, requested me to take it to 'Mr' Baker. I suppose I must have been seven at the time.

Hamble river was equally lovely then. There were just the brothers Luke with their yard at Hamble with quite limited capacity and Moody's at Bursledon, also quite a small establishment. The river may have held a dozen or so medium to small yachts and for many years Mr Shenley's steam yacht, *Triad*, lay near the entrance off Warsash. The training ship *Mercury* was there as also was the Ratsey family's houseboat just above her with what I termed 'the gardens of Babylon' hanging gaily from her flat upper deck; these were wired baskets of geraniums, gypsophila and moss.

Sixty-two odd years on and here we are plagued with the problem of trying to find a space to moor up our boat.

During the First War, when boats were prohibited in the Solent, our annual blackberry picking visit to Lepe in the family launch gave way to going by motor-car. When going in the launch year after year accompanied by our nannie and the cox we used to fill a large wicker hamper with these blackberries which in the Beaulieu area are as strawberries around the Hamble.

This trip by car once caused rather a dicey meeting with a gentleman who was to be a future client and to whom I refer under Power Yachts. My Father never took half measures and drove the Sunbeam touring car right up to the hedge which had had our autumn favours so often before. Picking commenced and all was well until a gentleman in a trilby hat and smoking a cigar arrived and, turning to Father, exclaimed, "What an earth are you doing on my land?" After due apology the car was removed to the lane and we were allowed to prosecute our market gardening, thanks to Mr Lionel de Rothschild's kindness.

After the last war Father, having sold *Flame*, decided to use the last of the little thirty-foot sloops that we had built in 1939 and 'put on ice' for him. He named her *Cinder* and, in his usual manner, gave her more lead on her keel. I had designed these boats to be lively in light winds and they had sufficient ballast and power of section to sail well in a breeze so I never thought that this addition to her keel was worth while.

He and my sister enjoyed a season or two in her and then a rather better boat came into the market, namely, *Sheba* which was owned by Captain Walker. He had bought her from Mr Addinsell for whom she was built and originally named *Tar Baby*; she was painted black and I shall refer to her again later. Father renamed her *Cinder*, painted her white and sold his first *Cinder* to Group Captain Haylock.

Father enjoyed a little time in her and kindly lent her to others, including my cousin Charles Blake who raced her a little for him, but it was noticeable that he spent many hours below and seldom emerged unless there was some racing to be seen. He used her only at weekends—never during the week—and in time my sister Mary, who looked after him so well and for so long, felt he might pass *Cinder* on to me. She must have shown great skill in choosing the moment to put this forward and I seem to remember the dear old gentleman concurring on the spot.

And so perhaps the greatest yacht designer of all decided to haul down his flag.

Before touching on my own activities I must refer to those of my uncles. Ben had quite a string of yachts of which the first I believe was *Little Nell*. I have a faded photo of her somewhere and believe she was a yawl in the old tradition with straight stem and long counter. Subsequently he owned the ex-8-metre *Endrick* and gave her a fine whale-backed coach-roof and, later, a small engine. He retained her racing gunter rig but gave her two headsails and she was a really slippery cruiser in which he usually took day sails.

He then acquired a splendid little yacht which was his great joy; this was the 16-ton cutter *Maeve* built by Arthur Payne of Southampton in 1907. This was the first of his boats in which I frequently sailed with him and, of course, those were proper white flannel days.

His paid hand was one Taffer Williams, a deaf-mute but a cracking good sailor; oddly enough when Taffer was in the forecastle a bang on the deck with the flat of the hand would bring him out as lithe as a cat.

Taffer had twelve children at the time my mother founded the Gosport Mothercraft Club and when the thirteenth child arrived Mrs Williams came to the Club to learn how to care for babies, bringing the child with her!

Ben married rather late in life (1909) and I cannot remember how long he kept *Maeve* but I think he married while he still had her. Later he owned one of the sweetest little yachts ever designed, *Mimosa III*, built by Herreshoff at Bristol, R.I., in 1904 and 15 tons. As he was getting on and was never blessed with too much energy Father designed a new sail plan for her—a sloop with self-sheeting foresail but retaining her bald-headed gaff mainsail. I remember on my first sail in her at the warning 'ready about' there was nothing to jump to but the runners. I think she was too fast for him at his age and later she was bought by Sir Fisher Dilke . . . perhaps I should have taken her on.

Ben's last boat was a miserable box of a thing whose name I shall not disclose. None of us knew why he had bought her; she was a poor attempt at a 50/50 with a small cutter rig and a Kelvin petrol-paraffin motor.

My Uncle Arthur was very fond of racing but was not too strong and he suffered rather a lot of illness in the more active time of his life. He owned one of the little family class dinghies referred to elsewhere and also one of the 16-ft Lee-on-the-Solent One-Designs in which he loved his racing, but it was not until we brought our 8-metre back from the Clyde that his real sailing life started. He and Father shared *Sagitta* but Arthur sailed her far more as Father was usually too busy and for a number of years *Sagitta* was Arthur's 'summer'. He also enjoyed racing in our 6-metre *Rose* around 1922 but it must have been then that he was not too well as I remember crewing my father in her very often.

Those were good days with names like *Jean*, *Freesia*, *Patience*, *Caryl*, *Flia*, etc., to cogitate over.

Thus it may be seen that I had plenty of sailing in family and clients' boats before I married in 1928 and bought the first of my own boats. This was *Tammie* owned all those years before by Father which I bought back from Colin Ratsey. He by then was one of our up-and-coming helmsmen before he deserted us almost totally for the States.

She was Bermudian rigged and needless to say had a fine wardrobe of sails but her solid Norway spruce mast did not please me; this I was able to change fairly quickly as, fortunately for me, an 8-metre had carried one away and I was able to acquire part of it from under-writers to our mutual advantage. I had Colin's white sails kutch-tanned but did little else for the first few seasons.

It was wonderful owning such a real little character. The saloon oil lamp was still there and so was the lack of headroom. Among the assorted items left by the late owner was a fine, albeit rusty, carving knife that I have to this day. It is real good steel—none of this stain-less stuff—with a dark bone handle and foolishly, when cutting up a salmon, I used to hit it with a small hammer and the handle was beginning to turn up away from the blade. It is now never used for such ignominious tasks and is reserved for the Sunday joint. After a season or two I took the plunge and gave *Tammie* a cabin-top but perhaps I made a mistake in using rather heavy teak coamings where mahogany would have saved that little extra top-weight. I also had canvas laid properly over her old decks and this and the cabin-top decks were painted a non-slip pleasing shade of green. This was before the days of non-slip paint and I used sand and a pepper castor before applying the last coat; this lasted for years.

By fitting the cabin-top I reduced the length of the cockpit by some three feet and used this extra space below for a good little galley to port and hanging cupboard to starboard. The following winter I gave her a good new engine. When I bought her I had her repainted to her original black topsides with green bottom in harmony with her decks; her metal tiller was canvassed over and painted white and, in all, she was a very smart and functional little ship.

Although only having the modest draught of 4·7 ft her beam was 9·5 ft and she went to windward well, particularly in medium-light weather and was a grand little sea boat.

During my many years of ownership I changed the sail plan twice. Firstly I shortened both bowsprit and boom but retained jib topsails to the masthead. Her new mainsail, cut properly on the diagonal, was loose-footed and being cut fairly flat one could regulate its flow by the outhaul. I adopted a splendid long-rope jib topsail with fair overlap and cut well up at the foot; it sheeted right aft and we must have sailed many miles with it set, particularly in medium to light weather. I also fitted a small wishbone bumpkin to take a standing topmost backstay and new runner slides on tracks which could be set up extra hard (when desired) by tackle and winch.

We relied all those years on a hand-bearing compass which fitted into sockets port and starboard at the fore end of cockpit and our only other 'aids' were a log and lead-line. When we changed to electric lighting with the new engine we kept the gimballed saloon oil lamp as it gave a 'warming' glow to the cockpit at night.

The second change of sail plan was inspired by a conversion we did for Miles Wyatt and his brother, from cutter to sloop rig, to their little yacht *Freedom*. I decided to do the same but for balance and to save shifting the mast I retained a very short bowsprit and, since she was due for a new mainsail, I adopted the orthodox foot with hanks to a rectangular box section boom. I suspect that ex-8-metre mast and this boom are still in service today. By a strange coincidence her present owner is a near neighbour of mine.

When Mr 'Bill' Stephenson was Commodore of the Royal Albert Y.C., he kindly gave a little trophy for evening races once a week throughout the season and in its first year it was won by Major Jack Blake (who later was Master of the Hambledon Hunt) and we were second. The evening turn-out was an average of five or six little cruisers and we had good fun.

Space does not allow me to dwell too long on our many races and cruises in *Tammie* but I will tell of one or two of the ones I particularly recall.

In her many races round the Island (we have five or six tankards) her most strenuous was that of 1933 when it blew a near SW. gale. We had a slashing sail down to the Needles and before we reached the Warden Ledge I warned my crew as to what was ahead but they all agreed to stick it out.

A sizeable yawl was returning with broken bowsprit, another yacht was aground in Alum Bay and with the strong ebb the sea at the Bridge was alarming. Our cockpit was rather shallow and, in these very steep seas, one had the sense of being left behind and I remember holding my wife on several occasions. At the buoy I decided to stay her round rather than risk a gybe and by this time the water was up to the sofa seats and there was a vile smell of petrol.

Apart from bilge pumping we had little else to do until rounding St Catherine's, and that leg of the course was pretty nasty, but when we were in Sandown Bay with smoother water and blessed with sudden sunshine all was well. We found the petrol smell was caused by the tank having too short a vent pipe which, with a nearly full tank, had been allowing petrol to escape in the big seaway off the Needles.

As we reached the Bembridge Ledge my father was running a trial with the new ketch *Saharet* which we had just built for Wood-bury Parsons who was on board with him. Father picked up a megaphone and shouted, "Don't break her up my boy."

We had a hard turn to finish, against the tide but in smoother water, crossing the line around 6 p.m. and after a square-up we went ashore to sign our declaration. Finding the Island Club nearly deserted and with no hot soup as per instructions we dined at the Gloster where the winner, Ike Bell, was at the next table. He had recently acquired the nice Fife cutter *Rosemary* and, with rather scanty opposition in those days, he was cleaning up the class which whet his appetite for the sport of yachting.

Ike Bell was a distinguished master of hounds but unfortunately a nasty polo accident caused him to give up hunting. He ended his great hunting career from his charming place, Castle Hill, Shaftesbury, when he was Master of the South and West Wilts.

Reverting to that dinner, among his guests was a lady who shall be nameless and who had dined rather well. She was describing to Ike how her husband was to sail a match race to Hanko, Norway, having been challenged by another prominent yachtsman. She went on to say that he was fitting an enormous water tank under the saloon table, adding that she couldn't think why as he never drank water and never washed.

While on the subject of Isaak Bell I must digress for a moment from family craft and tell the story of *Foxhound* and *Bloodhound*.

Bell decided to build an offshore racer but his first wish was that he wanted his yacht to be good to look at and not necessarily built entirely to R.O.R.C. rules of that time. The result was the 33-ton cutter *Foxhound* which we built in 1935. She was more to the international rule, rating 12 metres, and her R.O.R.C. rating was 43·40 ft. She was a very successful boat and, when Comte Georges de Gasquet-James wanted to buy her, Ike agreed and decided to build an almost similar yacht which worked out at precisely one Thameston larger and was still of 12-metres rating. This was the celebrated *Bloodhound*, without doubt my father's best offshore racer.

By this time Ike was 'right in the money' and in one year he won nearly every major R.O.R.C. prize. It was at the conclusion of the La Rochelle race, which he had won, that he was called on to speak at the dinner. In his speech he said that he felt he should not have signed his declaration having had two engines installed; one ran on milk and the other on gin. He was referring to two members of his crew for that race, namely Rod Stephens and Ducky Endt.

Ike was one of the most gracious and charming sportsmen we ever knew.

Bloodhound was later owned for many seasons by the late Sir Miles Wyatt, Admiral of the Royal Ocean Racing Club, who sailed her with considerable success in both British and American waters. His trophy, the Admiral's Cup, for competition between international teams, has now become second only to the America's Cup.

My father would have been very proud had he known that *Bloodhound* was also later owned by Her Majesty the Queen and H.R.H. Prince Philip. I was privileged to refer to this subject when meeting Her Majesty one Sunday at Romsey Abbey and to hear her gracious reply of, "Yes, isn't it exciting now the children are growing up."

One year my wife and I took *Tammie* to the West Country or rather, she took us. My cousin Charles Blake was with us; he and his two brothers often sailed with us in *Tammie*.

When going to the West in smallish craft the only real hazard is Portland Bill although St Albans race can be nearly as trying. On this occasion our timing at the Bill was all wrong and we were rounding on the last of the flood with next to no wind. A fisherman was tending his lobster pots off Church Hope Cove and as we passed him he replied to our question about the Race without looking up and simply said, "Summer weather." The wind fell away so we started up our unreliable two-cylinder motor, which usually only ran on one, and could hardly stem the tide; in fact, after running a good two hours the Bill was still abeam some five miles distant.

Our destination was Brixham and it was near three o'clock but as the tide turned a nice breeze sprang up and all seemed well. After an hour or so the wind began to freshen up and expensive noises came from below. With wind over tide a nasty sea was building up and, thinking that we should get smoother water inshore, I decided to make for Exmouth where we had never entered before. Although it was smoother, the nearer we got to the land the more the wind headed us and we had to tack several times before making Exmouth. With the hard wind in our faces and the unreliable engine running, we fumbled our way in with the aid of a torch and the Pilot's Guide to the English Channel.

We dropped the hook in what I thought would be the right spot and cogitated a little on 'the timing round Portland Bill'.

6. FAMILY CRAFT. *Flame* with cutter rig racing at Cowes.

7. FAMILY CRAFT. *Deb*, with the author and his sister, Mary.

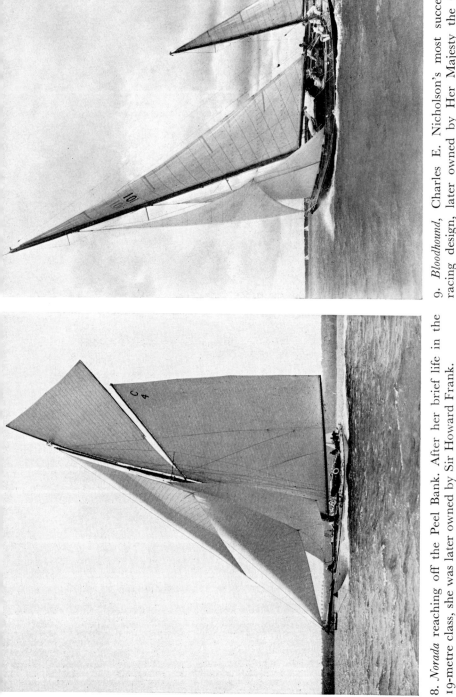

8. *Norada* reaching off the Peel Bank. After her brief life in the 19-metre class, she was later owned by Sir Howard Frank.

9. *Bloodhound*, Charles E. Nicholson's most successful ocean racing design, later owned by Her Majesty the Queen and H.R.H. Prince Philip.

Next day Charles left us to join our doctor at Dartmouth on his Bristol Channel pilot cutter *Seafarer*. The Harbour Master requested us to move under The Warren off Starcross and I told him we would do so the moment my brother-in-law arrived—we had been waiting a long time for him.

David, an accountant, duly arrived in his city suiting and I explained to him that we had to move. I started the motor, hauled up the anchor and told David to let go again when we found our next berth. When I did so he unfortunately slipped and went over with the anchor. I rushed forward remembering that he couldn't swim and yelled to Mary to stop the engine and get the dinghy alongside. The tide was ebbing at high speed and luckily he emerged bottom-up on the port bow yelling my name once. I dived in and got him to the bobstay, thence to the bowsprit shrouds and then into the dinghy and on board. He was half and half and we tipped the water out of him, gave him Bovril, whisky and aspirins and put him in my berth in the saloon. I slept in the forecastle.

He must have been knocked out by the fluke of the anchor which luckily did not get him in the eye and apart from a bruised nose he was as right as rain next morning. I made him promise to learn to swim, but he never did.

Following the theory that after a crash the pilot should get in the air again as soon as possible, we took him for a hard sail round Start Point and back to Dartmouth and our friends in *Seafarer*. Next evening they gave us a splendid dinner and were so keen to receive us well that we saw a hand whipping newspaper hurriedly off the saloon floor, which had evidently been scrubbed for our benefit.

The next day we had a fine catch of mackerel off Prawle Point so invited them to join us that evening. It was perfect weather so we had a meal under way running up the Dart by moonlight under motor. Small, fresh split mackerel were passed up and much enjoyed. David had met our friends before and he and the doctor's wife were rowing about in the dinghy; as the tide was ebbing we decided to leave them to it and return to our berth off Kingswear.

Charles Blake dealt with the anchor, so we thought, and after the arrival of the dinghy we turned in. Later my wife had a hunch that we were dragging, so I shot up and saw riding lights slipping past; how she sensed this I never knew but thank Heaven she did. I veered

E

about another shackle of chain and all was well. On retiring again I remembered it was near low water when Charles 'thought' we were anchored and I prayed that it would not be foul in the morning. All was well in spite of all the other moorings, Dart steamers, etc., and when we all met ashore after breakfast dear Charles was more than apologetic.

One morning at that delightful place we sighted Fred Milburn rowing toward us to the distress of Mary who was cooking the breakfast. We had recently built his 50-ton cutter *Kyloe* and she carried this little easy-rowing dinghy that he much enjoyed. As my sister Mary had christened his first yacht, the schooner *Norlander* in 1905, so *Kyloe* was christened in 1932 by our niece, my sister Ruth's eldest daughter.

This is the problem in writing about boats—one leads to another and causes me to to digress once more from family craft.

Milburn called *Kyloe* his 'piebald' yacht as she was built of quite a variety of woods. Her planking was teak, her decks yellow pine and her deck trim was of mahogany; she had oak floors and cedar internal fittings with spruce panelling. None of her cupboards was lined as he liked to see her structure.

It is a fact that he built her with the sole object of giving his skipper an interest as he was worried when Captain Clark had nothing to do.

As he sat down in *Tammie*'s cockpit he quietly told us that he wanted to see how we fitted in! We returned his rather early call at about 11.30 a.m., and as he left he handed a white box to my wife, marked 'Epsom Salts', which we found were excellent peppermints. She became known as his 'peppermint queen' and received a box from him every Christmas until he died.

The years rolled by and we had several pleasant holidays at a house at Sandbanks or Canford Cliffs with *Tammie*, having great fun with the children in the lovely district with its miles of waterways. Our last was the year war was declared when Father was down there enjoying his last few weeks with *Flame*. I have already told how Father made for Gosport while I decided to lay up *Tammie* with my good friend Myles at the Sandbanks Yacht Company.

In '38 we had built a rather husky little sloop for Mr Gordon Selfridge Junior; a boat after my own heart with a waterline of 27 ft

6 in which after many hours of 'bottom-gazing' and discussion we assessed as the ideal length for single-handed sailing.

He had been taught dinghy sailing at Portchester in the little 'Ducks' and, having become very keen to own an able little cruiser, Commander 'Bill' Hammond sent him over to me. Selfridge told me he was tired of flying as it was becoming too fast. We both studied everything to do with this boat but I did not find any appeal in the name he gave her, *So What*.

During her first season a charming couple came to see me. Mr Jack Addinsell told me that his wife wanted to build a boat on the lines of *So What* but that he insisted on all teak (*So What* was mahogany planked), and wished the accommodation to be altered considerably. The result was the little auxiliary sloop *Tar Baby* which the Addinsells hardly used before war came.

During the war both yachts were laid up at Gosport. *So What* was bombed but her gear in store was safe; *Tar Baby* was not lost but her gear was destroyed. Neither of their owners wanted to commission again so when Captain Walker wished to buy *Tar Baby* he commissioned her by arrangement with the respective owners with *So What*'s gear.

He named her *Sheba* but unfortunately both Walker and his wife found that they were not immune from *mal de mer* and they decided to sell her. This was when I advised Father to buy her and how I wished that he could have been a little younger to enjoy what was, to me, the best little 10-tonner on the high seas. She had teak on oak frames and timbers, teak decks, teak flooring and teak panelling and all deck trim—what a boat and at that time no more than £2,000!

When my father gave her to me she was painted white and named *Cinder*. During my ownership I repainted her black and reverted to her original name of *Tar Baby*. Thus both my own boats were black and, with what was known in our family as 'the twenty-five bob gold line', they certainly looked far better than white, or any other colour. It is an old sailor's saying that 'a black ship never goes to hell', and I remember quoting this to Maldwin Drummond, chairman of the Sail Training Association Technical Committee, when we were designing the schooner *Sir Winston Churchill*.

We had our first season in *Tar Baby* under my ownership as she was originally arranged. Mrs Addinsell had her cabin forward with a small fore peak and sail locker and there was a 'loo' compartment between this and the saloon in which the owner had a comfortable sofa-berth to starboard. The saloon was far more spacious than that in most of her size as the table was offset to port with comfortable corner seats (just for Mr and Mrs Addinsell); galley aft to starboard, good stowage to port and hinged steps to cockpit. A folding 'root' berth over the table was fitted for an occasional sail with their son.

Our eldest son Michael never took to sailing. At his first Cowes Week in *Flame* his granny asked him how he had slept and he replied that he had had a tummy-ache in his throat. My wife and I whisked him home forthwith and, I fear, were not very popular in doing so. One cannot make a person a sailor and later little sorties that we attempted with him just proved that he was not one for the sea.

We retained that excellent offset saloon table—the sense of space was really exciting—but instead of the root bunk over the table we fitted a Pullman folding berth, which became my second son's berth, and a new single berth and folding cot forward. One thing we did find not so good as in *Tammie* was the galley to starboard—perhaps Mrs Addinsell was left-handed.

Tar Baby was the proper family man's boat and for some years was considered the 'queen of the river' lying as she did off Warsash under John Chamier's eye. It was noticeable as time went on that on Sunday evenings 'Bond Street Parade' as I called it, with everybody trundling up the river after the week-end, was quite something to watch. I must admit that 'cockpit gazing' can be jolly amusing and I have spent hours at it.

Now that we are approaching the times of not so long ago the memory is surprisingly dim but, so far as I can remember, we never cruised to the West in *Tar Baby* and, I suspect, the call of the fishing rod and the good country was getting hold of us. We did of course use her hard at week-ends and raced in the appropriate 'round the buoys' Solent occasions, the Round the Island, Nab Tower races and others and some of the best were from Cowes and Southsea. I remember too that being Commodore of the Royal Albert Y.C. for some ten years—and that was no sinecure—took much of my time.

I much enjoyed this office and the splendid backing that I received from a jolly good team of race officers and committee men. Above all I remember the fervent loyalty and great assistance of the late secretary, Captain Trevor Lean, who was virtually 'the Club'. He was splendid with the cadet members in summer, and in winter they did the pantomime, fish suppers and many things that young people enjoy.

Trevor never really grew up himself and within the Portsmouth Command it was refreshing to be guided by a popular senior Captain. His only vice was a bob or two on the horses, at which he was rather clever. I remember how he said I had overpaid in some quite trivial matter and, rather than refund to me the small amount, we decided to start a Club Fund with it, in absolute privacy; if it accrued—well, we'd just give it to the Club.

This tickled Trevor enormously and on Saturdays, as regular as clockwork, he would 'phone me at home to report the horses of his choice that week-end, naming the various meeting venues, the odds, those he had doubled up on (whatever that means) and always ending his summary with, "And jolly good luck, sir!" The next Saturday before describing his selections he would announce the state of the kitty.

He sailed with us quite a bit but, on regatta days, was racing with the youngsters in the whaler. Trevor Glanville and his twin brother Geoffrey were largely responsible for persuading me to take on as Commodore and, with their elder brother John, who relieved me when I retired, did much for that fine old Club.

The pendulum that swung so freely in the inter-war years, as a metronome, has been forced to lower its beat. The old club-house that I first knew with its croquet lawn, its card room and dining room disappeared in the last war. We merged with the old Portsmouth Corinthian Yacht Club, taking over their house, and that too has been disposed of. The revitalized Signal Station is now temporary 'head office' and I pray that this fine old Club will retain its identity for many years to come.

One hundred and six years ago saw its foundation at a meeting on September 21st, 1864, at the Portland Rooms, under the presidency of the Mayor of Portsmouth. In 1914 the Club Roll showed 292 members with a fleet of 58 yachts, having an aggregate of 5,976 tons. The Albert Cup, first competed for in 1865, was won in 1895 by King Edward VII with *Britannia*, and the following year it was carried off by the Kaiser with his schooner *Meteor*.

In the inter-war years the Commanders-in-Chief provided a sloop to act as committee boat to the south of the Hamilton Bank for starting the larger classes, a requirement which, unfortunately, no longer exists today.

To some extent a degree of parochialism has crept into the present Solent area yachting scene. Far fewer competitors visit the clubs' annual regattas and concentration is almost limited in these days to Cowes and the Hamble river area. Again the remarkably rapid development of offshore racing has had its impact on 'round the buoy' racing and, with the rat-race of life today and the sport confined to the week-ends only, it is not so easy to go in leisurely fashion to race at all those pleasant places as we used to do.

We decided to part with *Tar Baby* for a variety of reasons, one being that my son Christopher had sensibly elected to marry and so I lost my excellent and hard-working mate. I too had had the 'gipsy's warning', being advised to give up anything that could be termed strenuous, and after some thirty-eight sailing seasons in all manner of craft I sensed that my wife had had enough.

I sold the yacht to my old friend Commander Hector Dobbs who told me that she would be his last purchase. However, an owner once replied to my question as to why he changed his yacht almost every year, "You cannot do that with your wife," and this rather applied to Hector and *Tar Baby*.

She has since had two other owners and, although not of endurable fibre-glass construction, as Father said when he gave her to me, "She will outlast your great grandson." I expect she will.

5 *The great schooners*

The disastrous fire at our Gosport office in 1910, which I have mentioned earlier, destroyed most of the records of yachts built by William Camper in the first half of the nineteenth century. I have a record, however, of one notable yacht, *Anonyma*, which was one of four famous yachts of the Royal Yacht Squadron destined to end their days in the opium fleet.

Built in 1839 for Colonel the Hon. F. R. Greville, this 427-ton brig had a most ambitious sail plan which Lubbock in his book describes as 'lofty', and I doubt if any craft of her size carried more sail. Her portrait can be seen at the Maritime Museum at Greenwich. Colonel Greville sold her a year later and, in a matter of months, she was resold to Captain John Vaux of London. He intended to sail her himself but, on arrival at Bombay, he was persuaded to part with her for a very large sum and in 1842 she sailed on either the Bombay or Calcutta run with Jardine Matheson's house-flag at her main truck. She was lost with three other clippers in the typhoon off Swatow in 1858·

Of Benjamin Nicholson's great fleet of schooners a few that can be mentioned are: *Aline*, 216 tons, built in 1860; *Guinevere*, 304 tons (1868); *Elmina*, 344 tons (1874); *Chazalee*, 545 tons (1875); *Czarina*, 564 tons (his largest); *Waterwitch*, 159 tons (1888); and *Amphitrite*, 161 tons, his last schooner, built in 1899. As I write these notes the *Amphitrite* is nearly seventy-one years old and still in commission as a barquentine-rigged training-ship based at Port Grimaux in the Mediterranean.

Aline was built for Mr Charles Thelluson and varied from the

normal run of schooners as regards her rig. It was usual practice at
that time to give the masts an appreciable rake aft in the belief that
it gave more lift to the sails. *Aline's* masts were nearly upright and
her performance quickly dispelled the previous illusion. In the hands
of her able owner she proved a great success and was the type on
which many of the better-known schooners following her were
based.

She was owned some years later by H.M. King Edward VII when
Prince of Wales and in 1887 he raced her in the Royal Yacht Squadron regatta commemorating Her Majesty's jubilee.

I remember a print of yachts racing off The Kish in Dublin Bay
and some seven of the gamut including *Guinevere*, *Aline*, and *Bluebell*
were of my grandfather's build. This picture has, sadly, gone astray
but it is possible that my father may have presented it to some yacht
club.

Amphitrite had some fifteen owners and has been renamed four
times. To one owner, who used her as a mobile houseboat and wished
to do much work on her, we suggested that the removal and sale of
the lead keel would largely offset his expenditure. This was agreed
and he brought *Amphitrite* to Gosport from his base in the West
Country. We have recently been in touch with this gentleman in
view of *Amphitrite's* resuscitation and, with his approval, I feel that
one of his letters is worth quoting in part. He had not visited Gosport
since the war and it was on the pre-war area of our property that the
slipway and pub he refers to were located. He writes:

"We were aghast—no C and N slipways, where I remember the Js in
1925 and '30, but three sky-scrapers like multi-storeyed public lavatories
where the 'Thatched House' used to stand. When *Amphitrite* occupied
No. 1 slip the pub was most convenient for a midday pint and we referred
to it as the Bowsprit Arms. It had a particular charm on Saturday nights
when the full house had a regular contingent of chiefly retired music hall
'troupers' and, of course, pianists. On a fine moonlit night it was an
experience to sit quietly up by the knight-heads, looking down on to the
B.A., and to listen to the (first-class) 'Nellie Dean', 'Daisy Bell', etc.,
rolling out. Promptly at closing time a silence, then all hands joined in
that beautiful air, 'Haste ye back'."

All gone. Another thought has just occurred to me; behind the bar
and very well out of reach were suspended two broken champagne

bottle necks with gold foil and corks intact. I was assured from several sources that they launched *Endeavour* and *Endeavour II*.

He goes on in his letter as follows:

"Reverting to the slipping of *Amphitrite* at Gosport: your father took the keenest interest in the ship, very naturally, as it was he who was given the task of making her still faster after her first season in 1889. During the actual hauling out by winch I was ashore with my camera photographing the whole operation, and with me—very tense with interest—was 'Mister Charles'. When the ship was clear, and as the scrubbers went on, he turned to me and said in a low voice, 'I don't know how I dared to do it.' 'Do what sir?' 'Look, I raked the stern post to 45 degrees.' I had never heard of the two huge centre plates installed at, I presume, the same time... but I actually examined them, filled in, when the lead was removed.

Present-day yachtsmen would be astonished to know that her keel bolts were of Naval brass, as thick as my wrist, seven feet in length and in close-set groups of four!'

We fitted internal granite sets to give *Amphitrite* enough stability as a mobile houseboat but today, with her bold barquentine rig, I imagine she has much more internal ballast.

In those days we really had two separate yards at Gosport and the 'slipway' area referred to was almost self-contained as a repair yard. It was in that nice old part of the town where Trinity Church still stands and my grandfather's house should still be there (as a scheduled building of historical interest) had it not been demolished in error by the over-zealous town planners.

Those racing schooners thundering through Osborne Bay—that was my impression of them—were a wonderful sight to me as a youngster in the early twentieth century. The founder of that final schooner revival was in fact Kaiser Bill who originally owned the cutter *Thistle*. She was so well beaten by *Britannia* and *Valkyrie* that he got Watson to design him a 20-rater which was a failure and was given away to a relative.

His third venture was a different story. In 1896 Watson designed and Henderson's built the magnificent *Meteor II*, a cutter, but in a few years she was outclassed by *Sabyrita* and in 1901 he gave her to the Imperial Navy under the name *Orion*.

Meteor III was a schooner built in America in 1902 and many of her crew were British.

By 1904 *Meteor IV*, the great schooner of 400 tons, was built but she was not too successful. On one occasion during Cowes Regatta in 1912, when all her competitors were well reefed, she carried full sail and got out of hand when rounding the Warner lightship; her rudder was so far out of water that it was ineffective and her mainsheet could not be reached as it was belayed to leeward and was many feet below the water. Finally she sagged round before the wind and righted herself enough for the rudder to take effect.

After the first war, *Meteor IV* became the property of Mme V. Heriot, who renamed her *Ailée*.

The beautiful Herreshoff-designed schooner *Westward* was built for Mr A. S. Cochran who raced her in 1910 with great success, particularly at Kiel. She was later purchased by a German syndicate who bought up many costly yachts to provide sport for the Kaiser and was renamed *Hambourg II*.

Other famous boats racing in this great schooner class in the pre-1914 era included Herr Krupp's *Germania*, Major Cecil Whitaker's *Waterwitch*, *Cicely*, *Suzanne* (then German-owned), *Cetonia*, *Adela*, and the ketch *Cariad*.

Waterwitch, regrettably, was a failure and it was thought that her quarters were too full, causing bad wave form. Her owner approached my father, who advised him that he could not come into the picture until her designer, his old friend Bill Fife, had been consulted. He then suggested that a new hull was the only answer and that all existing gear and equipment from *Waterwitch* could be used in this hull.

Major Whitaker sportingly agreed to this proposal and the next season, 1913, *Margherita* emerged and I remember the trials of that longer, and slightly less beamy, lovely lady. 'Shrimp' Embling was her captain and he was due for a change of luck- always a trier, never crestfallen and a great little sportsman, he had picked a first-rate crew.

I think that *Margherita* was probably the fastest yacht ever built by my father in his long career. At Kiel regatta that year *Margherita* won five first prizes out of six starts racing against *Meteor*, *Germania*, and *Westward*. On the penultimate day of the regatta she carried away her fore topmast and, when back at anchor, the Kaiser—rowed by his officers—came alongside and suggested that they select a new spar in the dockyard so that they could race next day. This sporting gesture was accepted and by working overnight the spar was re-rigged in time for the last race, which she won.

Afterwards the Kaiser was again rowed alongside and was invited by Whitaker to come aboard. After the guests had been presented he took Father by the arm and walked forward to the foremast; pointing up with a sweeping gesture he exclaimed, "Not bad for made in Germany?" In the little chat that ensued Father praised many German skills and the Kaiser was pleased and grateful but said, "One thing we cannot yet do is to prevent babies being born." (1913!)

War 'I' saw the end of schooner racing and how grateful I feel for having been able to see its last chapter.

Margherita was purchased by Sir William Reardon Smith for conversion to a training ship for his shipping company; she was renamed *Davida*, given a three-masted rig and two diesel engines. Her owner impressed us all with his biblical quotations at which he was the equal of the aircraft pioneer Handley Page.

As a youngster one always remembers the spectacular and, when *Davida* was lying off the yard, it was decided to cut the old racing masts and let them go overboard; the steel bulwarks were protected and one always regretted that those two fine splashes went unrecorded.

This chapter would not be complete without mention of some other well-known schooners, their owners and stories connected with them. Those which I am now going to describe are, I think, of particular interest.

Auxiliary schooner 'Sylvana'

This fine schooner was built at Gosport in 1910 for Colonel Courtenay C. E. Morgan. She was 254 tons and had many owners and many names, including *Diane*, *Pays de France*, and *Orion*. In those days we employed the services of one Monsieur Billard of Havre who was our Courtier Maritime. I hardly remember him but we did a very fair business with him and on one occasion it was of rather a serious nature. When this yacht was named *Pays de France* and owned by the proprietor of the French journal *Le Matin* she suffered a bad explosion in the engine room. Billard called on us to assess the damage and my father and I went over—I was called in as Father knew nothing about machinery.

We crossed on a Sunday, staying at the little old Hotel l'Europe. On the Monday we all foregathered at the yacht store on the quayside; all the windows round the Basin de Commerce were shattered and the cost of their replacement must have been very large.

The cause of the explosion was the engineer smoking in a small engine room housing a petrol-starting paraffin-running auxiliary engine and a petrol generating set. There had been a large companion-skylight over the engine room. Luckily the engineer was unscathed but the whole of the companion was blown sky-high and the ensuing fire badly burned the mainsail, main boom and most of the gear in the adjacent sail cabin and bosun's locker. Much of the deck and deck gear over the engine space was also destroyed.

All was removed and laid out in this large quayside store. We were joined by numerous representatives of the owner and insurance assessors. The first lunch, I remember, started at noon. We were not back in the store before 4 p.m.

After the second day our damage assessment was concluded and Father and I went up to Paris. I remember we went to hear the new opera 'Harlequin' at the Opera House which was then the first building to be floodlit at night. It happened to be a gala night with everyone in full dress, while we were in day suits, mine a grey 'square-rig' suit, and wearing brown suede shoes. In such distinguished company we felt we had let Britain down.

This was the year the great French liner *Normandie* was commissioned and it was noticeable in many of the shops at Havre and indeed in Paris that many of the goods were styled 'à la Normandie'. As a youngster I was very impressed by the subtlety in blending art and commerce in the naming of all forms of household and domestic articles.

Before returning we dined two prominent French yacht captains at our hotel: one, the Merchant Service trained Captain Le Goiffre of *Pays de France*, and the other an ex-Naval officer and Captain of the S.Y. *Atmah*, of 1,746 tons, owned by the Baron Edmond de Rothschild. Father warned me that the start of the meal might be a trifle frigid and it was so. As time went on the barriers of distinction were brushed aside and after a most interesting and happy evening the two gentlemen departed together in a state of utter harmony.

Auxiliary Schooner 'Oceana'

This twin-screw auxiliary schooner of 206 tons, built at Cowes in 1880 and originally named *Thais*, was often at our Gosport yard for the winters around the early 1920s. Her owner, Captain R. Gordon Sillars, and his wife were good friends of my Uncle Ben. One rather unusual feature was that her auxiliary engines were of different horse-power but she was a vessel of great charm and character. She was later owned by Sir Charles Allom after he had sold *White Heather*, the 23-metre cutter, to Lord Waring and when he was Commodore of the Royal London Yacht Club for several years.

Allom being a great artist repainted *Oceana* a pleasing shade of slate-blue, and with her yards on the foremast she presented a fine picture. Later she was acquired by Lt.-Colonel J. Benett-Stanford who changed her topsides to a good shade of green and always laid up at our Southampton yard. He was a great personality and was usually accompanied by numerous charming young ladies and a leash of well-bred spaniels. He wore blue full-cut yachting suits of distinctive shades and used a thumbstick when coming ashore with his entourage.

One winter he arrived at the yard from his home on Salisbury Plain in a full gale in his very high and unstable Rolls coupé-buggy. Various modifications and estimates were discussed and he returned home stating that he would advise us later as to his decisions. Next day we received a telegram reading more or less as follows:

'Car capsized estimates accepted. Benett-Stanford.'

Auxiliary schooner 'Heartsease'

This grand old schooner of 224 tons was owned for many years by Sir Henry Seymour King, K.C.I.E. She was built in 1903 at Fay's yard and was later acquired by our firm in 1912 when starting our Southampton branch.

Sir Henry enjoyed many happy seasons cruising with his daughter and every May, so regularly that it became an institution, he dined my father on board off the Gosport yard. The dinner was always the same: consommé, chicken, strawberries and cream, and Krug. Father always returned to quote at breakfast next morning that Sir Henry, as usual when served with his strawberries, proclaimed, "God may have made as good a berry but NEVER a better berry."

The schooner's motif of the flower on the stemhead was ripe for improvement and I remember enjoying sketching a different hearts-ease for our painters one winter.

Sir Henry wore a fine beard and was of large stature; we provided special rings over his bath for easier exit but as the years rolled by he left the yachting scene. His daughter kindly left my father a set of lovely prints of Solent harbours but he never framed them; today they adorn our staircase and give a great deal of pleasure.

Auxiliary schooner 'Creole' (ex-'Vira')

Before leaving the field of schooners I must mention the sequence of three fine vessels and how the first influenced the sail plan of the other two.

In 1927 we were approached by Mr Alec Smith Cochran who was a very sick man and desired a large cruising auxiliary schooner with the minimum of crew. He had a suite at the Berkeley Hotel and, on the several occasions that I accompanied my father to visit him, I was impressed by the fact that when invited to smoke a cigarette one was expected to take a new amber holder as well. After one of these meetings Cochran agreed to adopt our proposal for a three-masted staysail rig having the advantage of most sails being self-sheeted thus reducing the crew to the minimum.

Thus the schooner *Vira*, as she was to be named, of 699 tons was laid down. Of composite construction she had double skin topsides to obtain a perfect finish and there was a stipulation that all deck fittings, where possible, should be of monel metal.

For a yacht of her size her bachelor owner's requirements were modest. The few cabins were spacious and the large dining saloon, with the entire bulkhead panelling and fixed furniture, were treated with the finest cedar veneers. This was a wonderful room.

The owner's stateroom and bathroom were fitted with sycamore veneered panels and furniture, and a guest's stateroom and bathroom, passage-way and lobby were of solid Cuban mahogany.

More Burma teak was used in the planking, decks, bulwarks, and superstructure of this yacht than in any in the history of the Firm.

When the time arrived for launching we were surprised to find that her sponsor was to be an elderly gentleman and, in fact, the christening bottle rebounded so freely off the copper sheathing that the foreman painter was called to apply a diamond cut to it.

A few days after launching the masts were stepped and Cochran visited the yard. As mentioned, he was in poor health and rather alarmed at the height of these masts and it was agreed to shorten them by 15 ft. It may be appreciated that removing these masts and restepping was quite an operation and on another visit the owner requested a further reduction in height to be made and another 15 ft was removed, making a total reduction of 30 ft in sail hoist.

After the usual trials the yacht left for the Mediterranean to be joined there by her owner and, within weeks, he cabled us complaining that she was most uncomfortable in a seaway. He was using her as a full power yacht running on both her auxiliary engines and, with her lead keel of some 90 tons, she was of course over ballasted under these conditions and her action was far too quick in a heavy sea. We cabled back suggesting the removal of a good proportion of lead and it was only some years later that we discovered that the yard in question had robbed him by removing far more than we recommended. Unfortunately Cochran died at about this time.

Vira was later bought by Major E. W. Pope and re-named *Creole* after his previous steam yacht. He retained her reduced sail plan and, to my personal disappointment, had the lovely veneers painted over. She lay on moorings off Hythe in Southampton Water and, as much of her passaging was across to the Royal Yacht Squadron, she was humorously dubbed, 'Pope's Ferry'.

Later this fine schooner was purchased by Sir Connop Guthrie. I remember meeting him with his friend Tom Thornycroft on his first visit to our Gosport yard and the look of immense pleasure on my father's face when Sir Connop agreed to put back the originally designed sail plan. From then on, and for the first time, this schooner was seen as she was designed and her owner enjoyed many seasons of extended cruising in her.

During the war she was taken over by the Admiralty and sent up to Scotland from our Southampton yard for conversion for depolarizing work on the Equator in connection with magnetic mines. She was gutted out and equipped with a large number of high-powered generators but due to the development of de-gaussing she was never used. She was given the ingenious name of *Magic Circle* and, strange to relate, her three fine spruce masts were 'lost' during this adventure.

Fortunately her Chief Officer was a yachting man and when plastic armour was being fitted to her superstructure he saw that it was hung rather than bolted.

After the war the Admiralty rightly returned all requisitioned yachts 'to whence they came' and I remember one afternoon running down Southampton Water in a yard launch with my father to greet *Creole* on her return from the north. I can only recall one small incident and that, oddly, was meeting the cook, who in peace-time was Lord Glentanar's chef, and enjoying perfectly-baked bread for tea.

Sir Connop had recently died and his family did not wish to use *Creole* any more so my Firm purchased her. She was eventually sold to the Imperial Shipping Investment Company and removed to Germany where she was re-rigged to her original plan, re-engined and had her accommodation drastically modified.

In our Firm and family we always regarded *Creole* as Father's sequel to Grandfather's *Czarina*.

Auxiliary Schooner 'Ailée'

The next of these three-masted schooners was *Ailée*, of 496 tons, built in 1928 for Madame Virginie Heriot. She must have been one of the finest sailors in France and was a popular member of the international racing classes, in the 6-metres in particular. Unlike *Creole*, *Ailée* was of steel construction and carried a rather different staysail rig; she was a beautiful cruising yacht and gave her charming owner a deal of pleasure for many years. After Mme Heriot's death *Ailée* was given to the *Ecole Navale* at Brest.

Auxiliary schooner 'Sonia II'

Lastly, in 1931 Miss M. Betty Carstairs placed her order for *Sonia II*, also of steel construction and 450 tons. When building, plans were made to seek treasure off the Cocos Island and so for ocean voyaging it was decided to give her an inner and outer jib—it was felt to be more fitting to set these sails over a cut-water bow—and she certainly was a striking and lovely ship. It is an interesting fact that her design was the basis of the Sail Training Association's *Sir Winston Churchill* built thirty-four years later.

I remember the occasion of *Sonia's* launch and the near late arrival

10. *Czarina*, 564 tons.
Benjamin Nicholson's
largest steam auxil-
iary topsail schooner.

11. *Margherita*, probably Charles E. Nicholson's fastest schooner.

of Sir Malcolm and Lady Campbell who were among her guests and from whom, as a christening present, she received a box of cigars. Mr Scott Payne was also there. It may be remembered that he started his career as office boy to the flying-boat pioneer, Noel Pemberton Billing, and steadily worked his way up the organization, eventually taking it over as the Supermarine Company.

Miss Carstairs was very much to the fore in motor-boat racing so it was not unnatural that several of that fraternity should join this very gay party. Lunch on board, as soon as *Sonia* was launched, was the order of the day and I remember that the affair went on until after tea-time!

Sonia's accommodation was admirable and she was among the few yachts ever to be equipped with a small gymnasium with rowing and cycling machines and other gymnastic devices.

I remember my wife and I were aboard *Sonia* in Southampton Water at the time Miss Carstairs was competing for the Detroit News Trophy. We and others were watching the race from the launch. Unfortunately she capsized and both she and her mechanic, Joe, seemed to be under the water for a terribly long time. When they emerged rescue craft were standing by and we returned to *Sonia* and greeted Miss Carstairs and her mechanic at the gangway. She immediately gave her wrist watch to a friend to put in oil and was far more concerned for the welfare of Joe than for herself.

We never heard if the treasure hunt took place but later Miss Carstairs bought an island in the Bahamas and one at least of *Sonia*'s officers acted as agent.

To the best of my memory I believe we built only one schooner after *Sonia* and that was *Erix* of 89 tons for the Count Jean de Vogue in 1965. She was designed specifically for world cruising with a rig specially suited to the desires of her owner and she could be described, in fact, as a picture ship.

I believe the last big schooner race in British waters was a match between *Ailée* and *Sonia*. My father presented a trophy for the match starting off Ryde pier to Le Havre Light and back and deputed me to run up to Town and find a fitting prize. This became a nightmare as time went by and the taxi-meter mounted up. I had been to some of the best West End shops and, after some hours, I saw exactly what I wanted in the window of that well-known Danish silversmith in

F

Bond Street. Stopping the taxi, as one could in those days, I bought a superb silver dish, or shallow bowl, with a mermaid peeping over each handle. My selection was greatly admired at the office and I must say it seemed eminently suitable for two great sailing ladies.

Various guests joined each yacht and among those in *Ailée* was that fine Solent helmsman and friend of Mme Heriot, Joe Hannen. Among those in *Sonia* were Sir Malcolm Campbell and Sir Charles Allom.

Nearing the finish *Ailée* was comfortably ahead and as they were standing in to Dunnose, during breakfast, Hannen heard sounds of going about. He rushed up on deck to advise the captain to stand on inshore to check the tide and that piece of local knowledge ensured victory for *Ailée*.

Mme Heriot was so delighted with the trophy that she had an alcove made in the saloon for its permanent display.

By and large, schooners of all shapes and sizes were more popular in America than in British waters. I remember how this impressed me when over there with *Shamrock IV* in 1920. From about that time onwards those grand little 'Malabars' from John Alden's drawing-board made a great name in offshore racing.

I believe I am right in saying that the last time a schooner raced in the Fastnet was in 1933 when that fine little bald-headed schooner *Brilliant* came over and we had such a small entry. To me *Brilliant* was near my ideal husky little schooner: short-ended, good beam but full of character, with eyed splices on hardwood cheeks for her standing gear, baggy-wrinkle in the right places for chafe and all that goes with 'a proper little ship'.

Thirty-four years later, in 1967, we find an ultra-modern schooner again in the money, that very strange schooner, *Pen Duick III*.

6 Ketches and yawls

I find that in this chapter I have written almost exclusively about yachts designed or built by my Firm in Gosport for which I must ask the reader's indulgence and hope that it will not be found too tedious. The chapter could not in any case have been written but for the great help received from John Henderson to whom I am most grateful.

As a matter of statistical interest I mention that there are records of eighteen ketches totalling some 1,620 tons and twenty-five yawls totalling 1,520 tons built at our Gosport yard between 1876 and 1959, but I know that there are many omissions. The largest 'pure-bred' ketch designed and built at Gosport was the 254-ton *Sylvia* for Mr Alan Butler in 1925. The largest yawl discloses a dead heat between *Ada* built in 1876 and *Brynhild* in 1899, both being 153 tons. I see that the yawl *Glory* of 205 tons built in 1901 for Sir Henry Seymore King tops that rig but she was designed by Arthur Payne.

Few of these yachts were designed for racing but two at least became famous as racers whilst a number tasted the fun of handicap racing. The ketches *Sylvia* and *Kathleen*, when owned by Sir Alfred Goodson, both took part in at least one race, the first Morgan Cup which I have described in the chapter 'Family Craft'.

In the more modern times, on which I touch only scantily in this book, there can be little doubt that the offshore racing yawl *Bloodhound* carved a name for herself that must be nearly as famous as that of her celebrated elder sister, the '40-ton class' *Bloodhound* designed by Mr Fife Senior and owned by the Marquis of Ailsa. The Marquis also owned *Foxhound*, *Deerhound*, and *Sleuth-hound* but his

Bloodhound, the most famous, was referred to as 'The Hound'. There is little doubt that, of this fine collection of yachts, two were outstanding and I will deal with the oldest first.

The yawl *Florinda* was built by my grandfather for a Mr W. Jessop of Butterley Hall, Derbyshire, and her plans appear in the Badminton Library publication of 1910. She was 126 tons and built fundamentally for comfortable, fast cruising but here I will quote from an inscription on the back of a splendid lithograph of the yacht that my good friend Rear-Admiral Morrice McMullen kindly gave to me some time ago:

"She showed so much speed in her maiden races and beat such celebrated vessels so handsomely that her owner determined to give her more chance of distinguishing herself, *et vires acquirit eundo*, and he raced at all the regattas in the south of England and at Havre.

"*Florinda* has proved herself not only a fast and weatherly vessel amongst her own rig and size when going to windward, but has put the *Arrow* and *Kriemhilda* to the pin of their collar when trying to squeeze out on her weather, and she reaches so fast as to make it a troublesome matter for even the best of the large schooners to go handsomely through her lee."

Her enthusiastic owner took Grandfather's advice and gave her another seven tons of lead on her keel and the best possible sails of that day and she was outstanding in her time.

At the yard she became known as 'the Gosport mistake'. Her model is still at the office and was among a few kindly returned from the Royal Victoria Yacht Club of Ryde, arranged by our good friend Mr Ricketts. Having observed that model many times a day in the passage to my office, I am sure that *Florinda*'s secret was her long easy 'run'. She had a lovely tail and was among the last of the good old straight-stemmers with deep fore-foot, black hull with copper bottom and set off by a 'twenty-five bob' gold line.

She was later owned by Sir James Pender who, incidentally, also owned for a few seasons the next 'old lady' I shall describe. The old *Florinda* became and remained for many years the flagship of the Royal Motor Yacht Club and finally was destroyed by enemy action when lying alongside Poole Quay.

The second gracious and not so old lady was *Brynhild*, 153 tons. She was, perhaps, my father's sequel to his parent's *Florinda* and was another remarkable yawl that later became a ketch. Built in

1899 for Major Selwin Calverley and, again, intended for fast cruising, she was a beautiful sea-boat and soon showed her good all-round performance in a keen handicap class.

In her long life she had some eleven owners. Sir James Pender, Bart., then of Thornby Hall, Northampton, owned her for five seasons and I refer to him again when describing the tragedy of his later cutter *Brynhild*. In 1907 she was sold to an Italian owner and from 1912 until 1922 she was owned and sailed in British waters by a gentleman named Frederick Schwann (who later changed his name to Swann). During his enthusiastic ownership she was altered to ketch rig with more sail and was one of the forerunners of a fine fleet of yachts racing in the large handicap class including such celebrated names as *Cariad*, *Valdora*, *Sumurun*, and others.

Brynhild was owned by Major A. W. Foster from 1928 until 1936 after which she changed hands (and names) several times. She became *Black Swan*, *Changrilla* and again *Black Swan* under which name she was eventually sold in 1958 to a Mexican yachtsman and is believed to be still in service.

I remember her best in Mr Swann's time and consider she too must have been among my father's 'top ten'.

The ketch *Joyette* of 89 tons was, perhaps, his prettiest cruising boat and her model also hangs in that office passage. Some years ago we removed her lead keel for an owner who proposed to use her as a mobile houseboat and only recently has she been recommissioned for cruising.

Another fine ketch, *Gwendolen*, of 113 tons was built in 1927 for Mr Nutman who was in the timber trade, hence every effort was made to ensure that the timber used for her construction was the very best of its kind. She too had a string of owners and is still in commission in the Mediterranean.

Talking of timber merchants reminds me of the late Claude Worth, the great amateur yachtsman and ophthalmic surgeon who wrote those splendid books on his various cruises in his many yachts named *Tern*.

He was a perfectionist in anything to do with yachts and when he asked us to build one of his *Terns* my father declined in spite of Worth offering to look after his eyes for the rest of his life. He knew that that owner would scrutinize every inch of timber that was used and might criticize much which was perfectly serviceable.

After Worth and his contemporary, Warington Smyth, had passed
on I asked the latter's son, Nigel, where his father's grave was and he
replied, "He's dropped his hook alongside Claude Worth at Mawnan
Smith, with a fine view down Channel." Later we visited that charming little churchyard and saw both graves; Worth's simple cross of
Cornish granite just had inscribed on it 'Claude Worth' and nothing
else.

Tom Worth, of course, out-cruised his father and the last time we
met was at his place in Berkshire when we went over to advise him as
to structural maintenance of his nice little teak-planked composite
Dutch-built yacht. He had a wonderful collection of pistols and,
taking us to lunch at a well-known hotel, he described the exact part
of the Helford River that each oyster had been dredged from.

It would be fun to write on and on about these yachts but it might
well be less fun to read. I must, however, mention one other fine
ketch built just before the war. This was *Blanche Neige* of 132 tons for
M. Rene Combastet, a gentleman who excelled himself on all
matters concerning safety at sea. One felt that it was all very prudent
and certainly good for trade. This yacht—like the ketch *Aries* built
some years later—had three forms of steering gear including the
Chance system of remote control, an American development whereby one could steer the vessel from anywhere on deck.

The family were delightful and I remember on the launching day
how my cousin Norman Blake, who was supervising the yacht's
construction and was a splendid amateur gardener with rather a
flair for floral decor, elected to adopt the simple violet and anemone
for the lunch table in what was 'the silly season' for flowers. Madame
Combastet was charmed with this. I also remember when sitting
next to her how she circulated her menu for signatures of the party.
I was the last to sign and when I passed it back to her I was surprised
at the remarkable way she described the characters of those sig-
natories. I felt when it came to my turn that it was, perhaps, a trifle
too flattering.

In those days we had several good friends who enjoyed wandering
round the yard; they were far too expert to be classed as 'time-
wasters' and one of them was Hanson of the Cruising Association—
a most accomplished sailor.

The day we lifted the large deckhouse aboard *Blanche Neige* happened to be one of his visiting days. We used strops and the overhead crane to hoist this fitting over the stern and, as the twelve o'clock whistle had blown for dinner, this structure was left right on the stern. During lunch Hanson, who was in this building shed, noticed this fitting sitting almost on the stern and later asked me, "Who was building that nice yacht with the gazebo on the stern?"

One much enjoyed the company of visitors like Hanson, many unable to afford anything but a small craft but with immense enthusiasm for and knowledge of the larger ones.

I see the smallest of this category of yachts was the little yawl *Thetis* of 8 tons built in 1906 and this reminds me that her owner, around 1920 when I had just joined the Firm, was among the first of our clients that I ever met. He was a Naval officer with great yachting experience, but somehow I felt his opinion of me was still very much as of the snotty, though my stock improved a shade after recommending that if the cranse-iron and jib-traveller were re-served with raw-hide it would be kinder to the bowsprit.

7 One Designs

I imagine that the Redwing must have been one of the first One-Design classes in the country. The Redwing Club of Bembridge ordered their celebrated little fleet in 1896 when fourteen were built and the number increased to twenty-four in 1901.

Perhaps more accurately they should be referred to as a 'restricted' O.D. class as, although the hulls were identical, sail area was limited to 200 square feet and owners experimented with sail plans in great variety. Most adopted a gunter or gaff rig and some indeed were cat-rigged without any head-sail and experimentation thrived as the seasons passed.

These bonny little yachts were 22 ft 1 in overall with a beam of 5 ft 2 in and their draught was 2 ft 11 in with a cast iron keel of 10 cwt. Construction was orthodox with yellow pine planking.

The Fiftieth Anniversary was celebrated by a luncheon attended by my father and the menus each had little handpainted sketches of all the different sail plans. I still have the copy of the original class book, 'The Redwings and their Home', presented to Father by the Commodore, Blair Onslow Cochrane, all those years ago.

I believe that a few of these old boats are still in commission and we have heard from at least two owners since the war, one at Plymouth and one in Jersey.

In 1938 the Club decided to replace the class with a new one, again with the 'do as you like' sail plan of 200 square feet. These new boats were 27 ft 9 in overall with 5 ft 5 in beam and 3 ft 3 in draught, limited unfortunately by the harbour bar. Keels were of lead, planking was mahogany and every conceivable thing was done to produce a perfect standard hull. Their construction was my pigeon and I had immense fun meeting many of the owners. Tempting though it may be, I must not mention all those refreshing people but will single out one only.

Sir Hercules Langrish arrived one evening after having crossed from Ireland and driven over to Gosport from Fishguard. It was about 6 p.m. and my father unfortunately was away and unable to meet one of his oldest friends. This grand old gentleman, helmsman and huntsman throughout his life, was now in his eighties. His interest in his new boat was tremendous and I realized he was very distressed to miss my father.

When he took his leave, which seems the appropriate way to refer to the departure of such a fabulous character, I saw he was driving an elderly Ford V8 saloon in which his gear, including golf clubs, were in the 'stern sheets' and on the empty front passenger seat was a route scribbled on a large sheet of Bristol board and a bottle of whisky. He said he was off to Town for the meeting of the Squadron next day. I only hoped at the time that I might emulate some of his achievements.

This new class generally adopted the orthodox jib-headed rig and we produced a standard rig for any that wished to adopt it with high aspect ratio and some third of the area in the foresail. It seemed as good as any but, as usual, it was the helmsman or woman, so often the latter at Bembridge, who was as important as any sail plan.

Two adopted the Lungstrom rig and one of these was the late Lord Brabazon. He, I suppose, experimented with more extreme rigs than any in the history of the class including the Flettner rotating cylinder 'mast', and also a rotor-rig on helicopter lines. It was found that the Lungstrom outfit was the best to windward but fell off reaching and running as the 200 square foot limit prevented the 'goose-winging' of the sail downwind.

Lord Brab. wrote a splendid article on his Redwing research in the Aeronautical Society's journal at the time.

The last time I met him was at a Boat Show at Earls Court when he was moving round at high speed followed by his breathless secretary. Thus we find I have, inadvertently, mentioned two owners of this delightful class—perhaps two of the greatest sportsmen of all.

The Royal Naval Sailing Association dinghy was one of the larger O.D. classes for years. These 14-ft boats were originally designed by my father for the Island Sailing Club and were also used by a vigorous local club founded by my cousin Charles and others and known as the Centre-board Sailing Club, sailing off Cracknore Hard in Southampton Water.

Meantime, when Vice-Admiral Sir Geoffrey Blake was Commodore in H.M.S. *Hood*, that wonderful battle-cruiser, he ordered four of these sailing boats to be carried aboard and they proved so successful that the Admiralty, realizing they were robust enough for service use, prepared a complete specification and some hundreds were built. They were, in fact, discarded only a few years ago.

I gave a trophy, a plated model of one of these boats, to the Royal Albert Yacht Club in my father's memory for annual competition at their combined regatta with the Royal Naval Sailing Association. Amongst the winners of this were a civilian tug master, the Captain of the Dockyard, Bertie Pengelly—a member of that great Cornish family of fishing and sailormen—and indeed it was almost won by Admiral Salter when sailing with his daughter when he was Admiral Superintendent at Portsmouth.

I omitted to mention that Vice-Admiral Sir Geoffrey Blake, who died in 1968, was the doyen of the R.N.S.A. and did much to foster recreational sailing in the Royal Navy. I've always considered that Paul Hammond was his counterpart in America and he too is an honorary member of the Association.

Lee-on-the-Solent Sailing Club, that thriving little institution hard on a lee shore, was founded in 1909. One always marvelled at the sanity of this concept, where a class of some twenty boats or more had to be hauled out whenever it blew up hard and that was pretty frequent. I cannot remember the size of the first class of centre-board boats which we built for the Club but think that they were 16 ft overall. They had gunter rig and were admirable for this breezy location.

In 1914 we designed a new 16-ft class which were built by Percy See of Fareham and I doubt if any dinghy hull form was ever more powerful or better than these. They were clencher built with good floor and tumble-home and equipped with a jib-headed mainsail,

rather a novelty at that time, and a roller jib fitted to a small boom
for guying aft when running.

The class lay on moorings under the lee of the old pier and rode
out quite heavy weather provided the boatman kept their bilges
reasonably dry. As youngsters we learned a great deal from sailing
our boat, known as Number Eleven, this being her sail number, and I
remember collecting the first boat with Joe Hannen from Fareham
Creek. Off the 'Kicker' we had a white sea with fresh westerly wind
over a foul tide and the boat amazed us. After bringing up off the Lee
Pier we had lunch at Joe's father's hotel and heard that his splendid
German waiter had to return to his country, war being almost
declared.

This vintage of seagoing sailing dinghy had a long and successful
life and after that World War we had many wonderful seasons with
them. It was much of a 'parochial' class as dinghy classes were few
and far between and inter-club racing had not matured in those days.
We had some of the best Solent helmsmen and competition was very
keen between my father, my uncle Arthur, Fred Blake the Commodore and Jack Blake his brother who turned up with a hefty paid
hand in hard weather, much to our annoyance. Others included Joe
Hannen who was very hard to beat, Rex Curtis and the Misses
King who kept their boats at Hillhead.

My sister and I crewed Father through thick and thin and it was
my good fortune to be his sheet hand for many seasons. His directive
'check a shade my boy' meant the slightest spring to the sheet and
I was often soundly rated for easing it as much as an inch!

Between the wars the Club adopted two other O.D. classes both
designed and built by See of Fareham. One was a sixteen footer
whilst the other a seventeen-foot class that had many good qualities
and was retained until the Second War.

After the war we designed and built a new class of twenty boats
for the Club, which were eighteen footers and known as Seagulls.
We could not obtain a building permit to purchase mahogany in
1946 so we were forced to use anything we had in stock and adopted
silver spruce, reverse clencher, for their construction. They proved
to be excellent boats and, after some twenty-four years hard service
and continual beaching, a good few are still racing as a class.

For many years this vigorous little Club had no sea view, being located in one of the main streets. Some years ago we purchased a good property on the sea front and built on to it over its garden area. It is now among the nicest of the smaller Solent clubs with commanding views to the south embracing Spithead, the whole of the north side of the Isle of Wight and right down the Solent to the Needles.

The Lee-on-the-Solent dinghies I have mentioned really sprang from the family class of boats called the 'Shellfish' class. Although it comprised only five boats it must have been one of the earliest O.D. classes, at any rate in the Solent area.

These little Shellfish class boats were all named after crustaceans and ours was *Limpet*. They were 14 ft overall with a near vertical pram bow which I learned later was something of a 'rule cheater' in those days and, at all events, most of her length was 'sailing length'. Of clencher construction, they had gunter rig with a roller jib and were equipped with a kapok-stuffed all-round fendoff for buoyancy which was discarded as we children matured. One day a stranger inquired of Uncle Ben what class of boats they were; he was the eldest of the three brothers and a passive but deliberate old chap and his reply was, "They are a family class."

A great many years later my second cousin and colleague Charles Blake owned *Limpet* when he was working with the shipwrights in the Gosport yard. His immediate associate, one Alf Cresdee, was among our most skilled craftsmen at his trade and he and Charles built a new and pleasing stem in place of the pram bow.

At that time the late Commander 'Bill' Hammond was the Pooh-Bah or 'Lord-high-everything-else' to the little Portchester Sailing Club at the top of Portsmouth Harbour. He built a little class of scows known as the Portchester Ducks and all were named after the various species. He conducted the races, serviced the little boats and had great charm and affection for all his fellow creatures. At the Christmas parties he was a good shantyman and a splendid companion for a cruise or a short day sail. He was wise enough to let another wear the Commodore's hat and over a long and happy period this little Club flourished under the castle walls. They had a menagerie handicap class and it was in this that Charles Blake excelled with *Limpet*.

I had my first sail with Father off Bembridge in one of these family class boats when I must have been about six years old and in the days that we rented Foreland Farm at Bembridge or took a house in the bay at Seaview.

In those days Seaview was a paradise for old and young. The houses overlooking the bay have now completely disappeared due to erosion and a strata of 'blue slipper' clay. The largest, at the south end of the little promenade and named Hawstone Point, was the summer home of the Garnet family. The Garnets 'ran' Seaview; they organized hockey—of a sort—on the lovely sands at low tide. When the tide was up Mrs Garnet could be seen distributing coloured ribbons to all and sundry and, when it was low-water, these tremendous games took place. If one side was winning some would join the losing side and once we had the thrill of playing with the great rugby international, R. W. Poulton, who later became Poulton-Palmer and he with his international jersey with number on the back!

Before the First War and during the inter-war years our business was generally recognized as one for building the 'one off' or 'custom built' yacht and was little concerned with a standard product. Personally I had toyed for some time with the idea of producing what we termed 'batch-production' rather than mass production and I prepared a design for a little cruiser-racer, 30 ft overall, for a small family or four adults. I was very happy with the whole little conception but worried by the opposition I should meet when presenting the project to my seniors.

My father definitely felt that it might effect our custom built trade but, by discreet persuasion, I won the day, explaining my view that these craft were not designed for the owner of a Rolls or a Ford but more for the Rover type of owner. Oddly enough four of the ultimate owners had Rover cars.

I was granted permission to build six which I felt was, at all events, a start to my theme of batch production. This was in 1939.

Standardization of hull, uniform engine harness and plumbing and standard accommodation, except for variations in forecastle arrangement, were the order of the day. They were known as the Thirty Footers, were classed at Lloyds and planked with mahogany. With a first-rate specification they were sold at that time for £875 all-in, including everything to the bathing ladder but excluding owner's bedding and cutlery. Had not the cloud of war been so near no doubt many more would have been built.

Boat number five was sold and Father instructed me to put number six 'on ice' as he doubted, if war came, that he could maintain his cutter *Flame* after it was over. As things turned out this was so and number six was named *Cinder*—his grandchildren's sailing dinghy was *Spark*.

I believe all these little boats are still in commission under different ownership and perhaps the greatest yachting contrast happened after the war when Mr Bill Stevenson bought one and used it in the Poole Harbour district, having a house at Canford Cliffs—rather different from owning the J class *Velsheda* and the 457-ton motor yacht *Malahne*.

Apart from the International 14 Footers and a few other dinghy classes there was almost no estuary sailing before the war. The then Y.R.A. did not cater for dinghy racing until Sir William Burton and Stewart Morris persuaded the Council to foster its development. Now in all these harbours and estuaries we see immense activity in any British port of call and perhaps the following little description epitomises the scene almost anywhere.

My wife and I were at Instow one evening when I had some business in the district. After tea in the hotel we went off to try to get a paper and, passing the nice little yacht club, we noticed that a signal was hoisted and race officers were in evidence. While we were in the little shop there was a loud report and we were told it was the first gun for the evening race.

As we returned towards the hotel we saw, with some amazement, little red-sailed dinghies emerging from gardens and private houses in Instow and in Appledore across the estuary. This, of course, was the local class of Redwing dinghies designed some years before by Uffa Fox. Another gun was fired and several boats were afloat and making for the line with very little wind from north of west funnelling up the river with a young flood tide.

At the start several boats were minutes late but that did not seem to matter as the tide was stronger than the breeze and all were hanging on the line. The last to join the struggling fleet hailed from Appledore and we suspected he was one of their star turns as, immediately he crossed the line, he reached back across the estuary and we knew his object was to check the tide. This chap also seemed to pick up little free puffs from the quays and buildings of the town and soon worked into a nice little lead; others followed suit, but not all.

The mark-boat was well downstream but as we had to meet friends we had, reluctantly, to leave this fascinating scene and thus missed seeing the first boat round that mark but whoever it was must have been the winner with the falling wind and increasing tide under him.

This vast development in dinghy racing everywhere has now become one of the many and varied issues within the scope of the ever-expanding R.Y.A. Wherever we go, including inland with all the lakes and ponds, we see the last word in the latest dinghy creation, generally well sailed and bringing the finest recreation to thousands who never saw a boat before the war.

Not so many years ago Rod Stephens gave me his opinion that the long-term future of yachting would see the steady increase in One Designs and standardization of many racing and cruising craft, with which I agreed. Only recently do we see the ousting of the 'rule designed boat' from the Olympic regatta and it would appear, from the racing yacht designer's point of view, that the offshore racing field may be his only battleground excepting the odd 12-metre challenge for the America's Cup.

Times indeed have changed and whereas in my day the British citizen was more individualistic, be it in his car, his boat, his pipe or his bicycle, the American accepted standardization as slick high-efficiency production. Now here we are 'all in the same boat', striving to condition ourselves to the new yachting scene which, as an old 'un, seems to be charged with a most exciting future.

Another near One Design class with which we were closely associated from 1947 was the International Dragon class. This, to me, has been the greatest small racing yacht surprise in the history of yachting.

Many years ago during Cowes Week our good friend Alfred Mylne dined with us ashore and, since he was Father's guest, he thought he should wear a dinner jacket. Not having brought one with him he hired one and when we greeted him he was prolific with apologies as to its fit. He reminded me of that brilliant French comedian, Grock, with very baggy trousers the top of which were some inches above his waistcoat.

We had an amusing dinner during which the advent of the Dragon was a topic and Alfred surprised me by squeezing my leg rather hard under the table exclaiming, "John, my boy, the Dragons are knocking at the doorr!" His vision then was far greater than mine and one never anticipated that the class would prove so popular for so long.

Designed by the late J. Anker around 1929 with shake-down accommodation for cruising some of these earlier boats performed heroic deeds in the matter of distance cruising. Gradually any semblance of cruising fitments disappeared and for a long time now they have been pure racers. We built some twenty to this class of which two, at least, were Solent champions.

I was never a statistician or even a diarist. People and boats came and went and, to me, that was the spice of it all. I suspect my good friend John Henderson knows more of these historical statistics than most and, maybe, one day something from him may come up from the well.

12. *Creole* with her original sail plan, when owned by Sir Connop Guthrie.

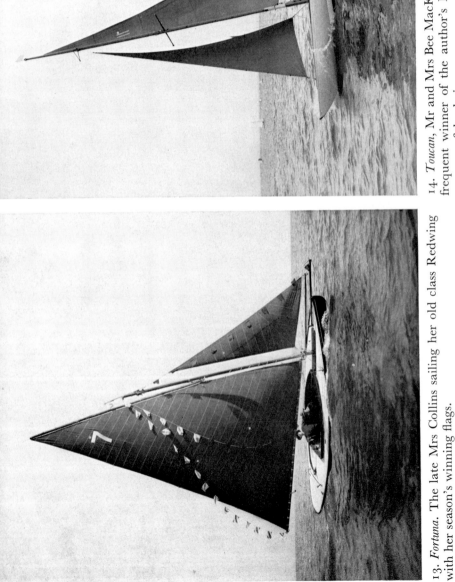

13. *Fortuna.* The late Mrs Collins sailing her old class Redwing with her season's winning flags.

14. *Toucan,* Mr and Mrs Bee MacKinnon's new class Redwing, a frequent winner of the author's Royal Albert Y.C. trophy in memory of the designer.

8 Captains and skippers

I have pleasant memories of many fine sailors and great characters with whom it was a privilege to have worked, sailed, or just to have known.

In this age of smaller yachts, with owners and their friends doing everything, the passing of the professional skipper and paid hands is no longer regarded as a calamity. If there were again a large demand for them the matter would be more serious due to the passing of the sailing fishing fleets from our inshore waters.

If some madman elected to build a J class cutter today he could never find a full professional crew and the possibility of finding some thirty good amateurs for six months or so would seem very remote.

When we reflect on the inter-war period with the 'Big Class'—be they 23-metres or the J class—embracing some six large cutters and, for many seasons, the schooner *Westward*, the classes of 12-, 8-, and 6-metres and a very large number of sail and power cruising-yachts, one can imagine that the professionals employed in the big class alone would probably outnumber those engaged in the whole of British yachting today.

While we always had a backbone of good amateur cruising yachts-men in the pre-war years, anyone owning something around 10 tons or over in those days invariably engaged a professional. Today, with many thousands more medium and small yachts than before the war, we find an ever-growing body of first-class amateur seamen.

Since these splendid professionals played such a great part in the past, particularly in my hey-day, I shall enjoy reflecting for a while on them, their employers and the yachts in which they sailed.

G

Most of the captains of the larger power yachts had Merchant Service experience and a few were retired from the Navy. It was not unusual for a captain to join his owner for recreation such as golf, shooting, or fishing.

Many good sailing yacht captains graduated from fishing as youngsters and employment as deckhands in racing yachts in summer; subsequent promotion to mate often ended with a captain's appointment. A few of the large yacht racing captains came from the Merchant Service and I will tackle them first.

Let us join the 12-metre *Flica* for a race at the Royal Albert regatta on the great day that *Britannia* and *Westward* had a dead-heat.

Sir Richard Fairey had kindly asked me to sail her with his friend, that great American yachtsman Sherman Hoyt, whom I had known since 1920 when he sailed in *Shamrock IV* as observer for the New York Yacht Club.

I joined skipper 'Grannie' Diaper and his small crew of four deckhands off Gosport. The rule limit of those days—five professionals in a 12-metre—is something of a contrast with present rules!

We sailed out to Southsea and, as arranged, Sherman joined us off the Club, wearing a trilby hat and a belted trench-coat. Diaper had never heard of this great little man and gave me a critical glance.

I offered the helm to Sherman but he preferred me to take her on the first round. We had a fair start and succeeded in keeping ahead with Sir William Burton's *Veronica* close astern. The breeze was freshening and I knew there was more to come on the second round with the tide turning against it.

Sherman took over and then I knew that Diaper was worried. He showed this by his habit of brushing-up his short moustache with a damp chamois leather and taking up a position on the lee side of the cockpit, one hand on the coaming. Sherman looked far more like an Army officer on leave than one of the greatest sailors of all time and Diaper mopped his moustache time and again. We were if anything dropping *Veronica* a little and I think he was somewhat appeased by our conversation on yachting.

When we arrived at the Warner Shoal there was a white sea running and we had to gybe. Sherman took us round as though we were on a millpond and Diaper winked at me—the chamois leather wasn't used again. Running into the finish was quite a warm business; as we got our gun Sherman said he felt like a bride in June and we celebrated with an aperitif which I knew was both the owner's and Sherman's favourite—gin and French.

I first met Diaper when he was skipper of the 6-metre *Patience* in 1922; he was one of the nicest fellows to sail with and, as he developed, so did the yachts in which he sailed. He remained with Sir Richard all his sailing life.

The assessment of the greatest professional sailing master is always a topic for fireside gossip. I never met the great Charlie Barr who I suspect was the 'King' and, although he spent much of his life in famous American yachts, it is good to know that he hailed from Scotland.

I rate Captain Sycamore among the most dashing and talented of all British professionals. An artist to the finger-tips, he had nerves of steel and was surely the doyen of them all. He served Sir Thomas Lipton for many years during his ownership of the 23-metre cutter *Shamrock*.

I often remember how Sycamore handled that fine cutter at the start. As cunning as a fox, he bemused his opponents by the most astute tactics and, as a youngster, I sensed that some were scared of him. He sported a sharp Captain Kettle beard, which was sometimes, perhaps, a trifle too auburn, and he had the energy of a far younger man.

Sycamore was undoubtedly champion of all those splendid sailors whose winters were spent inshore fishing on the East Coast.

When racing with *Shamrock V* on the Clyde in 1930 with Ted Heard (referred to later) as captain we had a splendid opportunity of studying the methods of Archie Hogarth who was captain of the gaff-rigged cutter *Lulworth*.

Archie got the better of the start to wind'ard in a soft true breeze and under those conditions *Lulworth* was remarkably close-winded. After about twenty minutes he had us nicely under his lee and to attempt to romp through would have been fruitless in that weight of wind. Several times we saw Archie leave the helm and, strolling along the lee side, he would give his own instructions for trimming the head sheets. He reminded me of those very skilful 'sailormen' handling their spritsail barges and of one day, in particular, when we were racing at Harwich and visiting Ipswich for lunch with my father and 'Uncle Malden' Heckstall-Smith.

Hogarth proved his skill and complete knowledge of *Lulworth*'s capabilities year after year; he seemed to prefer a rather flat cut mainsail and, although virtually a hard weather vessel, there were times when she went like a train in light airs. This, I suspect, was when the tide was under her and when many heavy displacement craft appear to ghost so well. One Cowes Week, when Franklin Ratsey won all the major trophies in his old gaff cutter *Zoraida*, I congratulated him and he gave me an honest look and said, "It was the turn of the tide, John." It so happened that every time they came on a wind the tide was under them.

Reverting to that Sunday morning on the banks of the Orwell en route for lunch at Ipswich, we sighted some five barges trying to save their tide. We got out of the car and soon realized that, although we were attending Harwich regatta with the cream of British yachts, we were watching with amazement some of the most skilful sailing in the world.

Not one barge had more than two on deck and one, which I put my shirt on, had only her helmsman. The light air was blowing downstream and the tide was on the turn. All had their bowsprits struck and the masterly way they slipped round, tack after tack, was perfection in seamanship. All were watching each other, playing cat and mouse, their movements akin to a shire horse with grace and power, stately and serene.

My hero was doing very well, quietly leaving the wheel to trim his only headsail, a long-rope jib-topsail, and back to the helm again.

Our rumbling tummies suggested it was time to press on and we had a very late lunch.

Among my favourites was Captain Fred Mountifield. I do not know if he had a predecessor in *White Heather* but, to me, he 'was' *White Heather*. Captain for all the seasons that I knew her, he was kindly, quiet and had sufficient evidence of humour to draw one to him. As a youngster I used to love watching his tactics before a start; how and when he elected to break-out this or that headsail; how soon to make for the line and if, as was often the case, he had a good start how he would let her go a good full. If it was a light day he would settle himself on a large canvas pouf to the leeside of the wheel and concentrate, leaving the second mate for'ard to trim the headsails.

Mountifield was captain during all the seasons that *White Heather* was owned by Sir Charles Allom and later by Lord Waring. In the spring of her first season under the latter's ownership I remember Fred's quiet and sad comment when Waring decided to combine the saloon with the amenities of a library and hundreds of books arrived from Town. Being such a senior member of the decorative profession many changes took place below but that saloon, with glazed syca-more-veneered book cupboards either side, was never appreciated by Fred.

Bill Randall from Emsworth was rather in the mould of Mounti-field—quiet, willing and a great sailor. Neither of them ever swore but both had the complete respect of their crews. This business of 'blazing' at sea has no effect on a good crew.

Bill had a long sailing career and, like so many, was a fisherman in winter. His first big-yacht appointment was the 19-metre *Norada* when owned by Sir Howard Frank and when there was a slight revival of that fine class of 100 tonners. Three out of the four were resuscitated, *Corona* being owned by Herman Andreae and *Mariquita* by A. E. Messer. *Norada* had gaff rig and her rivals Bermudian.

I remember several incidents when sailing aboard *Norada* with her delightful owner and his charming wife. One day in Cowes Week with a fine sailing breeze my father had the helm and it must have been one of his happiest sailing days. On the second round we were short tacking to cheat the tide under Stone Point after rounding the Ryde Middle buoy and bound for the West Lepe. It was so close that there was little to choose between the three of us and the crews worked so well and were so keen that these large cutters were being treated almost as 8-metre yachts.

Another day we witnessed a tragedy. We were running through the Roads to the east and were about halfway from the Consort buoy to Castle Point when someone shouted and looking astern we saw the 12-metre *Lucilla* and *Lulworth* locked together. This fearful collision was caused by *Lucilla* claiming starboard tack and *Lulworth*, running dead with everything set, being unable to anticipate the situation.

Bill Randall later became captain of *Velsheda* and had several good seasons with Bill Stephenson. In 1935 when we were aboard *Flame* at Brixham we were invited to race in *Velsheda* at Torbay. This was the great year that Gerry Lambert brought *Yankee* over.

One morning we were in the launch proceeding to join *Velsheda* off Paignton. There was little wind but quite a heavy scend in the bay and Father thought that a nosebag would be the thing to drag her through it rather than a double-clewed jib or a Genoa. On board he put this suggestion to Stephenson who replied that it was O.K. if Randall approved. Bill did agree but slightly under protest, we felt, and when the ten minute gun fired, still with the wind next to nothing, we hauled up the balloon jib in stops.

The rest of the fleet were breaking out their head-sails and, with little to go and *Shamrock* on our weather tending to bear down on us below the line of the mark off Torquay, we broke out our 'surprise'. In a matter of minutes we drew clear and had a nice lead at the mark off Torquay. On rounding we set the double-clewed jib and re-tained first place all day. Randall was generous in his thanks to Father.

Following the demise of the J class Bill Randall became captain of the 12-metre *Trivia* which we had built for Mr MacAndrew in 1937 and which had several good seasons.

In 1939, when Mr 'Mike' Vanderbilt brought *Vim* over from America, we had the good fortune to be invited to sail *Trivia* while her owner was abroad. This was also, incidentally, the year in which we built the last 12-metre for British racing—*Tomahawk* for Sir Thomas Sopwith, and the last year in the history of 12-metre racing in this country.

We had *Trivia* for all the East Coast regattas and all foregathered at Harwich. Rod Stephens had joined the Vanderbilts for *Vim*'s early races.

On the evening before the first race 'Uncle' Malden Heckstall-Smith, who as usual was my father's guest, was very concerned over *Vim*'s new alloy mast, the first ever used in a Twelve; he feared that it was curved, contrary to the measurement rule. In the evening I rowed him over to *Vim* and discreetly approached near enough to sight up the after side of that splendid mast. It was dead straight and the cause of Malden's fears was an optical illusion due to the method of tapering on its fore side.

The first race was virtually won by *Vim* but as she omitted to round one of the marks she did not cross the finishing line and gave the prize to *Trivia*.

Next day, only a short time before the ten minute gun, it was noticed that *Vim* had a foul kedge; she used a wire instead of chain and as the minutes ticked by we were all worried for her. Eventually Rod, stripped to his birthday suit, went down the wire and was under water for an alarming time. He managed to clear the trouble and *Vim* was successfully under way.

One of my clearest recollections of this series was seeing *Vim* in a fresh breeze with two reefs and setting a large Genoa as heavy as her mainsail. The mainsail was all alive, flapping and, we thought, doing no good at all. This was an early approach to present-day technique with ridiculously small mainsails and vast nosebags that seem to explode the 'slot' theory.

The first day at Southend was the only time that Bill Randall and I ever had a tactical disagreement, but since he was MacAndrew's servant I gave way.

At starting time there was next to no wind and a young flood was making; there were cats-paws off the pier and *Vim* sensibly kept milling around in these ripples. I thought we should get out there with her but Bill was all against 'getting out in that tideway'. At the start *Vim* gave us all the slip and had the prize in her locker within half an hour.

During the war Bill Randall was in the Firm's employ and must have conducted very many trial trips in Admiralty craft. I often enjoyed his quiet companionship when we went back over those great days together.

A smaller class, which in my view was next in appeal to the Twelves, was the 8-metres. Here was a fine fleet of delightful yachts with an unusually pronounced sense of friendship among owners and skippers. Certain yachts would be sure to win if it were their particular day and that was accepted by all whereas today, in round-the-buoy racing, so many expect to win all the time. One design racing makes this more possible, of course.

In our case with the family yacht *Sagitta* we were sure to do well if we had a fair tide under us when turning to wind'ard; *Wye* would usually get a flag in light weather and the Scottish boats, being more powerful, were 'in the money' in hard weather, and so on.

The skippers knew each other inside out and local knowledge played a great part. For instance, ours was a Portsmouth fisherman in winter and was better around Spithead than Bob Bevis or Joe Oakley whose respective hunting grounds were around Southampton area and at Cowes.

There was that great family of Parkers, one of whom was captain of *Britannia* before Captain Carter and Albert Turner. It was a Parker who when acting as pilot in *Britannia* was asked by H.M. King George V as to why the weather was so bad during a Cowes Week and replied that, "It must be that thar labour gomonent" . . . Itchen Ferry to a man and wonderful sailors.

For a time there were two in the 8-metre class, naturally known as 'old man Parker' and 'young Parker', the latter being the greatest talker I ever met. He sailed with Major Laureston Lewes, among other owners, and his incessant conversation was always humorous, kind and pleasant.

Old man Parker was at one time skipper of a 12-metre whose owner, a charming gentleman but not very experienced, often kindly invited me to sail her for him. I remember one day at Cowes when we were doing well and just coming up to the mark, when it was a matter of 'down spinnaker, in main-sheet, up Genoa and up runners', the owner suddenly emerged at the companion entrance carrying a tray of coffee and enquired, "Nicholson, do you like black or white and one or two lumps"?

I also remember that owner doing a standing gybe after a running start—fortunately with little wind. Old man Parker tendered his resignation on the spot but soon simmered down.

Our skipper, Jack Gawn, and his piratical looking brother Steve, sailed with us for many years in the 8-metre class and the way they addressed each other was anything but brotherly. Steve was splendid on the bow and Jack was among the best in the class. They had another brother, Ben, who never raced with us but was, perhaps, the finest small-boat sailor we ever knew, as the following story may show.

Years before, I was bailer-boy in the 5-metre *Cordella* designed by

Morgan Giles and built by the Firm for the One Ton Cup races against France, to be sailed from the Royal Thames Yacht Club's signal station on Ryde pier. Being an international event we all wore white flannels and the crew were Dr Sabaston (helmsman), Colonel Clutterbuck and myself.

The little boats, which were to a bad measurement rule, were virtually hip-baths and when running in a hard breeze the bow tended to go under. We won the first race, nearly sinking on the run back to the pier from the Peel Bank. Next day we wore grey bags and sweaters.

Having won the trophy we were greeted by that splendid secretary Captain Orr (the weather kept any spectators away) and we felt that we had earned the bubbly that he kindly produced.

It was Ben Gawn who sailed *Cordella* over from Gosport each day single-handed and pumped her dry for us which, in my view, was sheer bravery. He was a remarkably kind and gentle man who was never heard to swear.

One day, again off Ryde and in the 8-metre class, I was racing with Jimmy Robertson (of Lloyds) as guest and how keen he was. At the end of the first round, we, on the starboard tack, just managed to cross *Wye*, then owned by Mrs Pitt-Rivers who had not been sailing very long in the class and whose skipper was that dear old rascal, Bob Bevis.

Jimmy was excited and brim full of encouraging chatter and as we set off on the second round our skipper Jack said, "Bob's sulking, sir," and I asked how on earth he knew, to which he replied, "You can see how he's standing, sir." I looked back and there was Bob with his chin in his hands and elbows on the cockpit coaming.

As I mentioned before, these chaps knew each other inside out.

Joe Oakley, skipper of *Saskia* and other yachts owned in partnership by Sir Kenneth Preston and Mr Robin Steel, was another great Solent skipper. One day in Cowes Week we were racing for the Marchioness of Camden's Cup (one of which, dated 1937, I happily possess). We were leading on the second round and running up to the South Bramble which, on rounding, only left a close fetch into the Squadron line.

Saskia was to leeward of us but had she had occasion to tack we would have cleared her, thus she was not ahead. I warned Jack that at all costs we must not get on the putty and he replied, "Look where Joe is, sir. If any one goes aground he will."

In a matter of seconds we came to a grinding halt and the tide was ebbing. *Saskia* won the cup and our launch came to collect my wife and me.

That evening we were dining on board H.M.S. *Sutton*, *Britannia*'s escort sloop, and being Friday it was firework night. After dinner we went on the bridge and there we saw *Sagitta* being towed in by Ratsey's bumboat. She had been aground for some five and a half hours and the cause was old Joe Oakley sneaking up a little creek he knew on the south-west corner of the Brambles—as clever a move as ever we saw!

I am sure that I am right in testifying that the great friendliness and sportsmanship in those happy 8-metre days were among the best features in the whole history of British yachting and it is good to see today that a strong class of 8-metre cruiser-racers, and a goodly collection of the old class, are reviving in strength on the Clyde.

I have already described the ketch *Brynhild* and some of her owners. Her penultimate one was a Mr Sidney Greer who died in Ireland. He was a very happy bachelor and his will indicated that he wished his ashes to be scattered near the Nab Tower, in the waters where he had so often enjoyed his sailing.

A friend of his approached the Firm and, as it was summer, we offered our family launch for this rather unusual purpose. I got in touch with his captain, Allan Cooper, who was devoted to his owner and a very splendid sailor of a rather quiet disposition.

I arranged a chicken picnic lunch with the right beverage and, on the appointed day, we awaited this gentleman at the harbour pontoon. He arrived with a parcel which we placed under the little saloon table with Mr Greer's house flag over it and proceeded to Fishbourne. The lunch was most successful and our friend said it was just as Mr Greer would have wished.

There was no wind and it was getting foggy so I went forward and told the coxswain to proceed at funereal speed, which worried me as the Daimler engine was apt to oil up at slow speed. We had only a small box-compass and crept along the Sand's Head and through the Forts which we could not see. After a time Cooper suggested that the Nab must be very near so we stopped the engine and drifted a while.

What little wind there was was north and poor Captain Cooper was naturally overwrought. After sliding the lid off the precious box he threw it overboard only to be covered himself with fine ash. Cooper, like his owner, was of the type we sadly missed and I only mention this episode as an example of the variety found in yacht building.

In 1924 we built a 301-ton motor yacht named *Endymion* for Sir Herbert Samuelson who would not take our advice as to her engines. After her first season he brought her back to the yard with instructions to install the engines we had recommended and, on completion, to run a trial of 1,000 miles non-stop.

We found that from Gosport to Loch Fyne was around 500 miles so prepared for this cruise. I was representing the builders, Hugh Gardner the engine makers and Captain Len Routh was in command.

As we proceeded to St Catherine's fog set in and we wirelessed the owner at Sunningdale for instructions, receiving the reply that we were to remain at sea with a speed consistent with safety. Very annoyed we carried on down Channel and conditions deteriorated appreciably.

Routh suggested that we steam to and fro between The Lizard and St Catherine's as long as the fog remained which it did for the whole passage. We were so bored that I was reduced to cutting the silhouette of a tramp steamer and sticking it at eye-level in the saloon window. When lunch arrived I pointed at it exclaiming to the captain, "It's lifted." He shot out of his seat and made his way to the bridge before he realized the plot.

When we moored up at Gosport again I vowed that that would be my last cruise in a motor yacht.

Routh was a splendid fellow who started his career as a ship's boy in an Arctic expedition. Later he was with Mr Lionel de Rothschild for several seasons before the war in his 709-ton motor yacht *Rhodora* which, unfortunately, was sunk off Lundy Island by collision in fog. Routh was chief officer under an ex-Navy skipper and happily all hands were saved.

Sir Thomas Sopwith engaged George Williams as skipper of his first 12-metre, *Doris*, in 1925 and Williams remained in his service right through Sir Thomas's sailing career including that in the 12-metre yachts *Mouette* and *Tomahawk* and the two J class cutters *Endeavour* and *Endeavour II*.

Williams was strictly the mate in charge of the crew, and really akin to Jim Gilbey in *Candida*, as both Sir Thomas and Mr Andreae were the helmsmen.

Apart from Sir William Burton who sailed *Shamrock IV* in America in 1920 it was not until Andreae sailed *Candida* and Sopwith *Endeavour* that amateur helmsmen emerged in the big class of racing yacht in British waters.

Williams had a quiet manner and could be relied upon for a second opinion when racing. He wore a somewhat unusual moustache and his friends knew him as 'Brusher' Williams. His greatest friend was 'Grannie' Diaper.

Sir Thomas built his first 12-metre *Doris* in 1925 to the revised measurement rule and after three seasons he built the celebrated *Mouette* in that class. She was an outstanding yacht beautifully sailed by her owner and top of her class for several seasons.

I remember when my father, my wife and I were guests of Sir Thomas at Dartmouth Regatta we had a perfect young autumn day for the last race and Sir Thomas opened up a tremendous lead at the weather mark, the Mew Stone. On the reach into the finishing line he hardly touched the helm at all and the moment the gun fired Williams had all *Mouette*'s winning flags hoisted up through the fore hatch and we wondered when the string would finish.

I refer to Williams again later and show a photo of him (*Plate 17*) with his crew.

After one Cowes Week I again found myself racing in *Doris* at Bournemouth with Sherman Hoyt who invariably attended the regatta as he had a relative in Dorset on whom he called each year. *Doris* was at this time owned by M. Breguet, the French aircraft builder, who came over occasionally to race in the class.

The Committee had planned a course sending us three times round starting from the pierhead. It was a miserable day with steady rain and little wind and when running in to the line after the second round Sherman and I hoped to see the flag to stop the race but it was not hoisted and we were both quite irritated. Sherman's French vocabulary was somewhat limited and being annoyed at the prospect of another wet round and the crew equally despondent he shouted to the skipper, "Regarde le god darn halliard trailing sur la mer."

1934 saw Williams as skipper-mate in his first large racing yacht when Sir Thomas built *Endeavour* to challenge for the America's Cup, and again in *Endeavour II* in 1937.

Reverting to skippers in general and their natural enthusiasm for winning, there are of course black sheep in every family.

I remember sailing a Twelve with my cousin Charles Blake—it was the boat with the charming coffee-serving owner, previously mentioned—when we were all kedged off the East Lepe buoy. One of our rivals set a nylon spinnaker (the first year that this material was used) and as it filled she began to move over her kedge rope. We saw the rope slipping between the foot of the sail and the covering board and it was obvious that the kedge was foul and they could not hold the rope against the pull of the yacht; then we saw the end of the rope go overboard.

As she sailed past us we heard the deep rattle of the large anchor being tapped with its stock, obviously to give the impression that they were stowing the kedge! We asked our host if he had seen the incident but he had not so we had to explain the rule to him.

Our dishonoured rival crossed the line taking first gun.

When back at moorings we called on others in the class who were near but none had seen the incident and one dear fellow told us that he was a fatalist and felt sure the culprit would not win many more races that year. He was right!

Next morning we had an inquiry made at a well-known chandler's to ascertain if 'so and so' had purchased a kedge and the answer was in the affirmative. I may say we were convinced that the owner knew nothing of this; in fact his guest was a well-known politician with the loudest voice in the House, much of which we heard when kedged.

Once in my own boat when starting the race for the Muriel Gretton Cup a well-known gaff cutter with jib-topsail aback seemed to be holding a much better wind than we were and as she drew ahead we saw exhaust smoke coming from her stern. On enquiring whether they were running their engine we received the reply, "I'm only charging my battery"; quite quickly she fell astern and to leeward!

During a race the next day we were running from East Lepe to the South Bramble buoy and an infuriating lady helmsman kept bearing down on us below the line of the next mark. My son reminded me afterwards that I called her, "My dear good woman", when shouting across to request her to desist whereupon she dived below and emerged with a copy of the R.Y.A. rules!

So one felt that some amateurs were black sheep and others should learn the rules.

Luffing is a favourite sport with some and I remember during a race off Harwich in the 12-metre class when two of our greatest but most embittered helmsmen, Jim Barry and Colin Newman, engaged in the fiercest luff I've ever seen. We were sailing *Iyruna* for Sir William Burton and Colin Newman was sailing Sir Thomas Glen-Coats's *Iris*; I don't remember Jim Barry's craft. We saw them roaring away towards France and they had not returned long after we had stowed up!

Arthur C. Connell built *Westra* at Gosport in 1934 and she was top of the 12-metre class for several seasons. Unfortunately her skipper's name escapes me but he was a very pleasant fellow and I sailed with him often for several years.

One year Mr Connell invited me to race her at Plymouth regatta and my wife and I stayed ashore with friends who, by a strange coincidence, were also entertaining my old friend John Scott Hughes. I always enjoyed talking to him with his quiet and thoughtful manner and I regarded him, with his pleasant easy style, as one of our best marine journalists.

Our first race-day was bright with a fresh whole sail breeze and Plymouth Sound at its best and, since that great light-weather helmsman Johnny Payne never cared for sailing his lovely Fife *Vanity* in fresh weather, we invited his nephew to join us as he was a fine strong fellow.

We had a good start with a short turn to wind'ard outside the breakwater to the Knapp buoy which we rounded just ahead of some six others. As we were freeing our sheets for the Tinker (the next mark) in a jumpy sea young Payne slipped to leeward grappling first with the outhaul under the boom, then the skylight rods and finally the lee rail, and overboard he went. We could not execute the usual gybe with a gaggle of boats close astern so we shot up into the wind, observing that Payne was buoyant and breast-high.

Sir William Burton, the last of the fleet in *Marina*, gybed and collected the Channel swimmer and the race was abandoned.

I enjoyed several visits to Le Havre regatta with *Westra* as Mr Connell did not care to go and very kindly let me take the yacht. On two occasions I was joined by Admiral Sir Cyril Fuller and Lady Fuller who was Mr Connell's sister and we had very happy times.

I remember the last of these visits was in the year that Gerry Lambert came over with *Yankee* and *Atlantic*. On the day of our first race it was so hazy that one could not see the mark ahead and there was a light wind with little windward work. Our chief rival appeared to be *Flica* with Hugh Goodson now maturing into one of the best helmsmen in the class.

The Admiral acted as navigator and was remarkably efficient in plotting our course round such a large number of buoys. Lady Fuller had decided to stay ashore that day.

We won and as soon as we had brought up the Admiral suggested we should go to the Palais de Regatte to sign our declaration, so off we went up the long hill in a tram. After much browsing over the race chart and questions as to our satisfactory rounding of each 'numero bisque', to which the Admiral replied very smartly, we were advised that 'we 'ad de prize'. On our downhill journey back to the harbour the Admiral confided in me that had Hugh Goodson preceded us he might have ''ad de prize'!

At this particular regatta the Mayor of Havre gave a dinner-dance at the Club which was a trifle unusual and none of the guests were quite sure what was going to take place. Gerry Lambert was seated on the Mayor's right; I was next to Gerry, whose French was somewhat limited, and we both noticed that the Mayor spent much of the evening bending over the back of his chair watching the dancers. Suddenly Gerry turned to me and said, "I've got it now, John, this Mayor is having a night out!"

It was tragic when *Westra* and *Ornsay*, another Twelve built for Mr Connell just before the war, were both written off when a stick of anti-personnel bombs hit our laying-up area. We made a cigar box for *Westra*'s owner out of her cedar covering board but had the good sense never to send him such a melancholy souvenir.

When the Twelves joined the regatta fleet across the Channel they were sailed over by their crews and their owners either went across in their power tenders or by steamer.

One year we sailed over in *Flame*, then yawl rigged. My brother Richard was just down from Oxford and somewhat tired after his exams and it was agreed to let him sleep on the passage. Passing the Nab I noticed scud over the moon and as the glass was falling I suggested a reef or two before it might be too late but my suggestion was unheeded.

We had a new skipper, Jack Grist, who was with us for many happy seasons; it was the first time our deckhand had crossed the Channel and our cook-steward was a poor sailor. During the night the weather changed for the worse and a northerly gale was building up astern. The cook was ill already, Richard was gently cursing the increasing movement from his bunk and then the skipper came below.

As I scrambled up the companion I saw a pretty steep sea astern; my father had had his fill and the deckhand was at the tiller. I could just see the loom of the land and as Father went below he gave me the course and orders 'to avoid gybing'; we were running slightly by the lee then. Mizzen and staysail had been stowed but, of course, the whole mainsail was far too much canvas and the boom end was dipping in the sea. As every yachtsman knows, that rather shallow coastline with a northerly gale can cause an ugly sea.

The deckhand was now tiring so I sent him below and never had I a more unpleasant three hours at that wretched gunmetal tiller which swept the shallow cockpit. Luckily the morning was sunny and we had a good dry-out on arrival.

I cannot remember more than that Father and I sailed *Iyruna* for Sir William Burton and at Deauville Tony Heckstall-Smith and I danced with the Dolly Sisters who were guests of Mr Gordon Selfridge.

Alf Diaper was another great skipper in the Sycamore tradition who had a long and splendid career.

I first sailed with him when he was skipper of the celebrated

15. *Gareth* and *Carolla*. Two very successful small racing yachts which most influenced Charles E. Nicholson's career were the 5 Rater *Dacia* and the 2½ Rater *Gareth*, the latter shown in the foreground of this picture.

16. Mr Macomber and Captain John Evans fishing in Scotland.

17. *Right:* Skipper Williams and *Mouette* crew.

15-metre *Istria* which we built for Sir Charles Allom in 1912. She was a phenomenal freak with a powerful mid-section and tumble-home, very lightly built and 'hollows' in her ends, and she went like a train.

She was the first yacht ever to be equipped with what was dubbed the 'Marconi' rig; this was the fitting of her topmast in a socket, like a fishing rod joint, instead of 'fidded' down the foreside of the lower mast, and was so named as Senator Marconi had recently invented wireless and high sending and receiving masts were appearing in the countryside.

Another feature was her 'cockpit-dinghy', a specially built little craft with a 'hat-brim' that fitted over the cockpit coaming and in which the owner, skipper and guests all sat: it left more deck space clear and created less windage.

Istria's racing record could only be described as fabulous and two other sisters that joined her in this class were *Pamela* and *Paula* after whom Chris Ratsey named his daughters.

I seem to be dwelling rather long on Sir Charles but one cannot describe these wonderful professionals without writing about their owners. He was a tremendous artist, blessed with a fine physique and he told me that, while studying in Paris it was desired to make a plaster cast of his body and how, due to lack of breathing arrangements, he nearly died.

He played rugby for his county and one evening after inspecting *Istria* building I remember how he overhauled a tram to take him up the road to a garage. He had missed the London train so bought a Calcott coupé for the journey. . . . Times have changed.

Later Diaper succeeded Captain Sycamore and took over the 23-metre *Shamrock* for Sir Thomas Lipton. This yacht was trial horse to *Shamrock IV* in 1920 and went to Sandy Hook with the challenger. After this series Diaper elected to join the New York Police. In those wild days of prohibition there must have been some appeal to this rather dashing fellow, but even he could not stick the racket and returned a year or so later.

Then followed another great experience for him. He was appointed captain in the schooner *Westward* recently purchased by Mr T. B. Davis. Many, no doubt, can recall a variety of interesting events during this rather unusual ownership.

H

Westward preceded her owner to Gosport and I was delighted to meet Diaper again some eighteen years after I had had my first sail with him in *Istria*. He had grown more piratical than ever. His face was never beautiful, the flesh was that of a true shellback and his nose was an indescribable shape. This we felt was an occasion for a little refreshment and, to our surprise, he refused. Knowing him of old we asked him why and he replied that when working for his new owner he felt that a clear head was the first essential, and how wise he was.

Mr Davis was due next morning and, knowing how he liked to give his own instructions, my father arranged that the respective foremen should call on board. Later, one after the other came into the office; all were scared of meeting him again and none wished to take his orders.

My office was next to our reception room and when Mr Davis came ashore the next morning I heard him ask if Mr Charles was in. My door was ajar so I hastily pushed it to as Davis entered the room. Father came down from his upstairs office and then the fun started. I shut the door.

The slanging match was on and I never knew that Father had such an excellent vocabulary of swear words. After some five minutes conversation became normal and they seemed to be having a long talk. Later I heard that Mr Davis was surprised at Father's stand. They ended their talk on most friendly terms and Davis kindly invited him to sail aboard *Westward* whenever he cared to.

Many distinguished guests raced in *Westward* and perhaps the Jellicoe family were aboard more often than most. When Diaper relieved the owner at the helm Davis would amuse his guests by teaching them knots and splices. He made a suit of sails for *Westward* at his home in Jersey, built a launch for her and kept the mates fully engaged during the winter.

I remember after that great race when *Britannia* and *Westward* dead-heated from the Royal Albert Yacht Club how we had reserved a buoy from the King's Harbour Master for *Westward*. It was blowing hard from the West and she came into harbour with all plain sail set. She bore away to the railway jetty and shot into the wind with far too much way on, hitting the buoy a resounding crack on her port bow. The buoy jostled along her topsides and sprung away from her counter, the stampede ending as she grounded her forefoot well and truly into the Coldharbour mud. The whole scene was over in a matter of minutes and the shouting, amplified by the presence of that great sailor Franklin Ratsey, was a never to be forgotten din.

A friend of mine had sold a Rolls to Mr Davis and was invited by him for a sail at any time in Cowes Week. I took him alongside in the family launch when they were setting sail at mooring. Davis was supervising the setting of the fore topsail and was standing by the foremast as my friend leapt aboard. There was no greeting beyond a 'get hold of that gantline' in order to relieve the deckhand for more urgent work. Luckily my friend was something of a sailor and handled the rope round the bitts in able fashion; had he not done so the masthead man might have been in considerable danger.

I believe *Westward* was Alf Diaper's last command and before Mr Davis died he arranged to emulate H.M. King George V by having *Westward* taken out to sea, regrettably to be scuppered.

Diaper had a wonderful personality: he was a very buoyant and tough fellow and I am sure had many encounters in his long association with his owner. I doubt if any other family had more sailors than that of Diaper and I wish I had their family record. It only remains to refer to one other, namely Bill, who had a long sailing career before joining our Firm as a yard boatman and O.C. moorings.

He was very well known by some thousands of yachtsmen over the years, not only those who kept their craft at Gosport but by the large and ever-growing number of those participating in the offshore races sponsored by the R.O.R.C. and starting off the Royal Albert Y.C. starting line. He was a demon for work, obliging, helpful and could turn his hand to anything after so many years of racing and cruising. His colleagues made him an 'Admiral' and he would appear at the Firm's Christmas parties with his dress cocked hat.

Bill was for many years skipper of the little 16-ton *Iota* when owned by Dr and Mrs Atkins of Weybridge. In his younger days he was in the crew of the 12-metre *Mouette* and is to be seen in the photo of her crew in *Plate 17*, looking over Bill Williams's shoulder.

For a season or two he joined the Gawn brothers in our 8-metre *Sagitta* and, of the many incidents I remember, one of the clearest is that of a very hot day racing from Southsea in the year that King Alphonso had his *Hispania* racing in the class.

We were entertaining a young member of the building firm of Echevarrieta & Larrinaga of Cadiz who built the Spanish training ship *Juan Sebastian de Elcano* to my Firm's design. In fact it was the King who was instrumental in the order coming our way as he insisted that the ship should be designed by a good yacht architect.

During the race, on the humid run against the tide to the Outer Spit buoy, our young guest thought it was time for a snack and produced a sizeable wicker hamper with a strap and a bottle of good sherry from which he poured out a full tumbler for Bill who was leaning with his back against the boom to keep it quiet in the swell of the steamers. I was amazed to see him take it and, marvelling at the speed of consumption, I waited to see the effect. There was none at all and I could only assume that Bill's fondness for rum immunized him from any impact a long sherry might cause.

This was in 1930 and *Shamrock V* which had just been built was in dry-dock in Portsmouth Dockyard. After the race the Duke of Miranda phoned from their hotel in Southsea to say that His Majesty would like to inspect *Shamrock*. My heart sank as none of my seniors were available and off I went to the Dockyard. It was Navy Week and some crowds of people were boarding H.M.S. *Victory* near this dry-dock.

On their arrival I was greeted by the King with a smart, "Put your hat on quick", and realized he did not wish to be recognized.

After our inspection of *Shamrock* His Majesty turned to me and said, "Now I'd like to see your Arsenal". In despair I rushed off to the Harbour Master's office and when I approached a Petty Officer he nearly fell over backwards. I then guided our guests to the King's Stairs and along came the picket boat, brass funnel and all. His Majesty turned to his detective requesting him to remain ashore and we proceeded to Gosport.

In high summer few yards are worthy of inspection and I was relieved when my father appeared. He knew the King rather well, having assisted him over matters on his 15-metre *Hispania* some years before, and after inspection of the works and a long yachting talk in the office we escorted him back to the launch.

Back at the office I expressed delight at being invited to design a new tender for the 8-metre *Hispania*: that, my father said, was a gesture and not a line was drawn.

Before concluding my thoughts on Bill, I should mention that he frequently assisted the Royal Albert Y.C. on regatta days and in Cowes Week during the years that I was Commodore of that club. The younger cadet members were taken over to Cowes by Bill and Trevor Lean to see the fireworks. This was the highlight; the children received their quota of chocolate and ginger beer from me and Trevor Lean entertained them with shanties on his squeeze-box. That was also a great event for Bill who, with the captain, had his tot of rum.

In 1909 my Uncle Ben elected to marry, a trifle late in life and my aunt hailed from Yorkshire. He was a walking encyclopedia of yachts and captains, very different from his two brothers and most useful with his flair for 'knowing' these captains, their capacity and their general personalities.

On his wedding day he received a silver salver signed by no less than forty of the donors. My aunt very kindly gave me this wedding salver. It is quite beautiful and I am sure many contemporary yachtsmen would remember the signatures of some of those captains.

In the world of power yachts there were many great captains and only recently we heard of the passing of Captain Merryfield who handled many large yachts and whom I knew and liked well.

I believe Merryfield's last command was the 555-ton motor yacht *Sona* that we originally built for Lord Dunraven. Before resale to another great yachtsman, who was also a peer, a trial trip was arranged—from the vessel's moorings in Southampton Water down to Bournemouth Bay and back. On the bridge, after picking up her mooring, the captain turned to the peer exclaiming, as he rang down 'finished with engines', "You could not do that with steam, My Lord", and received the reply, "But isn't she steam, Captain?"

Another fine sailor was George Courtman, a Jerseyman, whose first big command was the 254-ton ketch *Sylvia*, built for Mr A. S. Butler in 1925.

While building, her owner was away on aviation affairs in Newfoundland and deputed his sister, Mrs Chester Master to deal with a great many issues including internal decoration and this and that. I had several outings in Town with this dear lady, going to a firm in the East End to select marble for a fireplace, to the Goldsmiths and other firms and she said what fun it was to spend someone else's money.

She also christened her brother's lovely ship and on that occasion we had very severe frost which in some way had affected the tallow used for greasing the launching ways. After the bottle was successfully smashed *Sylvia* remained ashore despite hydraulic jacks, etc., but just as we had decided to fit the retaining cleats to the cradle she decided to take to her native element and, with a curtsey, was afloat.

This curtsey, by the way, does not occur when launching a power yacht, but with a sailing yacht with her deep keel the cradle floats out, causing the vessel to dip.

Having qualified himself as a navigator Mr Butler did not want to engage a certificated captain and although Courtman was not 'ticketed' himself he was, with his fine physique and cheerful disposition, the ideal chap for this appointment.

Originally *Sylvia* had a gaff mainsail and jibheaded mizzen and was painted with black topsides. Her first long passage was to Newfoundland where Mr Butler became engaged and made the return voyage as his honeymoon. I remember on his return to Gosport how he, with Mrs Butler, came to the office to tell us that they had decided to repaint the yacht's topsides white and to give her a Bermudian mainsail as the slatting of the gaff was dreadful in the Doldrums.

Later George Courtman became captain of Sir Richard Fairey's 581-ton motor yacht *Evadne*. Sir Richard used this yacht very frequently and since she was always running at full speed she became known as 'The Wandering Jew'. She cruised extensively in Scandinavia and acted as tender to his racing yachts *Shamrock V* and the 12-metre *Evaine* in British waters.

Like so many power yachts *Evadne* saw a deal of war service. She survived and Sir Richard, who had suffered severe illness towards the end of the war, decided to recondition her.

I remember a little trial trip on completion of this refit, the party including Sir Richard and Lady Fairey, their young daughter, a couple of friends and myself representing the Firm.

Sir Richard was then Commodore of the Royal London Yacht Club and he decided to lay off Cowes while the launch went ashore to bring the Secretary on board for lunch. Before we rounded Castle

Point he asked Courtman to strike the Red Ensign and break out the Blue but George replied that, as yet, the warrant had not come through. Fairey then said, 'What's the fine?" and George replied, "£100", whereupon Fairey said, "Break it out." As soon as we were in the Roads the London cannons went into action firing the Commodore's salute and the moment this ended the Blue Ensign came down.

Evadne was Courtman's last command and unfortunately this fine, buoyant and lovable man died rather suddenly.

John Evans is an old friend of mine who has had a remarkably wide and varied career in craft of all kinds and who, I consider, is one of the greatest of all-round yacht captains.

Amongst his various private exploits was the sailing of the 47-ton cutter *West Wind* from Gosport to Buenos Aires which must rate as one of the longest of all 'run' jobs. This could make a story on its own and I give a very brief account of it later on.

After leaving school John Evans's first season was spent in *Coquette,* that celebrated member of the ½-Rating class started by a number of Bembridge yachtsmen in 1890–1. Then followed two seasons in the Luke-designed yawl *Grouper,* a season in the ketch *Little Mary* (of which he was in command for the first time), then three years in the 225-ton auxiliary schooner *Pampa* built at Gosport in 1908.

He then changed from cruising yachts and served in the 100-ton 19-metre class *Norada* for two seasons and then in the 23-metre class 179-ton cutter *White Heather* for another two seasons. Doubtless his experience was widened after four years in those two fine cutters.

After one summer in *Moyana* Evans joined the crew of the well-known auxiliary twin-screw ketch *Fantome,* of 303 tons, owned by the Hon. A. E. Guinness, for cruising in the Mediterranean just before World War I. This was the vessel whose owner was so fond of her that, rather than sell to purchase something larger, he decided to lengthen her by some 33 ft. When she was dismembered and virtually cut in half it was found that she was very rotten in parts and Father telegraphed her owner in Dublin urging him to desist from the operation. A grateful reply was received but with instructions to proceed.

During this conversion Mr Guinness came to the yard after the lengthening was completed and thought that *Fantome* needed a new shape of stem. On removing the original, more rotten timber was discovered, another telegram went to Dublin and the inevitable reply came back. When finally commissioning, Mr Guinness confided in Father that he was determined to complete the work as he had spent his honeymoon in the yacht.

A peculiar incident occurred one Cowes Week when the owner wished to give his guests a short cruise under power. The engines exhausted via the mizzen mast and, when started up, oil smuts covered the ladies' dresses much to everyone's distress. Mr Guinness then fitted an exhaust pipe of flexible metal and trailed it overboard. This looked like a sea-serpent and caused great amusement. When not in use the long pipe was coiled down on deck and lashed.

Later Mr Guinness owned the 611-ton auxiliary twin-screw barque *Fantome II* (ex-*Belem*), a picturesque craft which for many years was 'part' of Cowes Week with her spars floodlit at night. I remember we installed quite a large electric organ in her.

During the first war John Evans served in Naval Transport as quartermaster and, as he states, "Saw my mates studying, did the same and obtained my certificate."

After the war he was engaged by the Crown Agents for the Colonies to take the motor yacht *Pioneer*—which I describe elsewhere—from our Gosport yard to the Fiji Islands where she served as the Governor's yacht and had a long and great career as a 'maid of all work'. Evans told me that he gained valuable experience in reef navigation which proved useful in later years.

His next command was his briefest, ten days in fact, and on the last day the owner came to see his new purchase, the 135-ton ketch *Julnar* hauled up on the slip. This gentleman, who was not at all well, made an appointment to meet his captain at 10 a.m. At 2 p.m. he came up the ladder and Evans ventured a 'good afternoon' and was greeted with, "I don't want to talk, I want to eat"; Evans replied, "So do I," and went home. As he told me, he knew it was 'Trotski's goodbye' so he didn't hurry over his lunch; he also told me that in spite of it all he received from the owner a cheque for £100, which was 'not bad in those days', and a note that "he wanted a 'yes man'", which Evans was not.

Next came his appointment to deliver the 47-ton cutter *West Wind* from Gosport to the River Plate which I mentioned earlier. This lovely craft was purchased by a Mr Walter Mackinlay of Buenos Aires and was built at Gosport in 1906. The story is best told by the following brief summary of the Captain's report:

"A fine little craft. Experienced a SW. gale in Channel, steering gear worked loose on rudder head so put into Plymouth to have it fixed (cost 12/6!). Gale in Bay, then a wonderful run to Madeira in a week. Made one call at St Vincent. Hove-to in South Atlantic for five days, uncomfortable but never in danger. Fine weather going up the River Plate, dismantled all ocean-going gear, gave brightwork a coat of turps and varnish, cleaned brass, laid carpets and put mainsail coat over trysail and on arrival we looked as smart as any vessel off the Yacht Club. Owner was delighted; next day we bent the mainsail and went for a sail and got caught in a 'Pampero'. Having spent a year in the Plate in '*Pampa*' I was forewarned.

When in the Horse Latitudes 'calm' I rigged the spinnaker abaft the mast; having sewn doublings on the tack hanks and rolled and stitched up the foot and sheeted home to the boom end we were 'Bermudian rigged'. Total expenses to owner at end of voyage £5."

After his return John Evans had two seasons in the 79-ton motor yacht *Pearl* built at Gosport in 1921 for the well-known shipowner, Sir James Knott, a great and fiery character who started life as a cook's boy and ended a great career retiring to Jersey. For two years they cruised in the Channel and through the canals to the Mediterranean.

Then Sir James built the motor yacht *Princess* of 751 tons. She was built by a firm with vast experience of shipbuilding. Unfortunately she trimmed by the head and came to Gosport for many modifications but little could be done to improve her trim. I remember she had electrically operated w.c.s that did not always work the right way and, since the owner was renowned for his deep-sea language, Evans explained why these had to be changed for a more reliable type.

After Sir James retired from the yachting scene Evans was appointed to command the motor yacht *Crusader*, 545 tons, built at the Southampton yard in 1927 for Mr A. Kingsley Macomber. Two years later, this gentleman built a larger *Crusader* and both these yachts are referred to in the chapter on power yachts.

The captain's next command, after his long association with Mr Macomber who died just after the war, was the 581-ton *Zapala* (ex-*Evadne*) which I have already mentioned. After two seasons Mr Richard Reynolds of New York, the owner, decided in 1953 to build the 124-ton auxiliary ketch *Aries*, which is described elsewhere, and there is no doubt that Evans was largely responsible for a great many of her features and particularly for details of her rig.

Evans delivered *Aries* for the owner to the Mediterranean and remained as his representative and adviser on sailing matters until Mr Reynolds' death a few years ago.

To conclude this profile of Captain John Evans I must quote from his last letter to me:

"I have been fortunate in being in command of such fine seagoing craft with the finest equipment and picked crews; such a combination enabled us to weather many storms (wind over 100 miles an hour) without loss or damage and to keep to our schedule. Good team work and always a couple of knots up our sleeves!

In these days of motors, D.F., gyro compass, ship to shore telephone and the numerous navigational aids, coupled with frozen foods, etc., the finer points of navigation and seamanship are not necessary. This is applicable to most craft these days. In the early sailing days if anything went wrong the crew could put it right, nowadays a motor stalls and the lifeboat or a helicopter goes to the rescue.

One does not feel the same sense of achievement at the end of a long voyage in power craft as we did in sail; such is progress. However, each age finds its own level, but I am afraid that yachting, as it was between the wars, will never be the same."

John Evans has a brother, Len, who was also a fine sailor. I first had the pleasure of meeting him when he was captain of a nice little schooner lying at Galmpton, that charming sleepy little place on the river Dart.

The owner had died and my mission was that of probate valuation and I remember how helpful the captain was. While there I had the good fortune to meet Mr Peter Hoare and his daughter from Dawlish and they kindly invited me to join them for a picnic lunch in the yard. We sat on timber logs viewing the peaceful scene on a lovely autumn day and had cider from horn flasks.

They owned the trawler type ketch *Serena* which had been built by

Saunders of Galmpton ostensibly for fishing but which was converted to a yacht before completion. The redesign of accommodation had been conducted by my friend Sir Harold Clayton and the Hoares told me that with her heavy hull and displacement she was by no means fast and they felt that *Serena* was the right name!

Len Evans was for many years our special selection for delivering yachts abroad and, in particular, 12-metres that were sold to owners in the Mediterranean. He would refer to them as 'little darlings' and being so easily driven with a small sail area he found they were excellent sea-boats if not pushed too hard.

This reminds me that we too used to have an occasional week-end sail in our 8-metre *Sagitta* and 'shot' all over the Solent under trysail and jib.

Len was a boisterous and piratical looking character and, with his ear-rings, he was stamped as 'THE chap for run jobs'.

To write about all the splendid fellows we met would fill a book. There were people like Captain Harvey from the East Coast who had command of several pretty large steam yachts owned by a well-known member of Lloyds and who wore a sharply pointed waxed moustache and a splendid 'Albert' on his watch-chain. He ran these yachts with real efficiency, was quiet of manner, methodical and a fine sea-going master.

There was Donald McKillop who for many years was captain of Sir Thomas Sopwith's motor yachts. He had a charming personality and great sense of fun and, I suppose, must have been one of the strongest men I knew. He would outlast most, stalking on the hills, and I recall a scene during the war when Sir Thomas and Lady Sopwith brought him over to *Endeavour II*'s store at Gosport, just before this block of stores was bombed flat. The object of the visit was to collect blankets, pots and pans and anything else that might be useful including some thousands of square feet of light Egyptian cotton headsails for conversion to shirts.

Sir Thomas put the Rolls alongside the store entrance and we flaked these huge sails into the back of the car where Donald sat on them to compress them and make room for more. When this operation was over Sir Thomas and I went aboard his 12-metre *Tomahawk* which was hauled up with other yachts on our laying-up slipway.

She had been out of water rather longer than we cared and I suggested that she might go round to Hamble to a mud-berth in a less vulnerable position, a suggestion that appealed to Lady Sopwith who was thinking in terms of 'picnics' and 'house-boats' but she was reminded by Sir Thomas of their existing properties.

When we got back to the car Donald was fast asleep in the greatest of cotton-comfort.

Most of my working life was spent at Gosport. I have a deep interest in human nature and, since I have written mainly about those captains and skippers with whom I worked and sailed, I have found the subject a satisfying one. Many, I fear, are omitted.

Finally, it should not be assumed that there are none left today; there are of course many good fellows engaged in the larger yachts but they no longer 'grow on trees'. In all they are a very great band of competent gentlemen whose restraint, tolerance and seamanship were only learned the hard way and by living with Nature.

9 *Hired assassins*

Having written at some length on professionals it seems fitting that I should touch on their rivals of the times of which I write. Today, of course, the position is reversed and the number of amateurs far exceeds that of professionals.

I always thought the title 'hired assassin' or 'pier-head-jumper' was not too complimentary to those to whom it was applied but those who received it were invariably good helmsmen. Being rather out of touch lately, I am not sure if some more complimentary name has not been found but I am certain that these rare individuals are still in short supply.

In Solent waters in my time there were several very good helmsmen who had a deal of first-rate sailing without the expense of ownership and among the earliest I can remember was Major F. St J. Hughes. He was one of a very fine early Solent yachting family and when seen at the helm of one of our rivals in the 6- or 8-metre class we wished he wasn't there.

His sisters too were among the most celebrated Solent helmswomen of their day and my father enjoyed his long association with the Hughes family.

Strangely, this fine and somewhat dignified retired soldier—and how many soldiers are good helmsmen—had an unusual flair in his later life. Few, I expect, ever thought that he was rather an expert ladies' dress designer. He was always good at sketching and, somehow, this seemed to amuse him, and, I've no doubt, the ladies that he met too.

Lady Constance Baird owned an 8-metre for several seasons and her helmsman was a Mr Keele. He was first-class and respected by all his competitors but I always thought it unusual for such a dashing helmsman to be so shy and reserved ashore.

I remember a particular Cowes Sunday, when the church was always full. I was with my parents and had the misfortune to be in the pew just astern of Lady Constance; I do not think my family noticed it but I was constantly aware of the scent of angelica and was convinced I knew whence it came—a touch of scent, yes, but never angelica.

In the class Mr Keele was known as 'Grannie Keele' but we all knew him as 'the stepney'.

I remember too that on coming out of church there was always a good old hob-nob. On one occasion when I was almost twenty-four Sir William Burton was chatting to my father when he turned to me and, saying that he had to go to Town on Monday, kindly invited me to race his 6-metre *Victoria*. I, of course, was thrilled and, this being my second major invitation, I had become a 'pier-head-jumper' too.

Victoria was a flier in a zephyr but curled up in any weight of wind so I prayed for a light day. It was very light at the start and I opened up a good lead and was doing well on the first round. However, as so often happens in the Solent, when there is little or no wind at the start a decent sailing breeze gets up later and if it is a westerly one it often comes from leeward when it arrives. When it was 'flatters' down the Solent there would be a nice young wind building up off Hillhead and along the north shore. *Victoria* was last.

Since there is so little tidal effect on the Clyde the sudden breezes are largely due to mountain—or I should say hill—effects. In the Solent area I am sure it is the tides, and the tides only, that cause these vast fluctuations of wind and these very fickle conditions and, being at heart a light-weather chap, I do so wish that I had sailed more in tide-free waters.

I remember when racing our 8-metre *Sagitta* one day at Bembridge I was third after seeing, in detail, a classic race by the two in front of me. The helmsmen were Lord Forster and Sir Ralph Gore and, on a perfect sailing day, I felt that I had witnessed a miniature America's Cup race. This must have been the penultimate season in Lord Forster's sailing life. He was such a fine helmsman and so loved by all those who were privileged to meet him that his passing left us in the 8-metre class with an acute sense of vacuum.

Sir Ralph Gore had a long sailing career in the Solent classes, owning the Boat Racing Association 18-ft class *Prudence* among his earlier boats. He also raced Sir John Ward's 6-metre *Jean* and I often crewed him before she went to America with the first team of four boats in the 6-metre class to start the first of that British–American 6-metre series. As a youngster, lying up to wind'ard under the deck at the fore end of the cockpit with Sir Ralph above me sitting on the deck at the helm, all I could see was one foot braced to a slatted seat used for light weather sailing; the other leg was crossed and I marvelled at his beautiful instep—funny how little things 'stick' but I remember he had beautiful feet.

Sir Ralph relieved Sir Philip Hunloke in 1937 both as Commodore of the Squadron and President of the R.Y.A. and held these offices until 1956. He was also reserve helmsman in *Endeavour II* for Sir Thomas Sopwith and was undoubtedly a five-star H.A.

Claude Hapgood was a first-class Solent H.A. and a great friend of mine. On the occasion of that fine race between Lord Forster and Sir Ralph, the Bembridge Committee were operating from a marquee from Under Tyne and, having won third prize, I went ashore to declare, feeling a trifle embarrassed as I made my dis-honoured way up the slippery beach to that marquee with all eyes, including the ladies', focused on me. To my great relief Claude Hapgood was there and, evidently realizing my nervous condition, he remarked quietly, "Don't bother John, there's no one here who can really sail a boat". This was a relief to me but we both knew how wrong he was as not only are the Bembridge helmsmen renowned, and their ladies in particular, but most of them are good H.A.s.

Sir John Ward, whom I have just mentioned, seldom sailed his 6-metre *Jean*. I remember when she was new having a trial sail in her with her skipper Ned Pound, another of the Portsmouth fisher-men and a very good skipper but rather portly.

On coming ashore I met Mr William Rowe the yachting tailor who specialized in outfits for both owners and crews. He had evidently, while waiting on The Hard for a tram to take him to lunch, been watching our return to harbour and enquired how the boat was shaping up. In my reply I mentioned Ned as being a good chap with which he agreed, adding, "But he's too big for the boat John". Of course, he was right and years later, with the utmost respect, I thought of exactly the same thing in the case of Owen Aisher and his 5·5-metre *Yeoman.*

Another Solent helmsman, very much in demand as a H.A., was that splendid fellow Joe Hannen, Commodore of the Lee-on-the-Solent Sailing Club for many years, whom I have mentioned several times before. He often sailed Mrs Schnapper's 6-metre *Cresta* and I sailed with him in several Cory Cup races, particularly in Dragons.

Captain R. T. Dixon was another who had our greatest respect in the 8-metre class when, for several seasons, he steered Captain Dowman's *Cutty* to top the class. Another good H.A. in that class was Captain Tony Somers who sailed Mr Worth's 8-metres. I remember he wore a comfortable blue seaman's jersey (none of that collar and tie nonsense) and his tactics and helmsmanship were of a very high order.

'Boy' O'Connor had quite a spell sailing *Velsheda* for Mr Stephenson but I don't class him among the top H.A.s. I remember his father racing successfully in the handicap class, and how well his three sisters used to dance at Lady Baring's charity ball; indeed, I remember how embarrassed I became when these young ladies phoned me at my office from Town urging me to join them for parties. What must the staff think? etc!

I've mentioned both Major Jim Barry and Mr Colin Newman elsewhere and, my goodness, they were really hot stuff; and so one could go on.

My cousin Charles comes very much into this bracket as does his son Peter who perhaps, is just as good as Father was and, I feel, it was he who was the 'king' of hired assassins.

10 Unusual craft

I see from Lloyds Yacht Register of 1927 that the Hon. A. E. Guinness owned six craft of various kinds: they comprised two converted ex-war Canadian-built motor launches named *Amo* and *Amo II*, the 303-ton auxiliary schooner-ketch *Fantome* which we had lengthened for him some years before, the 611-ton auxiliary barque *Fantome II*, ex-*Belem*, built at Nantes in 1896, the ex-war Coastal Motor Boat (*C.M.B. 101*) designed and built by Thornycroft's in 1919 and named *Oma*, and finally the Saunders-built 30-ft hydroplane *Oma II* built in 1925 in which one of the engines I am about to refer to was later installed. It is the penultimate craft *Oma* that may well come under the heading of this chapter.

Mr Guinness approached us with a view to acquiring a 70-ft C.M.B. from Admiralty disposal. These craft were equipped with three Thornycroft petrol engines staggered to suit the restricted beam and it was his intention to install a fourth engine.

After studying the proposal we advised him that it was not possible but that an alternative was to install an engine on deck driving an aerial propeller, a proposition that tickled him immensely, so we purchased a 450 h.p. Napier Lion engine from Air Ministry disposal for the remarkably low sum of £100.

During the war my father and Sir Charles Allom had founded a small aircraft company, referred to earlier, and we enlisted their co-operation in the design of engine seating structure and propeller characteristics. When the work was completed and we had run basin trials we arranged to take *Oma* to Netley, where Mr Guinness was lying with *Fantome II*.

I

All four throttle controls were grouped for the helmsman and I remember when Mr Guinness took the helm he much enjoyed advancing all the throttles and telling us with a cheerful smile that he had shares in such and such a large oil company!

It is sad to relate that the increase in speed with the extra 450 h.p. was no more than three knots but we believe the owner enjoyed the novelty of the experiment and, in the ensuing Cowes regatta, *Oma* was the 'talk of the town'.

Round about 1910 the family launch was named *Constance* and I remember she was fitted with a cabin shelter with a top rather like a gipsy's caravan but was a sleeky, distinctive craft with light displacement and pleasing water-lines. Since Constance was the name of one of my aunts I suppose it was natural that both my mother and another aunt, Lucy and Gertrude respectively, were slightly jealous.

In 1912, when my father was concerned with the design of *Shamrock IV*, he built a prototype launch of 50 ft embodying several of his structural ideas for *Shamrock*. The launch was appropriately named *Gelyce*, these being the first and last letters of these three ladies. She was less than 8 ft beam on the waterline and built on this particular multi-stringer technique with laminated mahogany planking over fore and aft stringers and with laminated frames Where *Shamrock* had deep web frames the bulkheads in *Gelyce* served that purpose and the engine bearers ran right fore and aft as did the cabin and cockpit seats, in the same alignment, for longitudinal strength.

This prototype was a great success and the annual formula seemed to dictate a new 50-ft hull, with a 100 h.p. engine, to replace last year's model which was invariably sold after the summer. Only minor improvements were made; sometimes the sheer was altered or the cabin profile was modified; sometimes there was a change of engine but from 1912 until 1935 there was always this family launch

They were adopted for service by the Port of London Authority and the Tyneside Commission and four others were built to special order. One of these named *Eido*, built for an Argentine client, was the centre-piece of rather an unusual story.

Eido had a six cylinder Green engine installed. This was by far the lightest of all marine engines at that time and developed some 12, h.p.; the cylinders were separated and fitted with copper water jackets and they were good to look at; they were based on the little Green engine that was installed in the baby Avro biplane that was flown so well by Bert Hinkler in those days.

Most of the family launches had 100 h.p. Daimler sleeve-valve engines installed, and were beautifully quiet; these were ex-tank wartime disposal engines which we marinized.

Eido with her very light and slightly more powerful engine achieved 21½ knots; she had the standard layout but was fitted with specially large petrol and water tanks which, in the event, proved to be rather important.

Green's engineer asked me if we could have a short run one evening to test an adjustment and as my father and uncle had been racing our 6-metre *Rose* at a Solent class regatta at Calshot I thought we would intercept them sailing home. It was an early June evening with a bright and lowering sun.

As we returned through the harbour entrance I was in the cockpit and my seniors in the cabin when I turned to see how the tide was leaving Blockhouse Point. The next thing I knew was that the little saloon table was splintered all around and under me the two gentlemen were getting up with their faces covered in blood. We three went aft to the cockpit and I rushed forward to the steering cockpit to find that Green's engineer had a nasty gash in the calf of his leg, having been flung over the exposed engine flywheel, but that the cox, who was really to blame, was unhurt.

On rejoining the others I was about to collect Father's binoculars from the cabin but he restrained me, fearing we were sinking though somehow I felt we wouldn't.

The cause of the disaster was a heavy Naval picket boat, steaming out of Haslar Creek down sun, which struck us just forward of the engine. Our cox, who was always rather proud of these smart launches, was inclined to enter harbour with a flourish and too fast. This was his undoing but in spite of this he remained our cox for many more years. By this time two yard rowing boats were standing by (no yard launches in those days) and we all boarded one and returned to the office.

Those two almost empty extra large tanks in *Eido* kept her afloat. *Gelyce* was in service as the Nicholson family launch for year after year. I include her in this chapter as, although most functional, she was certainly unusual. Light construction, 100 h.p., 50 ft long and less than 8 ft beam at the waterline equals twenty knots!

I mentioned that the Port of London Authority had one of these launches and, after she had given some twenty-seven years' service, they approached us in 1951 for a replacement.

Requirements had changed with the times and, as twin-screw diesel engines were specified, we designed a 55-ft hull sufficiently wide in beam to accommodate these engines abreast—our suggestion of staggered engines to reduce beam was not accepted.

This second edition of the launch *Nore* was a maid-of-all-work and performed a large variety of duties as a V.I.P. launch, meeting distinguished foreign guests to the City and being used for entertaining visitors up and down the great river.

Later, we were informed that *Nore* might be required to fulfil the duties of a royal barge for ceremonial occasions and, after discussion in great detail with senior representatives of the Authority, we obtained the expert assistance of the late W. Howard Jarvis, S.M.A., and our proposals were submitted to the Palace. A good deal of criticism resulted and it was asked that she be made to look a little less like the Lord Mayor's coach!

Jarvis, who worked remarkably fast, prepared alternative sketches in full detail in next to no time and the proposals were finally approved. The canopy was designed to be fitted and removed quickly and every detail was carefully and artistically considered. Tridents and dolphins were cast in white metal, the Royal Cipher was inscribed and the Crown, gilded with mercurial gilt on its cushion, was fitted to the canopy top; blue and silver was the theme for decor.

On the first occasion of her duty as a royal barge, *Nore* was much admired by Her Majesty. After presentations by the Chairman of the Authority to a fortunate few of my Firm with Mr Howard Jarvis, Her Majesty, accompanied by H.R.H. Prince Philip, inspected the Royal Barge Master and Watermen in their colourful uniforms, before boarding the launch and proceeding upstream from Tower Pier.

This was a colourful and moving moment, and one that could never be forgotten, as the riverside cranes dipped in salute and ships' sirens blew a crescendo of welcome.

One little incident comes to mind when looking back on this rather novel and unusual duty. When we were constructing a mock-up of the canopy in a rather secluded bomb damaged cottage near the works, we received a visit from the Manager of the Authority, Sir Leslie Ford, and the Chief River Superintendent, Captain Coleman, and after an inspection we went to my house for lunch. Sir Leslie was looking rather sunburnt and when my wife inquired if he had been abroad he replied, "No, but our kitchen sink faces south."

Nore, beautifully maintained, still fulfils her many duties and I always look for her when the Boat Race is televised as the Chairman and his guests generally use her.

In 1950 Colonel Ralph Blewitt wrote to me enclosing what he termed his desiderata for a somewhat unusual yacht. He wanted a sloop-rigged auxiliary for use under power until it was blowing fresh, when he would break out his canvas. He described his other requirements and concluded with "Over to you, John."

The Colonel desired a mast fitted in a deck tabernacle for lowering when cruising in the European canals and waterways; his modest sail requirements called for a small roller-reefed mainsail, a working foresail, storm foresail and modest Genoa jib that could be boomed out downwind.

We soon had draft plans completed; these comprised a waterline length of 30·75 ft, slightly over 11 ft beam and 6 ft draught. Armed with these and copious notes, I pursued my way to Boxted, near Colchester, in my worthy Alvis car.

One could not meet a more charming family and I trust they would forgive me for describing the somewhat intimate impressions of a rather unusual evening.

Surprise number one was the arrival of a very gallant young soldier wearing a cherry-red dinner jacket suit and when he replied to the Colonel's comment of "Good Heavens what on earth, etc." I realized that he had a rather troublesome stutter. His explanation was that on his death his uncle had not included him in the will so he thought he would take one of his suits.

It must have been well into the next morning when, sustained by Scotch, we finished the scrutiny of my plans, and when we broke up the Colonel took me to my room. Flinging the door wide open and displaying a fine draped four-poster he exclaimed, "That's your bed

John and you can take it from me that no queen ever slept in it";
before closing the door, he announced that the gardener would bring
me a cup of tea in the morning. I slept well and truly.

Ralph Blewitt was Olympic Captain at the Torbay Regatta; he
was a fine whip and a Commodore of the Royal Artillery Yacht
Club. His daughter Mary Pera, known as Maria, is a fine sailor,
navigator and cook. She was navigator for several successful seasons
in the well-known yawl *Bloodhound* when owned by the late Sir Miles
Wyatt and raced her own boat in the Admiral's Cup series in 1969.

After satisfactory trials of *Larph*, as she was named (an anagram
on Ralph) she was entered for the Princess Elizabeth Cup race at
the Household Brigade Yacht Club and I was kindly invited to take
her and hoped for a good breeze. Our party in this handy owner-
driven yacht comprised the owner and Maria, Brigadier John Barry,
my son Christopher and myself.

We had a nice breeze and with our exceptional rating due to
such modest sail area I sensed that we were 'in the money' but
unfortunately the wind cut on the second round and, if my memory
serves me, the race was won by Chris Ratsey in *Evenlode*.

When her delightful owner died *Larph* was sold and has changed
hands several times since.

Not a 50/50 but more of a 60/40 motor/sailer and rather a lovely
family boat.

In 1933 Mr W. K. Vanderbilt introduced a Mr Woodbury
Parsons to us. This gentleman was curator of some of the leading
museums and art galleries in America; he was a bachelor of considerable charm and among the world's leading art connoisseurs.

He told us that he desired a graceful and pleasing craft with
limited draft for cruising in search of art treasures in all kinds of
places in the Mediterranean and Aegean seas and she was to be
named *Saharet* after her smaller predecessor. After the preliminary
discussions he returned to America, leaving us to build this teak
planked 90-ft auxiliary ketch with a canoe hull form drawing as
little as 8·4 ft.

During construction the time arrived for the owner to select the
shade of green he desired for bulkheads with the walnut fittings so
we sent him a cable and received the following reply: "Kindly
examine kernel of a pistachio nut—Parsons." This is a particularly

lovely shade of green and, I thought, the perfect way to describe his choice. Being a bachelor, Mr Parsons often sought my wife's advice on little details one of which was the question of loops or button holes for lavatory towels.

Parsons was a member of the Yacht Club Italiano and had to lay up in Genoa but fortunately for us he elected to cruise a little down the west coast before leaving for the Mediterranean. He asked us if we could find someone who knew the waters to join him and, happily, we found E. G. Martin. It will be remembered that George Martin, whose lines I have quoted at the beginning of this book, was the Founder of the Royal Ocean Racing Club and was also something of an artist himself, illustrating his book *Sailorman* in colour and playing his Strad violin beautifully.

These two had a splendid time together and one evening, at Plymouth regatta, my father and I called on them after dinner; we moved quietly alongside the gangway, stowing the oars gently, and heard that violin. We crept on board and waited on deck until the music stopped. Martin told us that the acoustics of that cabin were better than the Wigmore Hall and I dare say an all-wood room with a fine cabin-top was the chief reason.

I see in the Register that Mr Parsons still owned *Saharet* in 1947 but we have now lost touch with her. Having a teak-planked hull I suspect she is still in commission under some other name.

During the war, on those boring evenings when fire-watching, it was hard to find much to do before turning in and I used to sketch or doodle a good deal. I thought, when it is all over, no one will be able to afford a cruiser as well as a racing boat and I did a number of odd sketches of what I described as a cruiser-racer.

My earlier shots embraced an ogee or hump-backed deckline in elevation but eventually I adopted a broken sheer with a folding cabin top rather similar to those seen on the Broads.

This little craft, appropriately named *Phoenix*, was the first yacht to be built at Gosport when war ended. She was 32 ft 4 in overall and was rated as 5 tons in the Register. With a canoe-form body built over almost a fin keel she had poor stowage space and one had literally to live out of a suitcase. My cousin Charles used her for a season or two and did remarkably well in the small handicap class.

Next year we built three slightly longer but I was distressed that my father would not approve my proposed slight extra beam. The result was that, with their light displacement, they had near 8-metre performance and Charles Blake and his wife named theirs *Cinderella* and did remarkably well in offshore and inshore racing.

Neither the smaller prototype nor her three sisters were pretty and their broken-sheer treatment was not artistically conceived or executed.

Some years later we designed a really good boat to this theme for Dr J. M. Park. Named *Feng Huang* (Sacred Bird), she was 36 ft 6 in overall and, built in Hong Kong, she was consequently planked with teak and generally a shade heavier than if built with mahogany. Her charming owner described her unusual launching ceremony which had to take place at night because of, I believe, either a strike or a public holiday next day. He kindly sent my wife a delightful piece of most delicate embroidery of the Sacred Bird; it arrived rolled up in newspaper and rather creased. Our picture framer ironed out the silk most beautifully and for years it has been hung and gives pleasure to many. *Feng Huang* was a vastly improved model in every department and was the final outcome of those fire-watching sketches.

I have already described the ketch *Aries* which, although quite orthodox externally, had a number of unusual features which warrant her inclusion in this chapter.

Her American owner, the late Mr R. J. Reynolds, was a bachelor when the plans were first drawn up and the accommodation was arranged accordingly. However, before her completion he became engaged and modifications were necessary. The layout of accommodation was of a modest nature but it included some very interesting and unusual items. Among these was a variety of stainless steel 'safari' tanks to carry food for varying numbers of people; they were stowed under hatches in such a way that any one could be selected and used at choice. Another feature worthy of mention was the folding bed in the owner's cabin; when not in use this appeared as an electric fireplace with overmantel and, on pressing a switch, the bed descended surrounded by a floodlit alcove.

She was equipped with every conceivable kind of navigational aid including radar and, as I mentioned earlier, had three forms of steering. The nerve centre of all the instrumentation was the chartroom which was a breathtaking compartment.

On deck *Aries* was most functional in every way; her boats were based on the Banks fishing dories and were nested for stowage; her rig was all inboard and she had portable outriggers for squaresail guys. Her rig was designed to enable the owner to get under way single-handed when he wished and much thought was given to the provision of power winches, special sheeting and other items to facilitate this.

This fine ship was later presented to the American Geological Society and is still in commission.

Although this is a yachting book I feel that I must, in this chapter, mention some of the most unusual craft that were constructed during the Second World War.

During this conflict, and much under the jurisdiction of a good friend, 'Bill' Holt of the R.C.N.C., Admiralty, we built a wide variety of small craft and, since he was a fine sailor and cruising yachtsman, his appointment to handle these rather special top-secret small craft was very fitting.

It all started through a special requirement called for by a Major March Phillips, reputed to be among the bravest in the Army, who, as a friend of that great horseman and yachtsman, Ike Bell, was put in touch with us.

The first project was a small two-man canoe to be produced to suit specified requirements of a rather testing nature including very limited silhouette or outboard profile and the carriage of two occupants plus 30 lb of limpet explosive. Everything was weighed carefully and displacement was checked to the last ounce.

We adopted a special form of light but very strong 'planking' by using a new process known as Jablo which was heavily compressed wood, remarkably thin and supplied in sheets. The canoes, which were built by women, were 14 ft long and of panel section, that is to say, they had four flat sections each side.

After a time when the Special Boat Section Commando was formed we developed numerous other types and sizes of canoes fitted with 'catamaran' portable stabilizers. All had paddles, some had small sails and the last and most fascinating were electrically driven.

Some were designed to fit a submarine's torpedo-loading hatch and many were sectional in three parts joined by luminous plates and ski-clips as worn round the heel of the boot; buoyancy was obtained by filling in with ping pong balls under fore and aft decks.

For the electrically driven craft we used a half horse-power lorry starter motor driven off special batteries as the 'engine', driving a little propeller that would almost fit a watch-chain. The battery compartment had knife contact plates so that they would drop out in the event of a capsize.

Sorbo rubber pads were fitted fore and aft to take the chin of the forward occupant and the back of the head of the aft man; steering was by the continuous wire running either side under the half-decking.

The requirement was five miles an hour for three hours and, when running the first trial with hands holding me alongside a workboat, I was surprised that full speed was obtained within seconds of their letting go. During this rather tedious trial we were chased by the Harbour Police but the yard boat quickly advised them that it was Admiralty research and the Sergeant in charge could not resist coming near enough to hail me with a, "You must have a wonderful little engine there, sir!"

These electric canoes greatly assisted those gallant fellows in reaching their objective after a submarine had surfaced around the six fathom line.

Colonel 'Blondie' Hasler, then Major Hasler, was among the brave users of these craft, particularly in his epoch-making assault depicted in the film of *The Cockleshell Heroes* and General Mark Clark was landed in Africa by one of them.

An amusing incident occurred when we presented the Commanding Officer of a nearby active operational base with a flagstaff and the flag of the S.B.S.C. which was the clenched hand holding the dagger emerging from the sea. He was so pleased that he advised us that the flag would only be worn when V.I.P.s called at the Base and the Union Flag would normally be used. A nearby Royal Observer Corps station spotted the flag upside down and phoned the Base to enquire if they were in distress!

Another phase of vital smallcraft construction was that of surfing boats and in this we were associated with another old friend of the family, Nigel Warington Smyth, who was attached to a branch of the Navy known as D.D.O.D.I.

The landing of special persons in special places, often in surf, called for deep analysis and study and, as a great cruising yachtsman from the West Country whose father was the author of *Mast and Sail in Europe* and *Mast and Sail in Asia*, Nigel felt that this study was, at least, next to yachting in war-time.

We co-operated with D.D.O.D.I., and Nigel in particular, in the development of surf-landing techniques, and trials were conducted in surf off the Cornish coast. Nigel based his thoughts largely on the famous American whalers and after early experiments we realised that one of the prime factors in hull design was what we called negative buoyancy in the ends of the craft, in other words, hollow waterlines fore and aft but a powerful mid-section.

The optimum of all this research was a fine easy hull of 27 ft and at her trials she came roaring through the big waves as steady as a rock with the cox steering with a long sweep. These craft were used in many operational raids and landings including the Sark raid.

The last and among the most interesting boats we developed with Nigel was a 27-ft sailing and pulling craft for the Hydrographer of the Navy who, at that time, was Admiral Wyatt—a brother of Sir Miles Wyatt.

Our yardstick, according to hierarchy, was to be the well-known but somewhat old conception, the 27-ft Montague whaler. These boats served the Navy well for a great many years and were really designed by Arthur Payne; they were rather tender and by no means as powerful as they might have been but they served well as regatta boats and certainly rowed well.

Our 27-ft boat had a far more powerful mid-section but embraced many of the features of the Banks fisherman, her construction naturally being more up to date with double-skin planking and laminated stem and wood keel; she had a centre-plate and gunter rig, all spars stowing inboard. The mast was stepped well into the boat and the rather futile mizzen carried in the Montague craft was discarded.

This, in the middle of a world war, was a breath of fresh air and Nigel, Louis Jacobs our Chief Draughtsman and I went 'small-boating' a good deal. Our trial sails against the old whaler were most conclusive on all points of sailing but unfortunately, the day the Admiral joined us for a proving trial, a full gale was blowing when the harbour gusts are frequent and may come from anywhere. We tested the storm rig thoroughly and adjourned for a little special lunch that we had laid on in my office. Our dear good friend Meotti, who ran an excellent café in the Town, had contrived to make little pastry models of our 27-ft boat filled with delicacies seldom met in war-time.

After lunch, with a spring tide roaring out of the harbour, the wind fell absolutely flat and a yard boat towed us well up harbour where we found little airs in Portchester Lake but not sufficient to show the Admiral how well she moved. Coming back to a steel mooring buoy off the yard the Admiral, who was at the helm, asked the best way to meet the buoy and we advised him to shoot hard round. For some reason he misunderstood and we struck the buoy head-on down tide. The Admiral feared we had fractured our stem but I assured him it was laminated and very strong and on inspection all was well.

Turning to other 'odd' craft, we developed soon after the war a small 20-ft hydrofoil craft from a hull built by Hamper of Fareham, the foil itself being handmade of boiler plate.

The instigator of this little development was a Captain Hampden who was an old First War friend and associated with the Coastal Motor Boats in that war. Known in the Navy as 'Happy Hampden' he was so obsessed with hydrofoil technique that we told him we felt he suffered from chronic 'hydrofolia'! His technical assistant who was extremely competent was Lieut.-Commander McPherson, R.N.V.R.

A continental Ford engine was installed to drive the deeply immersed propeller attached to a special bracket taking the rudder and a small fin; the latter could be actuated plus or minus one degree to assist 'take-off'. After early setbacks including the shipping of a great deal of water, and the fitting of a water deflector round the bow we were beginning to lose a condition that Hampden dictated to his female secretary as 'bottom-slap' but with propeller modifications to increase revolutions we became 'foil-borne'. Had a variable pitch propeller been fitted we should have performed better as once we were foil-borne the throttle was no more than third advanced.

We demonstrated the prototype to all and sundry including

various Ministries but little enthusiasm was engendered and, as funds had expired, the project was dropped. Meantime other European countries and America have forged ahead and produced functional commercial craft.

In passing, we feel there are many applications for the foil but perhaps the danger of submerged objects discourages more general adoption. I still toy with the idea of retractable foils attached to a flying boat to assist take-off and increase pay-load; this might encourage the return of flying-boats which, long ago, were so foolishly written off in this island with its thousands of miles of free runways.

Another odd little war-time boat which we were asked to develop was a small towing craft, to be known as a Slug, for towing the Mulberry Harbour 'beetles' into position to take the causeways to the shore. This operation was controlled by the Royal Engineers from whom we had a full briefing on operational tactics.

I see from our records that these craft were described as 'towing boats' as the venture was top-secret. They were 20·5 ft overall and sixty-five of them were built.

A friend of mine was working on the marine side with the Austin Motor Company during the war and I believe he was the only chap in Birmingham to wear a yachting cap at that time. His war-time ambition was to get all commercial ships' lifeboats fitted with engines which we felt was a splendid objective.

Affectionately known as 'Hell's-Bells Helberg' and a pre-war owner of an old Rater, he provided the engines—two to each boat, fitted with propeller reduction gears for towing. Construction was orthodox with plywood planking and chine form for ease of production; they were fitted with crash-bars to protect the users under bridges and had a vertical lever instead of a wheel or tiller, this being thought easier for the uninitiated 'Pongo'.

Dwelling on the Sappers a little longer, I must digress for a moment on Service yacht clubs and their great impact on the sport. It is good to reflect that the Royal Engineer Yacht Club, the oldest service yacht club in the country, owned for a great many years the little 20-ton cutter *Ilex* which we built in 1899 and in which they achieved great success in the earlier days of the Royal Ocean Racing Club. It is good to know that this link still prevails and that they now own one of our latest G.R.P. craft.

At the risk of being a little indiscreet I cannot refrain from telling of a rather amusing war-time incident. The Royal Engineers were using one of our 50-ft 'family' launches, mentioned elsewhere, fitted with echo sounder over the bow for the survey of French beach-heads. This particular launch had a Daimler 'marinized' engine of right-hand rotation but later they installed a more powerful American engine with left-hand rotation. One can only assume that they installed the new engine themselves and after trials they reported that speed had fallen right off but that she ran very fast astern. Asked if they had changed the propeller they replied 'No' and obviously they had been running for a great many hours in reverse which speaks wonders for the reverse box!

Having 'told a tale' I cannot reiterate too strongly how we treasure the privilege of our long association with the various service yacht clubs.

A younger but most active club founded in 1933 is the Royal Artillery Yacht Club for whom we built the sloop *St Barbara*, and who now possesses one of our latest type.

Another smaller but most active service club is the Coastal Forces Sailing Club founded in 1951, now more important than ever as, since Coastal Forces have disbanded, this little body preserves a great name in the history of the Navy.

In my next chapter, Summer-house, I describe the last of these unusual war-time craft. This was conceived in rather unusual circumstances and surroundings and so I have thought it best to treat it to a chapter of its own.

I make no apologies for introducing these war-time craft into what is intended to be a yachting book as I feel they are of sufficient interest to warrant putting on record. If I have over-emphasized the part played by my Firm I can only plead that this has been unavoidable in the circumstances and it leaves me with the conviction that, in times of stress, the good all-round capacity of a yacht yard and the ability of yachtsmen to improvise and diversify can be invaluable.

11 Summer-house

A few months after the last war started we received a contract from the Admiralty to construct eight anti-submarine patrol craft for Turkey. Turkish Naval representatives visited us frequently and the Naval Attaché referred to them as 'our fighting yachts'. We felt sure, all along, that the Admiralty would take them over for a number of reasons, chiefly we thought as they were very able craft and, under certain conditions, were better than any other Coastal Force vessels at the time.

The inevitable occurred; alternative craft were, we assumed found for Turkey and the Admiralty took over their completion first as anti-submarine craft, later as M.T.B.s and finally as M.G.B.s. The Commanding Officer of the Gosport Coastal Forces Base, H.M.S. *Hornet*, jokingly called them his 'Heinz' boats as they had had so many varieties of purpose during building.

Just as they were getting into a complete flotilla for normal duties after a large number of modifications, five were singled out for a very vital assignment.

We attended a top-level conference at the London office of the shipping firm of Ellerman Wilson and were advised that Mr Churchill was behind the project and it was to be the most accelerated job of refitting we ever undertook.

The mission was to run the gauntlet to the Skaggerak from the port of Hull to collect Swedish ball-bearings of which there was an acute shortage.

Ellerman Wilson's provided the volunteer captains and some of the crews and Sir George Binney was appointed Commodore. After the preliminaries were over and we had a grasp of the facts we suggested weight saving wherever possible to increase weight of cargo—weather-cloths instead of bulwarks, hollow spruce derricks instead of steel to serve the holds, a strong but light ply-wood deckhouse for officers' cabins and many other small but important features.

This was so secret that no one else in the Firm was told anything and as our temporary Office and senior members of the staff were at my uncle's house in Alverstoke, some two miles from the yard, we decided to use the revolving summer-house in the garden, which was well placed for private discussion, as 'head office'.

The shipping company were most co-operative and their General Manager, Paterson, resident until completion, was a splendid fellow and extremely helpful.

We began to find that the craftsmen were naturally critical of gutting out a large amount of expensive equipment that had only recently been installed in these miniature 'light cruisers' but this predicament was greatly eased by a visit from Mr Alexander, then First Lord of the Admiralty. He was rather lame so I took his arm and asked him what he wished to see first and he replied, 'Anything'.

After showing him a few interesting craft under construction we went afloat in a yard boat to look at two of these 'blockade runners'. The men working on both came onto the foredeck of one and he gave them a stirring talk but said nothing of the mission. After his departure there were no more grumbles and I felt a deep sense of pride for the spirit of Britain's craftsmen, fighting as they were at that time with their backs to the wall.

Our summer-house talks continued. At one time a staff officer complete with red tabs turned up and the next time we met him he was on security and checking the pubs at Hull, wearing a seaman's jersey and a cloth cap.

One Friday a delightful young Swedish fellow, who had been flown in the belly of a Mosquito, visited us. He was, I learned, responsible for the loading of the cargo and I was envious when he told me that on the Sunday following he would be sailing his 30 square metre.

The requirements for these craft included a range of 2,000 miles and a speed of 20 knots with a cargo of 50 tons of ball-bearings. They were of round bilge displacement form and had Paxman diesel

18. UNUSUAL CRAFT. *Oma*, powered by three internal engines and one on deck driving an aerial propeller.

19. UNUSUAL CRAFT. The Royal barge *Nore*. The picture shows the Queen being greeted at Tower Bridge where the royal barge master and watermen were inspected and Her Majesty embarked.

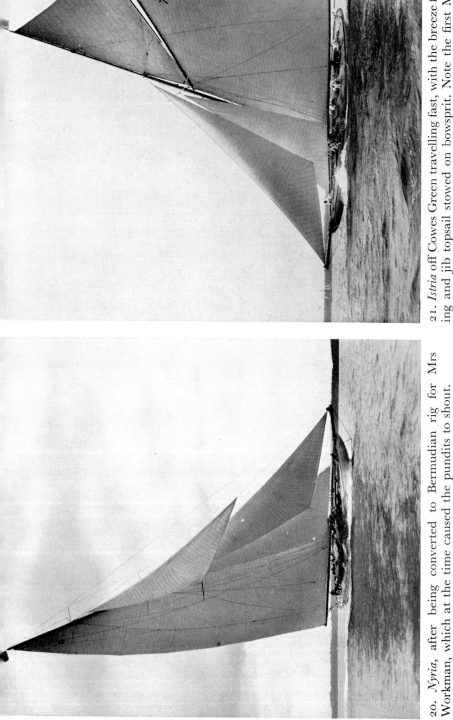

20. *Nyria*, after being converted to Bermudian rig for Mrs Workman, which at the time caused the pundits to shout.

21. *Istria* off Cowes Green travelling fast, with the breeze freshening and jib topsail stowed on bowsprit. Note the first Marconi mast.

engines, the latter being one of the reasons for their selection as they had greater cruising range than craft with petrol machinery.

When the first was completed Frank Murdoch and Paterson took her round to the Thames for trials on the Greenwich mile with illuminating results.

The trials were under light and loaded conditions using ballast for cargo. We had records of running angles or 'squat' in the fore and aft line of these vessels as gunboats when something in the order of 2½ degrees was averaged; in the case of these loaded trials the 'squat' was considerably more yet a slightly increased speed was obtained which proved that the displacement form of hull was virtually planing slightly.

Sir George Binney was very fond of playing patience and one day while doing so he decided to name these boats from *Pilgrim's Progress* thus they became *Hopewell*, *Nonesuch*, *Gay Viking*, *Gay Corsair*, and *Master Standfast*.

Since these blockade runners were to operate out of convoy and, of course, on moonless nights we arranged through my late brother-in-law, Air Vice-Marshal Sir Thomas Warne-Browne, as he was at that time, for their recognition photos to be taken. A Lysander pilot took immense trouble and got many illuminating photos; this, I felt, was a new way to study wave form and the wake form at varying speeds was extremely interesting.

One day when we were running one of these craft on the de-gaussing range off Portsmouth I noticed a youngster wearing the kilt and was told by Paterson that he was 'Sparks' and that he had volunteered provided he was allowed to retain his national dress.

As time progressed and the manning was completed I felt it would be nice to present the captains with good manly pipes so I wrote to the celebrated firm in Duke Street with my tongue in my cheek as, in those days, one had to queue up for a pipe. I stated that they were required for a handful of very gallant fellows and could they possibly oblige. We received them almost by return post.

Our little meetings in the summer-house were now all over as the last, *Master Standfast*, proceeded to Hull. We all felt we should miss Paterson's charm and humour and he confided in me how much he preferred the south to the hurly-burly of the north. "It was softer," he said, and he was a real countryman; he had lodgings at Fareham

K

and thought nothing of walking to Petersfield across country. One day at the yard we saw seagulls flying lazily at a great height and he told me that they were feeding on flying ants. The best present I could think of for his great assistance was a few years' subscription to *The Field*.

Operations commenced with a full measure of success but one day we heard that one of the flotilla had had a collision in fog just off Hull and Frank Murdoch went up to advise on her repair. We were told that she had extra cargo stowed on deck but she had remained afloat thanks to a good forward water-tight bulkhead and, within weeks, was back in service.

Regrettably one of the little fleet was captured by a German vessel wearing a neutral flag but doubtless breaking out her own flag before coming alongside. This was *Gay Viking* whose captain was killed putting up a gallant show of defence.

After the war one of these craft was purchased from Admiralty disposal and converted to an attractive fast motor yacht for a Mr Joe White who named her *Pimpernel*; later, I believe, she went to America.

As I write this I should mention that my uncle's house is now part of a large children's home and the summer-house has gone.

12 'Nyria'

In this and the immediately following chapters I have written about some of the famous large cutters, all household words in the yachting eras of pre-1914 and between the wars.

The lovely cutter *Nyria* rated at 21½ metres, was built in 1906 for Mr W. R. N. Young and was certainly one of my father's best designs.

She was unique at that time as she was the first large racing yacht to be built to Lloyds classification and, being of composite construction with teak planking, she had a far heavier hull than her rivals. She was 169 tons with a waterline length of 73·5 ft and a beam of 20·2 ft; her draught was 13 ft and her lead keel was approximately 50 tons.

Her designer studied the implications of 'sailing length' to a very marked degree; she had long easy ends and her bow was of quite unusual form but not at all ugly to look at. I remember our old friend Bill Fife, always appreciative of a good feature, expressed the view that 'that bow was awful clever'.

In her first season, first-class racing was at a low ebb and she only had the ketch *Cariad* and *White Heather* to race against. She beat the former easily and the latter with more difficulty but at the end of the season she came out on top with seventeen first prizes out of thirty-three starts.

The following year the international rule was introduced and against the new *White Heather II* she made a poor showing, being handicapped with a reduced sail plan. She continued to race and still proved she was at her best in fresh winds and not too much sea.

Memory cheats me here but records show that my Firm owned *Nyria* in 1911, possibly due to her owner's death, and that she had six subsequent owners from 1912 until 1953 when she was broken up in Italy.

In 1912 she was owned by Mr H. Peech, renamed *Lady Camilla* and given a ketch rig but it was not until Mrs R. E. Workman purchased her in 1920 that *Nyria* REALLY burst into fame and this wonderful lady owned her for nine splendid years. I always regarded Mrs Workman as the British counterpart of Madame Heriot in French yachting circles and she was loved and admired by her many yachting friends.

As a cutter once more and with many improvements *Nyria* was top of a far more formidable class in 1920 and a year or so later, as her owner was a lady, Father asked her if she'd like to start a fashion. In next to no time, Mrs Workman agreed to adopt his suggestion to try a rig that was a drastic change from the accepted topsail garb that had been *de règle* for a century or more. So next season saw *Nyria* emerge in a completely new frock, and what is best described as a jib-headed mainsail and became known as 'Bermudian' rig.

This of course showed considerable courage on the part of both the owner and her designer and though the pundits damned the experiment at the time, in a matter of a few years all cutters in the class had adopted it.

After all those years one is still alive to many of the cruising advantages of the old gaff rig and, to an artistic eye, there is no doubt that the gaff is more picturesque than the jib-headed sail. However, with the advent of aircraft and the science of flying and wing design in particular, the word 'aerodynamic' crept into sailing and, in the case of the pure racing yacht, the jib-headed sail had come to stay.

At that time, just after I had ceased to be connected with a small flying-boat factory, I was keen on flying and used to reinforce my views on the merits of the jib-headed sail by sketching a near bow view of a gaff-rigged craft with the gaff sagging to leeward and some third of the sail-area 'outside' the boat; I then turned the sketch sideways—as a horizontal aircraft wing—and proved how a gaff-winged machine could never leave the ground.

It is possible that the pointed head of our jib-headed sail is quite un-aerodynamic and that we may see the return of unusual head-boards or miniature curved gaffs so cleverly applied by the Dutch all those years ago but, in my opinion, the present ever increasing tendency to standing topmast backstays prevents any attempt to give the right small curvature at the top of this rather too pointed sail head.

The staying of *Nyria*'s mast was somewhat complex; the spar itself was to the existing measurement rule—solid to the jib-stay and hollow to the masthead, of spruce construction. At the outset her cross-trees and struts were rather numerous but as the season wore on some were removed and, in the end as *Plate 20* shows, her rigging was comparatively clean.

After a serious accident Mrs Workman was sadly crippled but she displayed great fortitude and so loved the sport that she kept *Nyria* in commission for many seasons. My father designed a special re-clining cockpit for her just forward of the wheel, so that she could keep her eye on everything from its sofa with canvas lee-board.

I doubt if any other large racing yacht had such charming decoration below. The saloon had a grey, blue and silver motif; panelling and fittings were of sycamore veneer and, being a lady's yacht, she had large mirrors sensibly placed with their bevelled edges treated a pleasing shade of blue and fastened by silver medallions.

When racing, whatever the conditions, the steward would come aft to announce that luncheon was served and down we went. This was always a full course affair most beautifully served, but I must admit that, as a youngster, I would have preferred to have remained on deck and shared the crew's bread and cheese snack, passed around in large enamelled bowls, and more than once 'Uncle' Malden and I went below rather ungraciously. It was quite a com-mon thing to hear someone at Cowes ask, "Have you lunched in *Nyria*?" rather than, "Have you sailed in *Nyria*?"

Tommy Workman was desperately keen and we used to tail on to the staysail sheet tackle during tacks but since in those days we were both in the lightweight mould I doubt if our efforts were as useful as we thought.

As a family we Nicholsons enjoyed wonderful hospitality from the Workmans. As well as my father, who used to take the helm on occasions, my sister Mary and I were frequent guests and had splendid times with Tommy and his two charming sisters.

I remember some of our best races in *Nyria* were at the West Country regattas and often Mrs Workman would say to me quietly at the start of a turn to wind'ard, "I wish your father would take her now." On one such occasion I remember how 'Uncle' Malden was the mediator between professional and amateur without distressing the former at all.

I recently received a delightful letter from Tommy Workman apropos of Father's helmsmanship. I always thought he was one of the best I have ever known and he probably had an advantage over his rivals deriving from a complete understanding of the performance, under varying conditions, of the yachts which he had designed. An extract from the letter reads:

"In my opinion there was only one person who could really sail *Nyria* to windward under her Bermudian rig and that was your father. I was always pestering my mother to persuade him to take over the helm but it was only very occasionally that your father could be persuaded to do so. On one occasion I well remember we were about a mile astern of *White Heather* on a mark off Berry Head, with a lightish Nor'westerly wind, and in the beat back to the finishing line at Torquay your father insisted on the tackle being put on to the mainsheet. We really bowsed it down till everything was bar taut and on the beat home we were pointing at least seven degrees higher than *White Heather* on every tack yet travelling through the water at the same speed and by the time we reached the finishing line we had pulled at least a mile ahead. There's no doubt *Nyria* could, if sailed properly, beat any of the 23-metres on the wind in a breeze up to force 5, under Bermudian rig."

I remember at an end-of-the-season regatta at Dartmouth, when owners, guests and crews visited the fair ashore and indulged in the bumper-cars, the coconuts and merry-go-rounds, that Father 'escorted' Mrs Workman down the spiral tower that ran round the outside of a high 'castle'. At the time I thought it was rather a risky procedure but have no doubt that 'the old man' skilfully applied some method to control their speed.

These great yachts seemed almost human even in winter, hauled out with their large canvas covers laced round their bilges and perhaps a flap set aside by the ship-keeper to admit air and a little dull winter sun; one would climb aboard and wander through those semi-dark cabins thinking of the fun of a past season or, better still, the season ahead.

There can be no doubt that the Workmans, their fortunate guests and the crew could never forget those tremendous days.

13 23-metre cutter 'Brynhild'

The story of *Brynhild* is, perhaps, one of the saddest in the history of yachting. The disaster which overtook her removed from that great class of large cutters a yacht whose name might have become as celebrated as those of her two great Scottish rivals, *Shamrock* and *White Heather*.

Sir James Pender who had a lovely estate at Donhead St Mary, near Shaftesbury, was a grand sporting gentleman and he and my father hit it off remarkably well.

At the time of our visit to Donhead Hall I was only eight years old but, surprisingly, the details of it are as clear as a bell.

It was in the days of our first family car, a grey Sunbeam touring model with brass embellishments, acetylene headlamps and the petrol tank under the driver's seat, of all places. I remember if the tank was nearly empty she was good for another mile or two if one went astern and the same applied on hills.

On arriving at the lodge gates, black wrought iron pointed in gilt, there was Sir James excitedly pleased to receive Father and dressed in his usual superb check with his inevitable bright blue collar and shirt. Lady Pender would be hacking in the park and on entering we were always greeted by the most gracious butler who, I know, had a soft spot for Father.

The entrance hall was a magnificent place with waxed oak furniture and parquet floor and, in the centre, a fine old silver ship model. I remember Lady Pender coming in wearing her side-saddle habit and thinking how awful it looked when unmounted. On going to the gallery along one side of the dining room she leaned over the banisters, looking down at the table, and told the butler that he had forgotten the preserves, which I thought was a wonderful name for jam.

Those gracious days seem like a fantasy today.

Brynhild, of 196 tons, was launched on a Friday and the superstitions of many were unfortunately confirmed quite soon. On her first trial sail the mast-head man fell to the deck and was killed. I always admired those fine seamen who spent their racing days aloft in the schooners and gaff-rigged cutters of that era.

During her first season *Brynhild* lost another man overboard and, when racing off the Warner in a fresh breeze, she carried away her topmast. When they had got the topsail down and cleared up the debris Lady Pender suggested to Father that they should give up and return to Gosport to see about replacing the broken spar and received the quiet reply, "I expect, my Lady, it is half made by now." In fact, whenever racing was in sight of the rigging loft at the top of a four-storey building—an old malthouse—the riggers had a commanding view over Spithead and any accident spread through the Firm like a prairie fire.

One day a very clever marine artist, C. M. Padday, was racing in *Brynhild*; he rather specialized in line and wash drawings and was almost a deaf-mute. During the race he made no attempt at sketches or notes and Lady Pender was obviously a trifle upset and told Father so. After the race, as Padday was leaving, Father told him that he expected he had made many mental notes and, indeed, within a few weeks, the artist sent him a delightful picture titled 'Hauling on the mainsheet'. Padday had not only captured the features of the mates and crew but had also remembered the exact shape of Father's binoculars stowed, as usual, inside the lifebuoy on top of the upturned dinghy.

Two of Padday's pictures were hung for many years in the Island Sailing Club at Cowes but had been removed the last time I was there—a pity I thought.

It was on May 23rd, 1910, that the great tragedy occurred off Harwich. There are two accounts of this, one from Tommy Workman with whom I have been in touch over *Nyria* matters and the other which I thought Father had told me afterwards.

Father had arrived the evening before the race and, noticing that the main shrouds were far too slack, had advised the fisherman captain to have them taken up before the race. It was never done.

Workman's account reads as follows:

"I can recollect asking your father about *Brynhild* and why she sank. He told me that he had had to step her mast on some wooden blocks to get a foot or so of extra height and that when the word went round that she was sinking he rushed down below when the others were abandoning ship to see that the mast had jumped off the blocks and gone through the bottom of the boat.

His insatiable curiosity to find out the root cause of failures and troubles nearly caused him to go down with the ship."

Be that as it may, the race was sponsored by the Orwell Corinthian Yacht Club and Henderson's records tell that she was leading at the time. Fortunately there was a Naval vessel standing by and her competitors soon had their dinghies afloat.

Father also told me other details of that sad occasion, one being that as the whole sailplan was lying flat on the water Sir James insisted on being rowed to the mast-head to remove his racing flag: this was quartered with black and red squares and he always raced in a red and black ringed jersey as worn by P.T. instructors.

Both owner and designer went straight up to Town on the earliest train still wearing their wet clothes and, on arrival, they saw a news-vendor holding a placard which read, 'Sir Thomas Lipton in sea rescue', or words to that effect—no mention of poor old *Brynhild*. Those were the times when Sir Thomas Lipton had the Press in the palm of his hand.

Lastly, Lord Dudley had given my father a fabulous travelling bag fitted with silver backed brushes and a very large silver watch which gave the state of the moon as well as the time; this was after his successful 5-rater *Dacia* had been built. It was known as the 'Dudley bag' in our family and its loss was keenly felt by its owner.

The last time we were near Donhead I enquired at the little butcher's shop and the owner, with his straw hat and striped apron, exclaimed, "You *are* going back a bit, sir."

The deer were still in the park.

14 'Shamrock IV'

This story is almost like a play in two acts. Sir Thomas Lipton came to my father for his fourth challenger for the America's Cup in 1913 and, due to the First World War, the races did not take place until 1920 off Sandy Hook.

For me personally the dreadful cause of this delay was beneficial as those four fearful years permitted my maturity and in 1920 I was able to be of some small assistance to Father in America.

I must admit that when she was building, my younger mind was occupied with faster things than sailing yachts, such as aircraft and fast motor boats, and sailing had not, as yet, crept into my bones. In fact my mother's sister (my favourite aunt) was quite cross with me when I displayed so little enthusiasm on taking her to the building shed which was always locked and had a permanent roster of watchmen.

Building a challenger in those days was no easier than today. The designer was flooded with correspondence that flowed through from Mr John Westwood, Sir Thomas's splendid secretary, and with letters from all over the world, mostly of course from America. His advice was sought on every single point and subject.

When his striking design was in draft he had a model made, coated with white polish and cut back to a marble-like finish; it was a perfect job executed by our joiner model maker Nobes. In the inter-war years I always found that the lady visitors whom one took to the yard on Sundays enjoyed the joiners' shop. The model maker's bench amused them as he made his own planes, some as small as two inches long and some with a radiused cutting edge for working in the tuck of a model.

I remember taking this model out to Father when he was laid up in bed after a heavy cold and I was instructed to borrow some of those lovely little planes. He sat up in bed and modified the bulb keel considerably and Mother was rather distressed at the shavings.

Shamrock IV had a slight hog-sheer for strength, excess tumble home, a very powerful mid-ship section with a hard bilge and flat 'floor', a rounded or bull-nosed bow, sawn-off counter stern and a pronounced bulb keel.

Known at the time as the 'Ugly Duckling' *Shamrock IV* was, I suspect, the fastest yacht of her size ever built for her own special conditions; these embraced really fresh winds but not too much of a sea, as her extreme bulb keel affected her 'speed of lift' in a seaway and her U-sectioned forebody was unkind in heavy swells.

She was by far the most lightly constructed yacht of her day with multi-skin planking on laminated wood frames, bulkheads, etc. Her web frames and floors were constructed of a special lightweight alloy known as Navalton and were deep and widely spaced; her deck was plywood covered with a rubberized non-slip material and all conceivable fittings were specially designed for lightness including fluted joiner work.

In those days lower masts were solid and the topmasts, gaffs and jackyards were of hollow construction. The particular tree from which her mainmast was built was shipped from British Columbia by slinging it outboard on S.S. *Minehaha* which, at that time, was the largest Atlantic transport liner to steam up the Thames—quite the finest log we ever saw.

Our craftsmen at Gosport gave Father a rather unusual present in the form of a round table; the top was the piece of plywood deck removed for fitting the mast, the outer rim was half an ash mast hoop, the legs were of mahogany as used internally and a four-leaf shamrock was carved in the centre of the stretcher rails under the table.

I last remember showing this table to an old chap who came to tea with old people one day and who loved his pipe. After tea it was raining and the elderly guests were indoors and when I asked him if he wanted to light his pipe he thanked me with the reply, "Not in here, Sir, because I spits so."

I seem to remember I had special leave from school to attend the launch of *Shamrock IV*. She was christened by the Countess of

Shaftesbury (as was *Shamrock V* in 1930) and our dear nannie was acting as her lady's maid in the office.

Sir William P. Burton was invited to become the helmsman, being considered the best in the country, and Captain Albert Turner who had been racing skipper with him for some nine years was appointed captain. Lady Burton joined them as timekeeper and observer.

During the war years Burton worked hard with the Food Ministry and it was thought, in some quarters, that the impact of those years had rather impaired his racing skill but I suspected that the humid climate around New York affected him as it did my father.

The navigator was Claude Hickman and I would say he was as good as any in the Cup challenger. He kept a diary of everything to do with the races and much else besides, such as troubles with the Press and internal friction that inevitably cropped up. Apart from his splendid navigational skill he was phenomenal at predicting the advent of thunder storms: he did not say, "We shall have thunder at about three o'clock," but, "We shall get thunder at ten past three," and he was spot-on.

I feel sad at letting the years roll by and not meeting Mr Hickman since 1920 as, without doubt, his diary would make good reading today.

Trials took place soon after launching and the 23-metre *Shamrock* acted as trial horse. Why my father ever gave *Shamrock IV* a sloop rig with a club to the foresail with jib-topsail set over it I never knew although the schooner *America* also had that large foresail boom. During trials off Calshot one day, with light wind luckily, my father was lifted overboard by this club or foresail boom but apart from his swim he was O.K. The rig, however, was soon altered to cutter.

As the trial races were nearing their end at Torbay and *Britannia* joined the two *Shamrocks*, the Mayor gave a dinner to celebrate the occasion at which my father received a gold cigarette case embellished with the borough arms while Sir Thomas received a rusty old teapot which pleased him well.

Among Sir Thomas's greatest friends were Sir Thomas Dewar and Sir Harry Lauder and by the latter they were known as Tea Tom and Whisky Tom.

During the trials the yachts were attended by Lipton's S.Y. *Erin* and I remember among his pets he was often accompanied by a monkey who unfortunately scratched my sister Mary rather badly although she was especially good with all animals; he also had some Cingalese servants and he loved to tell his friends that he was a bachelor "because he loved his single ease"!

Just before *Shamrock* was jury rigged for her transatlantic crossing and after seeing the vee-sectioned bow on the defender *Resolute*, Father decided to ease the flat bow form around the waterline and a partially new stem in that area was made ashore and fitted to *Shamrock* in the old Camber dry-dock.

When the yacht left Portsmouth Harbour for America with the usual blowing of syrens, etc., she was escorted by the 23-metre trial horse and the steam yacht *Erin* on which there was a small party of guests including that fine marine artist Charles Dixon.

War was declared just as the Lipton outfit was leaving the Azores and the New York Yacht Club cabled them stating that *Erin* could tow the yachts if they wished, it being understood that the challenger must always sail across on her own as a condition of the Deed of Gift drawn up when the America's Cup was instituted. My father, however, advised them not to, knowing full well *Shamrock*'s light construction.

Luckily they arrived without any enemy aggression and *Shamrock* was put away in a shed while *Erin* returned to play her part as a hospital ship in the war and was later sunk in the Mediterranean.

During the war the site of the laying-up shed was required for another purpose and shed and yachts were moved as one unit. It was not until the war ended and Father went over to the States to see how *Shamrock* had fared that he found this operation had altered her shape due to the removal of beams under her heavy lead keel; in fact her sections had been noticeably altered by this 'bulk removal'.

When the time was drawing near for the races our little family party—Father, Mother, my sister Mary and I—crossed in the old White Star liner *Olympic* and for my part it was a splendid voyage. The squash court was down on E deck; there was no air conditioning in those days and the Pro. lost weight on every voyage. The great Sussex cricketer Maurice Tate was aboard so we soon had nets rigged on a promenade deck and had much good fun every morning.

Among others on board was our dear friend Bill Fife, the designer of two previous *Shamrocks*, who always joined our table for dinner and invariably had a 'birthday' or some other excuse for a half bottle of champagne. On the last night on board at dinner I saw tears trickling down his cheeks and when later I asked my mother why he had been crying she replied that she thought it was because he had been so happy with us and was sad that he had no family of his own.

On our arrival at New York I was intrigued to see bottles of Guinness being handed out from portholes and stuffed into the trousers of the crews of some of the tugs. The first voyage of *Olympic* under her new 'White' system of oil-fired boilers was concluded and the power of Sir Thomas J. Lipton in New York was immediately apparent: our luggage was marked but not checked by the Customs and we were ashore in no time.

Due to the sad loss of *Erin* Sir Thomas had chartered the steam yacht *Victoria* and after a few days in New York we all joined him and his two charming guests Nita and Ella Weir, daughters of Lord Inverforth.

Before leaving for Sandy Hook for the races a number of interesting and unusual events occurred, some of which I will try to recall.

One day when Father and I were in the New York Yacht Club we saw a half model of the defender *Resolute* lying on a sofa. We did not pick it up but criticized it as it was lying there and I remember Father's comment that there seemed nothing about her to be frightened of and I quite agreed, but little did we know what fickle sailing conditions prevailed off Sandy Hook.

When the time for measuring arrived *Shamrock* was floated into the Morse dry-dock at Brooklyn. Father was not well and found the thundery heat rather trying but he was delighted to have met the great old man Nat Herreshoff who designed *Resolute* and so many other celebrated yachts. He congratulated Father on several of *Shamrock*'s features, particularly on a clever scheme we had of lashing a long strip of canvas from gaff to boom round the mast to create a fairing over the mast hoops; however, as it was included in the measured sail area Sir William decided not to race with it.

After lunch we repaired to the dock and to our horror saw a large party of mannequins parading on board; this, I thought, was something too American for words but evidently a large New York store thought it would boost sales. The distraction soon melted away and measurement was completed but unfortunately the Morse Company had applied pitch to the interior of the dock and, as *Shamrock* was floated out next day, her white boot-top was covered with thick tar. This misfortune necessitated another docking for cleaning off and, when refloated, the surface around the waterline was covered with hessian which was left on until well away from the oily area.

Before we rejoined Sir Thomas in *Victoria* for the races we had our fill of entertainments. Sir Thomas was given ringside seats for a heavyweight fight at New Jersey between the white Fred Fulton and Wills the negro and as he had no wish to go he kindly gave his tickets to me. I took young Larkin whose father was at that time High Commissioner in Canada. We went by the ferry, buying hot peanuts en route and, on arrival at the huge wood stadium which was known as the Armoury, I remember hoping the place would not catch fire and also that the negro would win as the place was full of them and a little dark boy had even climbed up to the rafters over the ring.

The supporting bouts were all good but in the big fight Wills caught Fulton with an upper-cut in the third round and that was that. The result, by law, was not announced but appeared in the morning papers.

I also took Ella Wier to lunch at, I believe, Delmonico's and had just enough cash to pay for it; I remember we had lobsters and strawberry shortcake.

We were taken to the Rumson Country Club for dancing and I remember that it was one of the best small bands that I ever heard; their rhythm was astounding as was the number of their gold teeth.

The outstanding affair, to me, was the dinner given to Sir Thomas at the Atlantic Yacht Club, Sea Gate, by the Commodore, Edward L. Doheny. This lovely Club had dirt tennis courts and many sporting facilities unusual in British yacht clubs and its flagstaff was the mast of one of the Cup defenders: I doubt if it still stands now.

The dinner was quite unique with a table in the form of a ring surrounding a sizable pond in which models of *Resolute* and *Shamrock* were afloat. During dinner I observed a slightly balding small gentleman right opposite me across the pond who suggested that the charming girl on my right was 'vamping' me, an expression that I had never heard before. This was my first acquaintance with one

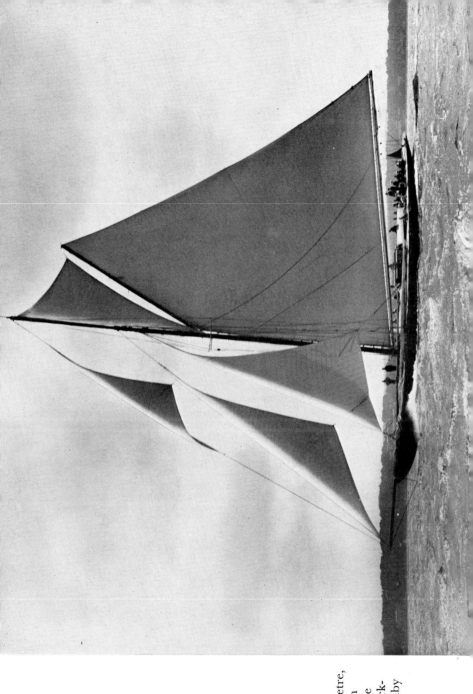

22. *Brynhild*, 23 metre, reaching in a fresh breeze off Osborne Bay. Note the working topsail and baby jib topsail.

23. Mr and Mrs J. Stuart Blackton presenting a 'tea' rose model to Sir Thomas Lipton.

24. *Right: Shamrock IV*, the 'ugly duckling'. Here her original sloop rig is shown, but eventually a cutter rig was adopted.

of the world's greatest amateur sailors, Sherman Hoyt, and I loved every moment of our many meetings that were to follow.

In his speech the Commodore referred to Sir Thomas Lipton as, "One who has walked with Kings but had not lost the common touch." This was indeed so; Sir Thomas was naturally proud of his association with many of the crowned heads of Europe but at heart he was the grocer and a 'master' one at that.

I played dominoes with him (given to him by the Empress Eugenie) and had it not been for Ella Weir he might have won every game.

These frivolities were soon to end and we joined Sir Thomas in S.Y. *Victoria*, towing *Shamrock* down to Sandy Hook. I had several morning swims from the gangway until one morning the captain shouted at me from the bridge to come aboard at once as there were sharks around Sandy Hook, a fact that I had overlooked.

Sir Thomas ate his porridge in the Scottish manner with a glass of milk in one hand and was so alert at breakfast that one realized that he was, for his age, a man of immense mental energy. Looking back I realize how amazingly fortunate we were to be his guests in those exciting times and I know that he developed a real affection for both my parents.

It would be inappropriate to describe in detail a series of races that took place thirty-seven years ago but I have before me the good book *Millions for Defense* by Herbert Stone and Alfred Loomis, given by the latter to my father in 1934. While I do not subscribe fully to all of Alf's comments on this series, all those concerned were agreed that, had the races been staged at Newport with its better sailing conditions, the story might well have been a different one.

During each race Sir Thomas entertained large parties of guests on board S.Y. *Victoria*. In those days of prohibition he respected the laws of the country and it was most amusing to note the shapes and sizes of hip flasks that came on board. I would hazard a guess that some fifty or more friends poured aboard each day and my mother and sister acted in some measure as his hostesses.

I think the Blacktons were his greatest friends out there. J. Stuart Blackton was a pioneer fast motor-boat racing man and had his film studios at Brooklyn. He produced the first colour film *Glorious Adventure* with Lady Diana Manners playing a major part. The

L

Blacktons arrived on board one morning with a fine floral model of a sailing yacht for Sir Thomas made entirely of 'tea' roses and he was very tickled at this novelty.

Mr Blackton took me to his studios where I saw the completion of a film that started on a yacht in California and the 'cabin' in this studio was a dead match of that in the real yacht; a girl was standing by a porthole and a small fan outside was blowing her hair gently whilst the overhead lamp was swinging realistically. I found all this clever and interesting.

At the start of the last race, in a fair breeze, when Father relieved Sir William Burton at the helm we opened up a good enough lead to cause Sherman to remark that it looked as though the Cup might cross the Pond; then the wind cut and our pilot advised working along the Jersey coast in hopes of more wind while *Resolute* stood out to sea, our courses forming a horseshoe. She picked it up long before we did and beat us by some nineteen minutes and the moment the whistle blew on the Committee boat Sir Thomas was searching for my mother to condole with her and to tell her he was going to have another go later which we thought was typically charming of him. Dear Mrs Blackton, a Carolinean beauty, quietly shed a lot of tears.

Throughout his four Cup challenges Father never ever expressed any word of resentment.

In concluding these notes on the 1920 races I must say a little about *Resolute*, that perfectly orthodox and quite beautiful cutter designed by the wizard of Bristol, as Nathaniel Herreshoff was often called. This was the last Cup defender he designed and built and her hull was of bronze.

She was built for a syndicate headed by Mr Henry Walters and her helmsman was Charles Francis Adams, Secretary to the Navy. A world class helmsman, he had a very calm natural temperament. One day when trial sailing, that great and artistic marine photographer, M. Rosenfeld, wished to get a close-up of Adams who, as was often the case, was at the helm wearing his Panama hat and braces, without his coat. Rosenfeld edged his launch *Foto* up the less side of *Resolute* and was closing near enough to get exactly what he wanted when Adams, who could stand it no longer, took off his hat in desperation and, waving it, yelled, "Rosy, get the hell out of it!"

I cannot remember her captain's name but he was a fine fellow; he and most of his crew hailed from Scandinavia as was always the case with these large American racing cutters during the inter-war period.

In the average pretty light winds and often an easy swell *Resolute* with her finer and more vee'd bow sections was a much better ghoster than *Shamrock* with her U-sectioned bow; it was also thought that the latter's bulb keel had a retarding influence in those trying conditions. Given a true sailing breeze *Shamrock* held her own as she proved in the second race, when she gave *Resolute* her rated time allowance and a good beating.

Statistically the following little table sums up these two totally different yachts:

	Resolute	*Shamrock IV*
Sailing length	83·5 ft	94·4 ft
Overall length	106 ft 3 in	110 ft 4 in
Waterline	75 ft	75 ft
Beam	21 ft 8 in	23 ft
Draught	13 ft	14 ft
Sail area	8,775 sq ft	10,459 sq ft

My father last saw Nat Herreshoff in 1930 when he was very blind. His visit was kindly arranged by Mr Harold Vanderbilt who told me that they just held hands together.

15 '*Astra*'

When in 1928 we were approached by Sir Mortimer Singer to consider building a 23-metre class yacht he suggested that he might build two, one for hard weather and one for light winds and we had to remind him that this was not horse racing. I remember having seen his horse take third prize in the Derby a year or so before, the only time I ever went to Epsom.

I must say the two-yacht idea rather whet my father's appetite!

Astra was built purely to the international rule and rated a shade under 23 metres; she was 164 tons with a waterline of 75 ft, beam of 20·2 ft, and draught 13·8 ft. She was of composite construction with all-steel frames and deck structure, mahogany planked with yellow pine decks with cedar covering-boards and deck trim and was built to Lloyds classification, as were all international-class racers after 1930. Many discerning critics thought that she was my father's prettiest design.

When she was launched Sir Mortimer, who was a pioneer balloonist, insisted on being launched on board and, standing near the bow, he looked down at the launching platform and gave the 'salute de ballonaise'!

During an early trial sail the second mate expressed the view that the jibstay band, of galvanized steel, was slipping on the spruce mast. We tried to convince him that it was 'settling' and Father, to reassure himself, decided to go aloft to inspect in a bo'sun's chair. He had a good head for heights but when about halfway up Sir Mortimer shouted to him, "Charlie, come down at once"; when I assured him that all was well the inspection was completed and it was confirmed that the band had settled.

That same day Sir Mortimer heard that I was about to marry and he took me down to his cabin and very kindly handed me a cheque for £25 with the advice that if my fiancée was a sensible girl she would buy one of his sewing machines. She did; we had it for years and now my daughter has it, ingeniously mechanized by her husband.

Sir Mortimer's constant sailing companion was Colonel Perry whose son, Colonel 'Stug' Perry, is such a prominent yachtsman today.

On a celebrated and sad occasion, when racing from Calshot, *Astra* beat *Britannia* in a good sailing breeze, the latter's best sailing condition. *Astra* had a brand new mainsail of Egyptian cotton—no terylene in those days—and when jilling about and taking in the headsails after the race she had occasion to go about just at the unfortunate moment that Colonel Perry was coming out of the deckhouse companion; the great boom came slowly over and, due to the stretching of the new sail, it was so low that it crushed poor Perry's head against the deckhouse hatchway slide. What might have been an appalling tragedy was luckily averted and some very wonderful plastic surgery enabled this good looking gentleman still to remain so.

Perry shared at least one 12-metre, *Noresca*, with 'Tiny' Mitchell, that great benefactor to yachting and for many years Commodore of the Royal Corinthian Yacht Club.

When Mr Hugh Paul bought *Astra* he was a very experienced yachtsman, having owned the beautiful 90-ton yawl *Sumurun* for many seasons and raced her in the large handicap class. Captain Ted Heard who was his skipper kept the yacht beautifully and the combination was extremely successful, winning many prizes over several seasons, particularly in medium to light weather.

Mrs Paul (Maudie, to her friends), took a great interest in the crew and at the start of each season she particularly inquired of the first mate, one of the many Diapers, how many children he had had in the past winter, he being the proud father of a young 'fishing fleet'; she was a true Wendy to her lost boys.

Each season one saw a minor ceremony take place in Portsmouth Harbour, usually on a Friday evening when the Pauls came down by rail from Town. The launch met them at the Harbour Station pontoon and as they came alongside *Astra* Ted was at the gangway, cap in hand; the moment the owner's foot was on the covering board the burgee broke out and yet another season had started.

Mr and Mrs Paul were true and respected friends among the owners in that great class and, indeed, among yachtsmen in general. Mrs 'Maudie' had a fine sense of humour in contrast to her husband who was a trifle reserved.

When the big class including Gerry Lambert's *Yankee* were at Torbay the racing was tremendous and a slight incident occurred one day between *Britannia* and *Astra*. After the race Sir Philip Hunloke called on my father aboard *Flame* at Brixham and we sat on that celebrated skylight seat over the ladies' cabin and held a technical discussion on a point in the rules. After analysis it was agreed to drop the matter and Sir Philip laughingly said to Father, "All right Charlie, we'll give the canary another seed!" (Mr Paul invariably raced in a yellow sweater.)

By and large there was a great spirit of friendship among the owners and all knew the rules inside out; I suspect that there were fewer protests in the big class than in any other of the many classes racing at that time.

When the Pauls were building *Little Astra*, the 12-metre, at our Gosport yard I used to meet them and invariably Mrs Paul would pull my leg on progress of construction. One evening we were standing on the staging looking into the empty hull between the deckbeams and, after listening to my report on progress, she suddenly asked, "What did I think about the owners in the big class?" There was no need for a guarded reply as they were all so charming and she concluded an amusing and complimentary chat with the remark, "I think my old man is the best of the bunch."

Astra was painted white in Sir Mortimer's time but one day when motoring down from Town Mrs Paul saw a brand new jade-coloured tarpaulin over a haystack and decided it was to be the colour for *Astra*'s topsides for the coming season, a colour that was much admired and was retained for the rest of her racing life.

Mrs Paul inevitably teased our foreman painter that it was different each season. By chance I was visiting my friend Ledwith at his well-known paint factory at Kingston-on-Thames and he showed me an ingenious device for paint matching, driven by a pocket-torch battery rotating a great many colour cards and by varying the segments of the cards one could match any given shade by holding it alongside the colour to be matched.

This, I thought, would at last give proof that *Astra*'s topsides were a constant colour over the seasons.

Regrettably there were no more seasons.

After the war *Astra* was purchased by Commander Hector Dobbs, an old friend of ours who for some years was a brilliant racing-car driver. He reduced her sail area slightly and sailed her with his wife and a handful of mechanics from his garage. One afternoon as they were reaching down Southampton Water I was on the Cowes steamer and we were in company nearly all the way, the steamer only dropping her as the wind eased off the Hamble Spit.

Like so many other good British yachts *Astra* eventually found her way to the Mediterranean.

16 'Candida'

In 1928, when Mr Herman A. Andreae owned the 19-metre yacht *Corona*, he decided to join the 23-metre class and when discussing the project he stated his preference for a yacht erring on the side of a hard-weather boat as he liked sailing in a good breeze. He also said that he did not need a captain but wanted a good mate to select and look after the crew.

We put him on to Jim Gilbey of Emsworth, a winter fisherman and mate with Fred Mountifield in *White Heather* and a first-rate fellow who was a fine sailor and respected by his crew. He remained with Mr Andreae throughout his sailing days.

Candida was a fully fledged 23-metres of 174 tons with a waterline of 79·4 ft, 20·5 ft beam, and 14·4 ft draught and was thus a rather more powerful hull than *Astra*. She was launched for the 1929 season.

When the yacht was building her owner often visited the Gosport yard, driving himself in various good cars, and on one occasion he arrived in a straight-eight Bugatti which I thought was the optimum motor-car of those days. As I owned a little modified Brescia model myself, Andreae kindly let me examine everything.

He was a great all-round sportsman, was Master of the Hampshire Hunt for many seasons and sustained it throughout the war. He also assisted the adjacent Hambledon by the drafting of a few good hounds.

He was a great skier but we never thought it wise to ski alone as much as he did at Pontresina; he was a good shot and keen fisherman for whom we built a little husky day-boat for his sea-trout fishing off his estate on the island of South Uist in the Hebrides. She was around 30 ft with a cabin and large fishing cockpit, built of Hampshire witch-elm clencher construction with a good robust engine and modest sloop rig with boomless loose-footed mainsail. He named her *Bumble-Bee* and I remember lunching at his great Hampshire home, Moundsmere, to discuss this little boat and his enthusiasm over every detail was refreshing.

All these 23-metre cutters had most spacious accommodation but, by and large, their internal decor did not call for the more careful attention applied to the cruising yacht. I seem to remember that *Candida*'s saloon was of dull waxed cedar and was unusually charming; *Nyria*, being owned by a lady, was, as mentioned previously, most charming and unusual with a blend of blue, grey and silver; Lady Sopwith chose a fine royal blue for *Endeavour*'s carpets and a blue non-slip material was fitted to table-tops, sideboards, etc.; but I am getting into the wrong racing class.

The passage of time dims the memory on what is among the least important facets of a racing yacht and I suppose the 'library saloon' that Lord Waring put into *White Heather* was quite unique.

Candida and her other sisters started their careers with spruce masts and during their racing years must have had their sail plans modified at least four times. The days of the long-rope and baby jib-topsails gave way to a higher aspect ratio of headsail distribution; steel masts emerged and double clewed jibs were 'in'; booms also came into the changing scene. Tom Ratsey introduced large holes in spinnakers to try to stabilize their behaviour under certain conditions but, with the arrival of the 'parachute' type of sail, the holes were dropped. These earlier spinnakers, being restricted by the fore topmast stay, were cut much flatter and the passing of jib-topsails saw great advance in spinnaker technique.

Candida took her full share of prizes, proving herself in hard winds, and Mr Andreae commissioned Stanley Lapthorn, of the Gosport branch of sail-makers, to cut him a mainsail of rather heavier cloth and about a reef and a quarter less than the full area; this was a wise move and I remember it paying off on at least two occasions, at a Ryde regatta and on the East Coast.

Although there was a deal of friendly rivalry between the Cowes and Gosport branches of the famous old sail-making firm, we always considered Mr Stanley Lapthorn as their best cutter, in tailoring parlance, and he cut and clothed these gracious ladies with a high degree of skill. His senior and, I suppose, the doyen of sail-makers, Mr Tom Ratsey, did not give Lapthorn too easy a time but he mellowed with age and we all loved him. His son Chris, whom I have mentioned earlier, became Chairman of the firm later.

One winter when *Candida* was laid up on our south slip at Gosport we decided to leave the lower part of her steel mast in her. These masts were provided with a drain plug, being veritable 'cooling towers' and subject to much condensation. Someone suggested we might remove the plug and at least a bucket and a half of water shot out.

As was our good fortune, both my elder sister and I had many fine races in *Candida* and although Mr Andreae never asked too many guests at a time, those we met were as charming as their host.

One of the outstanding yachting photographs was taken aboard *Candida* by Monty Spry, on the staff of the *Morning Post*, who must have been a great artist. It was on a day when Mr Andreae kindly gave the helm to my father, blowing fresh and the sort of conditions that *Candida*'s owner really enjoyed. The photograph shows *Britannia* under *Candida*'s lee with *Lulworth* just showing and *Cambria* astern.... A real Herman Andreae day.

17 23-metres in general

This wonderful class is now almost forgotten and when the sailing fraternity mention 'the big class' these days they all think in terms of the J class whose life span was far less than that of the 23s.

The class included *Nyria* (1906), the ill-fated *Brynhild* and *White Heather* (1907), *Shamrock* (1908), and the grand old *Britannia*. The latter, a 151-rater, who had been racing with those famous and celebrated yachts *Navahoe*, *Valkyrie* and others since 1893, was fitted into the 23-metre class and remained with it for many years after her contemporaries had faded away.

Terpsichore joined her elderly companions in 1920, *Astra* and *Cambria* in '28 and *Candida* in '29.

Like the gracious ladies that they were, they quite naturally endured many changes in fashion but none so daring as that of *Nyria* when Mrs Workman gave her the 'Bermudian' rig, later to be adopted by the whole class.

The great G. L. Watson, designer of *Britannia* and many celebrated racing and steam yachts, was considerably senior to Bill Fife, my father, and Alfred Mylne and although the latter was never commissioned to design a racing yacht larger than a 12-metre he was a great artist and designed many beautiful craft. These three, at that time, were 'out on their own', all great friends and with next to no other competitors in design.

When *Dacia*, the 5½-rater, was building at Gosport in 1892 my parent was honoured by a visit from the great G. L. Watson and after careful and thorough scrutiny his only comment was, 'That'll be a very fast boot."

Since we have touched on *Astra* and *Candida* it only remains to refer to my father's influence on *Terpsichore* (later *Lulworth*) and *Britannia*, in that sequence.

Terpsichore was designed by the brothers White of Itchen and built for Mr R. H. Lee in 1920. She had black topsides and it was known that her owner's ambition was to beat *Britannia* in her own weather; in fact, his choice of colour was criticized at the time as being a matter of mimicry or flattery.

Like *Britannia*, she was fitted with high bulwarks and her outboard appearance was rather more that of a cruising than a racing cutter, with ample freeboard and a semi-spoon bow.

The brothers White were not too well known in the field of design but without doubt *Terpsichore* had beautiful waterlines and was a very well balanced design. Her first season was a disappointment to all and that year in Cowes Week her owner invited my father to sail aboard to try to improve her performance, particularly to windward.

After a good sail with much of his time spent to leeward around the mast and studying her bow wave form from the bowsprit end he came to the conclusion that *Terpsichore* was sagging to leeward and, with her ample freeboard, might well be improved by additional ballast. He suggested that the yacht be sent to Gosport for the stowing of some 9 tons before the next race and the owner agreed. The result was a marked improvement and when she beat *Britannia* the owner was so delighted that he accepted our advice to give her a new and deeper keel that winter.

Up to that time all these large racing yachts were laid up and serviced at Gosport but since this proposal involved exceeding the draught capacity of our slipway the operation was carried out in our Southampton yard where the large slipway could handle her increased draught.

Right through the rest of her racing career and while retaining her powerful gaff-rigged sail plan, she was, as *Lulworth*, by no means too outmoded by her more fashionable rivals.

Reverting to the 'modernization' of the very beautiful old *Britannia*, it was felt at the time that perhaps this change had come too late. His Majesty King George V was intensely loyal to his servants and when it was suggested that perhaps dear old Albert Turner might be pensioned off to make way for a younger captain, it was not approved.

Sir Philip Hunloke was also 'getting on' after his long and splendid career as the Royal Sailing Master. History records that he had sailed her on 409 occasions, 109 times to win and 104 times to gain a place. She also had that dead-heat with the schooner *Westward* under the burgee of the Royal Albert Yacht Club on July 28th, 1932, the day I referred to when sailing the 12-metre *Flica* with Sherman Hoyt.

When my father visited the Palace he was most impressed by His Majesty's great knowledge of the details of the 'big class' and amused at the King's remark, "Whatever we do to improve *Britannia* we MUST beat that damned schooner"—referring, of course, to *Westward*.

Many felt that the inclusion of that fine schooner in a cutter class was a pity but there was no animosity among the owners. Her chances of winning under average conditions were remote but in fresh breezes with plenty of reaching she was a redoubtable competitor. She also inevitably raced on all days, many of which were more suited to the cutters, so she was accepted as a very sporting competitor.

His Majesty was gracious enough to accept all our proposals which, in addition to modernizing her sail plan, included the removal of her bulwarks—leaving a low rail, removing all unwanted fittings on deck including some fine brass-bound bitts at the heel of her mast, and finally removing her copper bottom sheathing which was very wrinkled with age and detrimental to fine weather sailing. The latter operation included the 'spiling' of thousands of tack holes; all her plank seams were raked out, recaulked and 'splined' with mahogany strips and the whole planed off to a perfect finish.

We found that her bottom planking was somewhat 'piebald' as mixed woods had been used and the streaks were unusually narrow. I've forgotten the length of 'splining' strips that we used but believe our foreman put it as well over a mile.

By the removal of the old gaff rig with its peak and throat halliard blocks, gaff and a great deal of rigging, some 2 tons or more were saved aloft. At that time we were developing new steel masts but did not care to take any chances in this privileged case and we built her a new hollow silver spruce mast of elliptical section some 2 ft in diameter at its major axis fore and aft. This was the longest wood spar we had ever built, being some 174 ft from heel to truck. I was never much of a statistician but believe the only longer wood

mast ever built was that used in the America's Cup erstwhile defender
Whirlwind during the Cup defence trials. I believe Nevins of City
Island built it and one of its unusual features was that, instead of
jackets or bands to take the rigging attachments, it was fitted with
very long bronze tangs attached to the spar with hundreds of screws.

It was tragic that His Majesty's sailing time ahead was to be so
limited and British yachtsmen understood and respected the under-
lying motives for this great old cutter being scuppered at sea.

We are now left with *Cambria* built at Fairlie in 1928 for Lord
Camrose by William Fife, assisted by his newphew R. B. Fife. She
and the schooner *Westward* were the only other yachts in the big
class that my Firm and, in particular, my father had no dealings with
except for the original fitting out of *Westward* when Mr Davis
acquired her.

Like all Bill Fife's creations *Cambria* was lovely to look at and, as
father once put it, 'round all over, fair and sweet', but unfortunately
her performance was not up to her looks. When reaching in a fresh
breeze she boiled up a rather steep quarter wave and it was suggested
that here Fife had erred, as he did with the schooner *Waterwitch*, by
designing her quarters on the full side.

At the end of her racing days *Cambria* was cut down in rig, given an
auxiliary engine and sold to a Frenchman who renamed her *Lillias*.

Westward, built by the great Nat Herreshoff of Bristol, R.I., in
1910 for Mr Alex Smith Cochran was a lovely vessel and in the same
stamp as her designer's *Elena* and the larger *Magdalene II*; all three
had modest overhangs, a flattish sheer and pronounced V sections
but they were great yachts, functional and thus good to look upon.

It is a nostalgic thought that those lovely Fife cutters *White
Heather*, 179 tons, built in 1907 and *Shamrock*, 175 tons, built in 1908
were both broken up in the same year, the former at Gosport and
the latter at Southampton.

Offhand I cannot remember this date but I suspect their racing
careers lasted all of thirty years and roughly five times the life of the
J class.

18 'Shamrock V' and J class in general

Whilst the 23-metre class yachts were built to the International Yacht Racing Union rules, adopted by the Yacht Racing Association in 1919 and embracing some twenty-two countries in Europe and South America, the United States applied their own formulae and the J class yachts were built to their Universal Measurement Rules.

Over the years the American authorities and the I.Y.R.U. have been interchanging ideas some of which have been adopted by the respective bodies in individual classes but there is still much variance in the two camps. This individuality is perhaps stronger in offshore racing in the two leading authorities, the Cruising Club of America and our Royal Ocean Racing Club and so it is splendid that these two great organizations have now been able to merge their rules.

When *Shamrock V* was built for Sir Thomas Lipton in 1929–30 it was his fifth and last challenge for the America's Cup and she was the first J class yacht my father had ever designed. Since the subject has been so well ventilated over the past thirty-eight years I propose merely to recall a few random facts.

Shamrock was of semi-composite construction with steel frames and deck beams, planked with mahogany and yellow pine decks; her plank seams were 'splined' by a process we had adopted with great success on many contemporary smaller yachts and which we also used when modifying *Britannia*, referred to in the previous chapter. *Shamrock* also carried the rig of the day and had a spruce mast of hollow construction and elliptical section. Little did we realize what was coming in the way of masts until we arrived in America.

During the early summer of 1930 *Shamrock* took her share of prizes in British waters. She seemed pretty fast off the wind but was not as good to wind'ard as I am sure my father had hoped. When racing during the Clyde Regatta *Lulworth* got a splendid start in a steady but light breeze and, try as we did, we could not outpoint her in that weight of wind. I have already described the prowess of Captain Archie Hogarth on this occasion.

That evening Colonel Duncan Neill took me as his guest to the Mudhook Yacht Club dinner and warned me of those round-bottomed decanters that just went on circulating. The Marquis of Ailsa was Commodore and of a great age; Mr Hamilton, for whom we had built the 8-metre *Sagitta*, was Shantyman and was later succeeded by Lord Glentanar.

Before sailing to Newport we were inundated with requests from amateur yachtsmen to join her in crossing the Pond and although a few were most worthy we dare not admit anyone and thus create a precedent.

On arrival *Shamrock*'s after-guard was to be Captain Ted Heard, Captain Paul as navigator, Colonel Duncan Neill as the owner's representative, my father, Stanley Lapthorn and myself. Had Father had the helm the result would have been the same but somehow I felt that Ted Heard was better sailing round the buoys than on a compass course and sensed that the ocean was too big for him.

Her passage out was uneventful but not so her return, described later. Father preceded me as we were expecting our first child and, if all was well, I was to follow on. This I did in the old *Carmania* with her triple screw, the centre one driven by a reciprocating steam engine and the wing ones by turbines. A lovely old vibrationless sea-boat which took eight days and, with the American youth that poured aboard at Cherbourg, we had a pretty gay time.

I arrived in New York on a Sunday morning and after meeting the parents of sundry Boston débutantes, one of whom had won the deck-tennis with me (she doing all the work at the net), I awaited Father's arrival. We lunched with a Mr Woods, a most charming man for whom we had just designed a nice sailing cruiser. He was a brilliant structural engineer whose stories of American bridge building were utterly fascinating but his comment that New York was within the earthquake zone was not too comforting on my second visit!

That Sunday was also my introduction to American Sunday

25. Charles E. Nicholson sailing *Candida* in a two-reef breeze. *Britannia* and *Lulworth* to leeward and *Cambria* astern.

27. *Candida* running with the mainsail well reefed. Note the effect of the fore topmast stay on the set of the spinnaker.

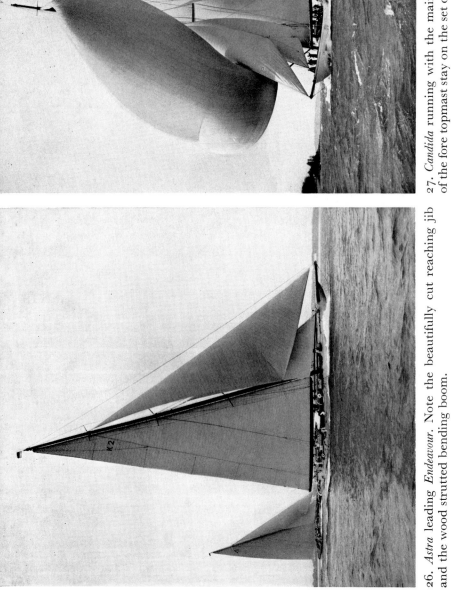

26. *Astra* leading *Endeavour*. Note the beautifully cut reaching jib and the wood strutted bending boom.

papers and in one there was a supplement entirely devoted to the defender, *Enterprise*. It described her 'Park Avenue' boom, with an aerial photo of two of her crew adjusting the stops on top of this triangular sectioned spar and her amazing ten-sided alloy mast. It also revealed the complete mechanization of halliards and sheets most of which took place below decks where slatted bulkheads and the minimum of accommodation were evident.

Father, always buoyant and cheerful, did not seem to be too disturbed at all this but, in my heart, I felt rather despondent.

That fatal year six American defenders were to appear. The four new yachts that were built included *Yankee*, for a Boston syndicate, *Whirlwind*, *Weetamoe*, and *Enterprise*; both *Vanity* and *Resolute* had been brought up to rule requirements. Eliminating races were finally to prove that there was little to choose between *Weetamoe* and *Enterprise*, in fact it was touch and go until the great genius of 'Mike' Vanderbilt displayed the final edge.

Enterprise had seven mainsails and I believe it was the last that was flown by flying boat to Newport, after the trials. This was a perfect sail and was the one that Vanderbilt used in this series and possibly later too.

All the designers including Francis Herreshoff (*Whirlwind*), Starling Burgess (*Enterprise*), Frank Payne (*Yankee*), Clinton Crane (*Weetamoe*), and the ageing Nat Herreshoff (*Resolute*), were on most friendly terms and the moment the defender was selected all in true American fashion offered assistance to the defender should it be needed in any shape or form. Thus my dear father faced the stiffest opposition of his lifetime.

When we advised George Ratsey that we expected service from his City Island loft his first reply was that he was far too busy with the defenders, but when Father reminded him that had it not been for Lipton's challenge he would not have enjoyed a record year's business, he changed his tune and he and his sons Ernest and Colin all assisted us whenever we needed them.

Sir Thomas had chartered a house-boat named *Killarney* for his after-guard, while he was living in his steam yacht *Erin*, named after his first which had been sunk in the Mediterranean in the war. We had two sail-makers from the Gosport loft with us and sundry other relevant bodies.

M

When *Enterprise* was selected *Weetamoe* was laid up at Herreshoff's Bristol yard and Father and I ran over to have a good look at her. We felt that apart from the great mechanical ingenuity displayed on *Enterprise*, *Weetamoe* might well have been the best hull of the lot. She, *Enterprise* and *Yankee* were all built with bronze plating as was *Resolute*, a technique largely favoured in the history of the later defenders. I have a paper-weight from the plating of *Enterprise* and it scales a shade less than a quarter of an inch thick—beautiful metal but surprisingly heavy for two inches square.

We enjoyed the usual kind American hospitality and one evening were entertained by Mr and Mrs Aymar Johnson at their lovely place on Rhode Island. Their humorous negro chauffeur collected us at the Signal Station and, stopping on a bridge with the sea on one side and a lagoon on the other, exclaimed "There you are gentlemen, the Atlantic Ocean both sides of the street."

Dinner was served on a verandah under a portico, the candles did not flicker and fireflies were droning. I was seated between two charming young ladies and when my father informed his hostess that I had recently become a parent she exclaimed "Hi!, this won't do," and a little game of general post took place. Father was between the charmers and I in his place!

The Aymar Johnsons owned the fine old steam yacht *Enchantress* and were very pro-British. It was the Aymar Johnson Trophy that the Royal Navy rowed for round the Royal Yacht at Cowes Regatta for a great number of years.

The impact of the Cup races off Newport was, of course, very good for trade and when the Mayor called aboard *Shamrock* all hands received a silver pencil suitably engraved: mine still works beautifully after forty years.

Prohibition was then still in force and it recalls many memories. George Ratsey took us out to lunch to a place noted for its home-brewed lager. We had a window table and with a fine great jug of this excellent brew it was amusing to see our host receive a big wink from a passing cud-chewing cop.

On my birthday we went to a play in New York. '*A Symphony in Two Flats*' by Ivor Novello, beautifully acted by four of our greatest artists and the silence throughout this play showed the audience's appreciation of good English. During the interval we thought we'd like a drink and, by habit, made for the bar. It was empty and carefully stacked bottles of Canada dry ginger ale formed the sole decor.

Colin and Ernest Ratsey owned *Gollywog*, a little 'character' sloop whose design was based on their grandfather's *Harrier*, originally used for ferrying canvas from Southampton to Cowes. One evening when Colin and I had had our usual quota of gin and ginger-beer, I felt that a swim was essential before dinner as the gin was reputed to contain tree bark and its kick was infamous. The swim was ineffective but we had delectable 'squab' which I assumed were young Rhode Island chicken and it was not until the meal was half through that I realized there was a child asleep in a pilot berth behind me. So much for synthetic hooch.

Reverting to Sir Thomas and his second *Erin*, he was getting on and it was noticeable that he did not entertain on anything like the 1920 scale. On the two occasions that I was aboard he took me down to his cabin to show me his mother's photograph in its large silver filigree frame. This ritual, as I expect many will remember, seemed to bring him endless pleasure.

It should be remembered that Sir Thomas made his many challenges for 'the old mug', as he called it, not to advertise Lipton's tea but because H.M. King Edward VII asked him to do so after the unfortunate incidents with Lord Dunraven's *Valkyrie* when the King desired to improve yachting relations between the two countries. As was known before the First War, the Kaiser could not understand why his nephew 'went yachting with his grocer'.

George Ratsey had imported five Lymington Scows and they were available in Brenton's Cove as playthings for the respective after-guards. This was a nice gesture and on several occasions Sherman Hoyt, 'Bubbles' Havemeyer, Ernest and Colin, Father and I had amusing little evening races. The contrast of sailing a 'limey dink', as Sherman called them, and a J class yacht was as pronounced as it was great fun. Sherman realized that they sailed better when upright and, in the usual light evening airs, he lay in the bottom of his using a hinging tiller which he had evolved.

I was privileged to bump into this great character off and on for many years as mentioned elsewhere throughout this book. During the Cup races he intended to wear his Breton-pink shorts but Vanderbilt insisted that he should not do so before they had won a race. He didn't have long to wait.

That year he chartered *Shimna*, an old 12-metre and I remember sailing with him and Major B. Heckstall-Smith up to Bristol. I had the helm for an hour or two and when on the wind and approaching a large Naval craft at anchor I asked him if we should clear her; his reply, "There is no tide John," came as a bit of a shock to one who has sailed nearly all his life in vicious tides.

One evening Mr Haffenraffer, Herreshoff's manager, who had a beautiful name, invited us all to a magnificent 'clam-bake'. It was all great fun but unfortunately Major Workman, back on *Killarney*, was frightfully ill and Father administered brandy, perhaps more in sympathy than hope. The Major was the Royal Ulster Yacht Club representative in *Enterprise*.

I doubt if in the history of yachting there was ever such a vast collection of fine power yachts, large schooners, and other craft moored in Newport's Brenton's Cove. The largest in the fleet was Mr W. K. Vanderbilt's *Alva* of 2,418 tons which he had just taken taken over from Krupp's of Hamburg. Colonel Neill and I did a great deal of evening calling on some of these craft. At first I thought it was rather cheek but he assured me that most owners expected callers at that great gathering, especially from the challenging party.

Glancing at the rough notes I made all those years ago I see that we called on *Lone Star* owned by a Mr Bourne. On being introduced to the guests I was amazed and pleased to meet a Mrs Huntington whom I had met many years before at Naples when her father, Mr Taylor, had chartered the 1,822 tons steam yacht *Iolanda*. My job on that fine yacht was to ply Miss Taylor with cigarettes when her dad wasn't looking and I remember when we called aboard the day they were leaving for their cruise, she threw a book on the cockpit gratings as we left calling out, "It's for you John, don't let your dad read it." It was the *Green Hat* by Michael Arlen.

I read in my notes on Newport, 1930, "I meet Mrs Huntington (*née* Taylor); she has a boy and a girl and says I am stouter!"

My scanty list of spectator yachts includes *Aloha*, *Corsair* with her war service chevrons on her funnel, *Iolander*, *Atlantic*, *Constellation*, *Guinevere*, *Enchantress*, *Erin* and others. Apart from *Shamrock* and *Erin* who wore the defaced ensign of the Royal Ulster Yacht Club there was only one other red ensign to be seen and that was worn by a little schooner that had turned up from Canada.

I do not propose to inflict all my rough notes upon the suffering reader but, to capture a little of the atmosphere of the moment, those on the first race read thus:

"We leave moorings at 9.35. Power yachts greet us as we tow out; H.M. Sloop *Heliotrope* gives us a rousing reception. Off Whistling buoy at 10.50. G Pennant hoisted on Committee Boat at 11.15 (Race postponed 15 minute intervals). Committee Boat is the Tug *Susan A. Moran*. Huge gathering of yachts including power, sail, racing and small craft of every type. Two American liners around 10,000 tons, 6 Coastguard ships and many destroyers and sub-chasers. Great difficulty in keeping small craft off the course; gunfire in some cases."

The other pages on this race describe every move of both yachts but for the sake of brevity I recount only the 'high spots':

"We had a running start, wind was light and it was fifteen miles out and return.

We were on the starboard gybe and, at times, as we exceeded the wind speed the foot of our spinnaker was often in the water; not so with *Enterprise*. Nothing in it at all and conversation on our rival easily heard. At about halfway down the run a little more wind came and more on the port quarter; we trimmed spinnaker further forward and *Enterprise* ran a sail in stops on jib-stay. She broke out a balloon-jib, lowered her big spinnaker and set a smaller one SPILLING the wind into her balloon-jib. (We had not seen this technique before and I do not think I ever saw it again anywhere.)

Nearing the mark we set balloon-jib in stops, downed spinnaker and broke out jib. *Enterprise* gained some two minutes by her headsail manœuvre. On rounding the mark and being on a wind she came straight at us causing us to go under her stern thus losing more time in rounding the mark. The leg home was a close reach and we finished with *Enterprise* winning by 2¾ minutes Mean speed 7·3 knots."

After the race we all thought that *Enterprise* seemed a trifle stiffer than we were and Father proposed trying a further 4 tons of inside ballast. We called on Mr Vanderbilt's tender, *Vara*, to congratulate them and to ascertain the form over the proposed ballasting.

Vanderbilt, 'Bubbles' Havemeyer, and Sherman Hoyt were all relaxing on a sofa going over the details of the race. They were quite shattered at the thought of this extra ballast but it was in order provided the marks were resighted after stowage. I believed we acquired the ballast from Manchester's yard, who serviced *Shamrock* at Newport, and when it was stowed all hands went aboard the dinghy and our 24-ft lifeboat while Professor Webb, the Official Measurer, checked the marks.

The second race, with a wind'ard start, made us realize in a matter of minutes what a fabulous craft *Enterprise* was to wind'ard in a good true breeze.

I will not enlarge on my notes on that race except to say that they confirm that we did all in our power to hold her though we did make one bad mistake in tacking to the mark far too soon when 6½ minutes astern of *Enterprise*. Ted Heard almost stopped *Shamrock* by pinching to fetch it.

On the next leg, a broad reach, we caught up a little before *Enterprise* picked up a smart breeze some minutes before us and again opened up on us. On the final leg with spinnakers and *Enterprise* tacking down wind she beat us to the finish by 9½ minutes.

That evening we made our usual congratulatory call on *Vara* and after dinner we attended the little Casino Theatre, filling an invitation box and listening to one of America's leading light music composers playing tunes such as the *Manhattan Serenade* most beautifully.

We turned in tired and discouraged and I, personally, terribly sorry for Father.

Secretly I felt that we should have had a far more efficient afterguard and I rather felt that the crew had rumbled to it.

Early that summer, when racing in the Solent, among the guests on board was a very intelligent naval officer. We lay up to windward together and I was bombarded with sensible questions—in fact I was immensely impressed that here was a great tactician. I refer to Captain John Illingworth whose impact on the sport, after leaving the Royal Navy, was pronounced. How I wished that he could have been with us at Newport, and his later achievements proved me right.

Reverting to the after-guard I would not hesitate to say that the most active member was Mr Johnson de Forest who was representing the New York Yacht Club and thus not authentically included in it. He confided in me at the outset that when sailing he always 'rooted' for the yacht he was on and, my goodness, he did all in his power to assist in so many ways. Being a great gentleman, his criticisms took the form of polite suggestions and they were always RIGHT. The greatest sea-lawyer we ever met among the top flight of helmsmen, he won the Seawanhaker Cup with his 8-metre *Priscilla* on the Clyde and I was told that he rented a small barn with ropes stretched across for hanging his sails as he did not like sail bags.

During these Cup races he was, I believe, a guest on board Mr Henry Plant's yacht and when young Mr Plant brought de Forest over in his launch for the first race the latter bumped his nose on the covering board coming up the side-ladder; he kindly leaned outboard telling me he could not dream of letting any blood soil it. Plant returned with a fine bunch of linen handkerchiefs tied up with good Irish ribbon.

Again, when de Forest noticed that Ted Heard enjoyed a banana with his snack lunch, he turned up for the next race with the largest hand of bananas one ever saw. Delightful people.

One day a thick fog prevented racing and we received a few pressmen on what they called 'an informal visit'. I remember leaning over the rail on *Killarney* chatting to a nice young reporter while the two rival yachts were just discernible through the haze. I explained to him that *Enterprise*'s alloy mast, most beautifully engineered with ten sides, thousands of small rivets and perfect taper was somewhere around $1\frac{1}{2}$ tons lighter than *Shamrock*'s and that if *Enterprise* had her starboard launch (as they call the owner's launch in America) hoisted about a third of her mast from the deck the yachts might have been more evenly matched.

To my horror a New York paper next day quoted me in an article 'Nicholson 2nd states, etc'. Had I known I would not have quoted such a true but somewhat odd simile.

That mast cost more than the whole of *Shamrock V*.

I've omitted to mention the day our main halliard broke, so we thought, at the start of one of the races. There was a lively sea and I was alarmed at the travel of the mainsail luff hanks, some two inches or so, up and down. That day *Enterprise* took the lee berth, but it was only a matter of a few minutes before she was nicely ahead when, suddenly, our boom collapsed to the deck, without, fortunately, anyone being hurt.

Our main halliard passed over a specially large sheave at the masthead and inside the mast to a winch at the base.

It was the pawl of this winch that broke and not the halliard, as we had suspected.

By the time we had hastily stowed up the main we passed by the Committee Boat and were hailed to inquire whether we could start by tomorrow. I was amazed to hear Father give a quick reply in the affirmative as I was thinking of that 'haddock's nest' in the mast and was wondering if the halliard would come kindly out through a not too large inspection plate. Luckily it did and the pawl was easily replaced.

To conclude my description of this fruitless and distressing invasion, we all realized that the academic and thorough ingenuity of American yachting science had us skinned.

Starling Burgess had had a sail with us before the races and gave me several mathematical formulae on far too many sheets of *Erin*'s beautifully printed notepaper. I still have some to this day and cannot begin to understand them! Unfortunately, I never had a sail in *Enterprise* but was aboard her several times. Having referred to her mast and boom I forgot to mention that, when sailing, over half her crew were below decks handling her many sheet winches; she was particularly 'clean' on deck, spinnaker booms cleverly stowed, her practical and very pleasing pram dinghy being stowed right aft when racing.

That dinghy was properly tested one day during a trial sail when, without warning, Bubbles Havemeyer dived over the side; it was he who relieved Vanderbilt at the helm down wind.

Burgess did, however, congratulate us on our blocks and seemed rather impressed with the outfit. These were things we had specialized in for many years with ash cheeks and well designed galvanized steel forgings—one of the many trades now gone overboard in these days of specialization in components.

After the series Father and I went up to Boston where, at Frank Payne's office, a series of meetings took place and the seed was sown for mast restrictions in future. We stayed a night or two at the Copley Plaza which I thought was a surprising place with powdered 'flunkeys'.

On a Sunday I strolled round the fish quays admiring some

splendid Banks fishermen hulls and was amused to see one husky little schooner named *Shamrock*.

Captain Paul brought *Shamrock V* home from Newport with a few Scandinavians who were among the *Enterprise* crew and although news was scanty we did hear that they were badly caught in the centre of a hurricane. When reported from the Lizard she was naturally followed up the coast and on her arrival at Southampton Father and I went straight on board. The first thing that struck me was the almost total lack of varnish on her spruce mast, boom, and deck trim. The crew were all in good shape and looked a pretty tough bunch of fellows, most of them with bristly beards, and Paul gave us a detailed description of their experience when struck by the hurricane. Apparently the ocean was flat but white with salt spray which nearly blinded them and they could move on deck only on hands and knees, holding on to anything at hand.

She was dry-docked after a few days and our inspection was a wonderful surprise; there was hardly a seam to be seen and one would hardly have thought she had sailed to the Isle of Wight let alone crossed the Atlantic twice including a hurricane.

Since so many challengers and defenders get broken up or fade away it should be recorded that *Shamrock V* remained in our menagerie 'big class', now only referred to as the J's, until the last war killed big yacht racing. Later she was converted to a cruising yawl with auxiliary motor and eventually found her way to the Mediterranean, later to be re-named *Sea Song*.

Little did we know that my father was yet to design the best challenger in the history of the Cup races.

It was five years later that Mr Gerald B. Lambert invaded our shores with his fine J class yacht *Yankee* accompanied by the gracious three-masted schooner *Atlantic* on which her owner lived. I have mentioned this 'invasion' earlier and I doubt if any year of big class racing history was more enjoyable for those who participated.

Gerry Lambert's book *Yankee in England* describes it all so well— the race across the Atlantic between the two totally different yachts with the cutter *Yankee* setting a generous jury rig and the whole British racing season from its start on the East Coast, Havre, the Solent and finally the Western regattas. There could have been no

more delightful and sporting ambassador and the impact of his visit
will be remembered by all concerned.

Lambert took everything in his stride and much must surely have
been novel to him and to his charming guests. I remember a small
group of persons seated on a pile of grubby timber stacked outside
my office—'Gerry', Mr and Mrs Potter, and Frank Payne—all
enjoying the novelty of the Portsmouth Harbour scene and watching
the nested dories being sent ashore from *Yankee*; the wind was east
and they 'sailed' so well with no one on board.

A year or two after this great Lambert invasion I met Sir Thomas
Sopwith who had recently been to the States and had been entertained to dinner by some five Commodores of the New York and
other yacht clubs. Sir Thomas told me that it was a terrific party
and he felt he should make a little speech. When he returned to his
hotel he wondered what he had talked about so 'phoned up 'Gerry'
whose reply was that he hadn't the slightest idea!

I have described earlier the Torbay regattas of 1935 and a race
from Paignton won by *Velsheda* starting with a balloon jib instead of a
Genoa. In another race, at Babbacombe, again in *Velsheda*, I had the
helm after Father had excelled himself by standing out to sea after
the first round when well astern and, getting a shift of wind, had
crossed *Yankee* and nearly did the same to *Endeavour* in the lead. On
the run with the *Endeavour* and *Yankee* playing cat and mouse I
realized the flood tide would be setting us up beyond the finishing
line, so, dinghy-wise, I steered a course to allow for the tide while the
other two were sailing a somewhat arc-like course.

That was my last sail in a J class yacht.

In her last race *Yankee* was dismasted at Dartmouth regatta and
the cause was never discovered; it was assumed that when well
reefed the large fore-triangle caused undue stress at a section of the
mast and it broke by compression. Among many messages of
sympathy her sporting owner received was a telegram from H.M.
King George V from Balmoral.

The final fling on board *Atlantic* must have been 'The Party of the
Year'. Father described how Lambert, when serenaded by an
excursion launch, dived down to his cabin for his harmonica and sat
on the rail playing back to them.

Designed by Gardner & Cox, *Atlantic*, of 532 tons, was built in

1903 at Shooters Island, N.Y. She was one of the most beautiful three-masted schooners and had won a transatlantic race before her visit in 1935.

When in British waters around 1928 the owner, General Cornelius Vanderbilt, sailed specially into Gosport to get Father to re-strike the top line of her green boot-top which was not 'right'; her topsides, by the way, were black.

I remember how he set about it with two yard rowing boats, the foreman shipwright with two others and some very long battens. He was renowned for his 'eye' and was often spotting little but important things in the shipyard.

His only criticism of that beautiful schooner was that her freeboard was a trifle low and I am sure that any knowledgeable critic would agree.

Now that this wonderful scene has gone for ever there are some who think that the America's Cup should have died with the passing of large racing yachts and that, perhaps, some other trophy should have been adopted.

Be that as it may, the present 12-metre contests create world-wide interest, but cost is so much greater today, with Twelve's many times the sum of a J in the past, and they are no longer a racing class for summer use.

With international economy as it is, I would like to think that, in the not too distant future, and with the full and complete blending of C.C.A. and R.O.R.C. rules could see this contest continue between far more utilitarian sea-going yachts.

19 'Velsheda'

This beautiful J class yacht was built for Mr W. L. Stephenson in in 1933 and was 205 tons. She was not only larger than *Shamrock V* but had several features gained in the light of experience in the Universal Rule over the previous four years.

Whereas *Shamrock* was of composite construction with mahogany planking and fitted with a spruce mast, *Velsheda* was of all-steel construction and equipped with a steel mast to a technique we were just developing, with internal diaphragms and all-welded steel shell, of which the plating was around $\frac{1}{16}$ of an inch thick. By then, and in agreement with America, these masts were built to a minimum weight and other sound restrictions were imposed.

Velsheda's all-steel hull had 'joggled' plate landings, a system which was adopted to save the weight of liners, as in flush plating.

Her rather pleasing name was formed by using the early letters of the three daughters names, Velma, Sheila and Daphne, and when, in 1937, we built the motor yacht *Malahne* for Mr Stephenson the last two letters were used with three from the name Daphne, and very charming girls they were too.

At the outset *Velsheda* was most successful, but as the seasons progressed and greater competition came, with *Endeavour* joining this 'big class' embracing 23-metres, *Britannia* and the schooner *Westward*, it was felt that *Velsheda*'s reaching speed could be improved by a most unusual operation. The idea was to lift her waterline bodily aft some eight inches and, before putting our proposals to Mr Stephenson, we made two large-scale models, one as she was and the other embracing my father's ideas of snubbing the bow around the waterline and giving her a new and, we thought, improved stern. We tested these models on the well-known Gosport model pond by using my little A.C. car with a towing boom fixed at right angles and, with a system of near-frictionless pulleys and sensitive spring scale, we set to work. Fortunately, there was a good gravel track near the south side of the pond and our runs were as near scale speed as we could manage. The revised model offered slightly less resistance and her wave form looked definitely better, but without confirmation in a proper testing tank we only had our 'rule of thumb' proof.

When we put these proposals to Mr Stephenson and suggested more academic research he surprised us by deciding to go ahead as he felt our trials were convincing enough. That winter this unusual operation was performed, working under special covers as *Velsheda* was hauled up on our slipway.

This bow 'snubbing' was not new and, *pro rata*, was in keeping with what my father applied around that time to several successful 12-metres. Latterly, since the war, my cousin Charles adopted definitely 'hollow' bow entries in some of his successful boats but I believe that phase has disappeared and, either way, I've always felt that it is not the detail of bow form that wins races but the far more important factor of 'delivery' aft by a clean-running tail. This is a most fascinating subject for analysis, but not in this chapter.

Next season *Velsheda* took her fair share of prizes including winning her most coveted trophy, the King's Cup at Cowes. When Stephenson went to the Royal Yacht to receive it from H.M. King George V, the King expressed his wish to look over *Velsheda* the next day as there was no race on.

Sir Philip Hunloke, as usual, made the arrangements and, after His Majesty had been greeted aboard, Mrs Stephenson and Captain 'Bill' Randall were presented and they went below. After a time His Majesty inquired of the three daughters and they all emerged from their respective hiding places, much to the King's amusement.

Velsheda was a very gay and happy vessel and the Stephensons were so kind and hospitable to Father and myself. In an earlier season 'Bill' Stephenson asked 'Boy' O'Connor to sail her a good deal. In 1937 Father sailed her on the Clyde and both he and I raced her at the Torbay regattas, as mentioned earlier.

In those days, in high summer, yacht yards were usually slack and, in order to keep things going, we used to lay down a 'stock' job, sometimes a power yacht and sometimes a sailing cruiser. In 1934 we had a twin screw 80-ft motor yacht under construction and when Mr Stephenson heard of this he came down to look at her.

One of the first questions he put to me was whether she was being built to Lloyds and when I gave him a negative reply, explaining that at that time Lloyds scantlings for motor yachts under about 200 tons were too excessive for words and went on about 'firms of repute', he gave me a funny look but ordered the yacht and named her *Bystander*. She was gutted out abaft the engine room and battened to form a hold for storing *Velsheda*'s unwanted or spare equipment when racing; she made a splendid tender.

With the crisis of war and the subsequent abandonment of large yacht racing, *Velsheda* has spent the past decade lying in a mud berth in the Hamble River. For many years she was well maintained by one of Lloyds' local surveyors and she is there to this day.

The impact of knowing the Stephenson family can never be forgotten.

20 'Endeavour'

Sir Thomas Sopwith's challenge for the America's Cup, through the auspices of the Royal Yacht Squadron, was accepted by the New York Yacht Club in the autumn of 1933 and we built *Endeavour* throughout that winter and spring of 1934.

Built to the Universal J class rule this fine cutter was of steel construction to Lloyds classification but her plating was not joggled all over, as with *Velsheda*, as it was felt that a flush-plated bottom was desirable; the slight additional weight of liners was not detrimental below the waterline, so her topsides only had these overlapping plate edges known as joggling.

Endeavour was, without doubt, my father's masterpiece. She looked 'good' everywhere and from any angle and was one of what I have previously called 'first-shotters'. By this I do not imply that he just 'dashed her off' as, for many days, hours were spent studying one of the greatest problems in all racing yacht design, that of reduction of wetted surface involving hours of planimeter work. It is tragic that all but a few of the less interesting drawings were destroyed during the war but I do remember that his original 'draft' lines were hardly modified and her above-water body was never affected by this study.

At that time tank testing in the American manner had not emerged in this country and, I suppose, it could be described as the time that British designers were 'getting warm' but no more. I always knew that Father was critical of model yacht racing as it could be very misleading if applied to a full-scale craft but that, of course, is not to be confused with tank testing. In 1930 I had an old Wykehamist friend who wanted to build a scale model of *Shamrock V* and he could not understand when I told him she would not sail and would blow over the moment he put her in the water; in fact he built but never sailed her.

We always held the view that the tank should be used as the servant and not the master. This proved so during the war when tank testing an air-sea rescue model for the Pacific along with models designed by several other firms. The tank experts built a model to their own ideas and theories and it was a complete failure. These perhaps rather sweeping remarks do not apply, of course, to the brilliant technique that was being developed for sailing yacht research by Dr Davidson at the Stevens Institute of Technology at Hoboken which I mention in a later chapter. Now, this country is far better equipped with its own resources for research which were not readily available before the war.

Reverting to *Endeavour*, it was decided to base her steel mast on the technique adopted for Velsheda, but we had been advised by our steel suppliers to use steel of a different specification. This added to strength without increasing weight but we had a difficult time in finding the right electrode for its welding; once this was solved all was well.

At that time Frank Murdoch was a senior member of Sir Thomas's aircraft organization. He was a very experienced yachtsman and an academic engineer whom we regarded as Sir Thomas's technical assistant in yachting matters. Murdoch was of immense assistance to my father in the development, stressing and rigging of this mast and designed many of its more important fittings, supervising their attachment. These fittings were constructed of special steel which, if suspended on a piece of wire and struck lightly with a stick, would ring like Waterford glass.

Frank was in charge of instrumentation and devised special strain gauges to record tension in runners and preventer backstays and, with his brother Bob, designed and constructed special sheet winches at their Antwerp works in Belgium; these were two-speed units with levers used as in rowing.

We also built a somewhat revolutionary boom, of deep section and hollow spruce construction, fitted with struts and tension wires whereby its curvature could be regulated on the weather side to suit varying wind speeds. Since Starling Burgess produced the triangular

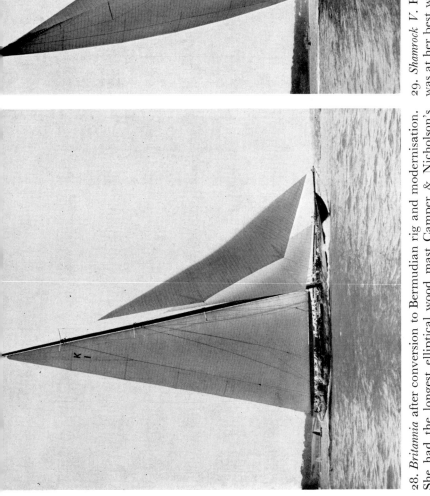

28. *Britannia* after conversion to Bermudian rig and modernisation. She had the longest elliptical wood mast Camper & Nicholson's have ever built. Also note the double clewed jib.

29. *Shamrock V.* Here she is racing close-hauled off Cowes, but she was at her best when sailing off the wind.

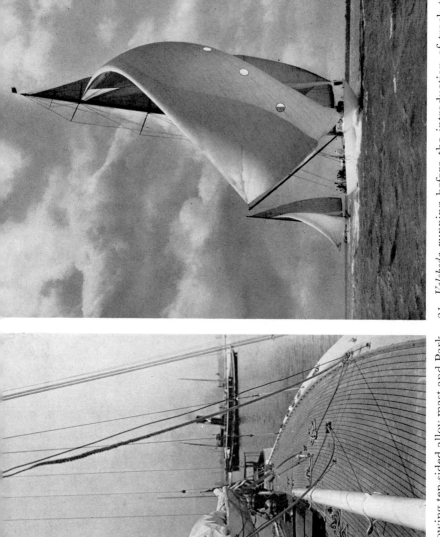

30. Deck view of *Enterprise* showing ten-sided alloy mast and Park Avenue boom and the towing strop.

31. *Velsheda* running before the introduction of track to raise the inboard end of the spinnaker boom. Note also Tom Ratsey's spinnaker holes.

section flat-topped boom for *Enterprise* in 1930 which was known as
the Park Avenue we described ours as the North Circular.

To this day I remember an unfortunate Sunday when Sir Thomas
was having a trial sail and Father, my wife and I, Uffa Fox and
Nigel Coleman were in *Shamrock V* with 'Grannie' Diaper, doubtless
combining a pleasant sail with, possibly, testing some modification
for Sir Richard Fairey. We were not flirting with *Endeavour* but
naturally had our eyes on her. There was a nice breeze but no more
and when somewhere off the Peel Bank we saw *Endeavour*, west of
Gurnard, lowering her mainsail. She made for Gosport under headsails and, as we converged, we saw the splintered boom. At a council
of war next day we decided that we had had enough of bending
booms and so, with little time to spare, we evolved the hasty construction of the Park Avenue boom.

Ironically, *Rainbow*, the defender, adopted a deep-section boom,
but without any struts to create a curvature and later, in the case of
Endeavour II versus *Ranger*, the former retained the triangular sectioned boom whereas the latter adopted our original style of bending
boom, but fitted with two sets of tensioning struts.

My thoughts are somewhat out of sequence here and I must return
to the day of *Endeavour*'s launch. On that day Gosport saw what was
probably its greatest crowd and we had to adopt a ticket system in the
yard as for a miniature Cup Tie. I remember that, for the broadcast
of the occasion, we fitted a microphone on a little raft to pick up the
'swish' as the launching cradle slipped through the water.

The Sopwith's decided to entertain their guests at a buffet lunch
on board *Vita III*. Though we expected that Lady Sopwith might
prefer to let a well-known London firm deal with the luncheon we
suggested that the rather celebrated little local caterer, a Mr Meotti,
be approached. I remember we left them to talk it over while Father
and I took Sir Thomas to the sail loft to talk with Mr Stanley
Lapthorn. We must have been there for fully two hours when one
of us remembered Lady Sopwith and Meotti. I went up to the little
Swiss café to fetch her and found them both almost in tears in their
artistic excitement after such a long gastronomic session. This was a
great feather in the cap of the Italian-Swiss artist who was so well
known among the yachting fraternity of those days.

It was a perfect spring day and Mr Herman Andreae made a

clever and charming speech on behalf of the many guests. It was he who owned the 23-metre cutter *Candida* at that time and who, later, was to own *Endeavour*. This had been a crowded and happy day and after it all I wandered down the little lane from office to garage admiring a wonderful sunset. That, I thought, was a great omen for *Endeavour*'s future.

Back to the yacht, we had a large-scale deck model of *Endeavour* at home in the garden, mounted on trestles which we used for checking sheet leads, etc. We conceived an unusual headsail which, I am sure, a great many people claim was their invention. The truth is that I had recently been to the Fairey aircraft factory at Hayes where Sir Richard's partner, Mr F. G. Dawson, had shown me their new high altitude machine. I was sketching a plan view of this machine's unusual wing with my father, near doodling in fact, and, thinking of the warped wings of the First War Caudron biplane, I added a number of clews to the wing sketch. We then sketched a three-clewed sail and both thought it was worth a trial.

After obtaining Sir Thomas's approval, we talked it over with Stanley Lapthorn and he, in turn, got in touch with Chris Ratsey at Cowes who always kept his boat *Harrier* in commission all the year round. A triple clewed jib was made to *Harrier* size and in no time we were experimenting off Cowes with Frank Beken taking a number of useful photos. I've always held the view that sail observation is better done off the yacht than on it.

After pretty exhaustive trials we decided to adopt a double-clewed sail and found that the best method of sheeting was to haul in the lower sheet first and adjust it by the upper sheet. It was so efficient that Frank's strain gauge registered some extra 2 tons or more on the backstays and the blocks were renewed after the original ones started to split.

Perhaps we all made a tactical mistake in setting this somewhat revolutionary sail in the Solent, rather than well out in the Channel, as *Rainbow* adopted it in no time.

Before departing for America and with little time to spare, Sir Thomas was embarrassed by an irritating strike of the crew who literally held a pistol to his head. Sir Thomas rightly refused to give way and with the active and efficient intervention of the Royal Corinthian Yacht Club, then based only at Burnham-on-Crouch, a splendid crew of amateur volunteers was quickly enlisted. Their training time was almost wholly limited to sailing at Newport just before the Cup races were to start.

When Frank and his wife were here a few months ago he produced a list of the names of that worthy band of amateurs which included A. Bacon, J. Bacon, Chris Boardman, Miles Belville (later, an M.F.H.), Henry Drew, R. Droop, Jake Martin, Roy Mitchell (son of 'Tiny' Mitchell, Commodore of the R.C.Y.C.), Beecher Moore, E. Moltzer, H. Richards, Bob de Quincey and Nigel Warington Smyth. These splendid fellows not only had the fun of falling into a great experience at the eleventh hour but they acquitted themselves, with so little training, in no uncertain manner.

It was in 1936 that two of these amateurs, Belville and Boardman, with Frank Murdoch and Charles Leaf formed a splendid syndicate for whom we built the 6-metre *Lalage* in which they won the Olympic Gold at Kiel. I secretly regarded them as the only true example in British yachting history of a syndicate that was, so far as one could see, in complete harmony. Charles Leaf, the tall Cambridge don, was the runner man and was given his own little cockpit with lower floor level to reduce windage; it was known as the coal hole. Incidentally, *Lalage* too had an unusual sail; it was neither a parachute spinnaker nor a Genoa and they called it the 'Paranoia'.

Besides Sir Thomas and Lady Sopwith, *Endeavour*'s after-guard included Father, Frank Murdoch, Mr Gerald Penney, and Captain Paul as navigator. I was not among the invading party this time and stayed behind to mind the shop.

So much has been written of those races thirty-three years ago that it would be futile to describe them again. I do, however, remember the evening scene each race day at our Gosport office and how we arranged for cabled reports to come at regular intervals. The office staff, and any others who cared to, all clustered round the outer office where the phone was located. One Rhoda Smith, my secretary at the time, sat glued to that phone and somewhere I still have that precious collection of orange-coloured slips. It was rather like a crowd watching fireworks, with cheers for the good and groans for the not so good ones and at times our hearts were almost crying out for those amateurs and the loyal members of the crew.

To me, they were quite the most emotional hours ever spent at

the office. It was the nearest thing in all Cup race history and the
world knew that Father, bless him, had done his stuff.

When all was over, the Press Club gave a luncheon to Sir Thomas
and, with Lord Camrose in the chair, it was a very gay affair. I
happened to be the guest of a great old local journalist, a Mr Bennett,
who for many years represented *The Times* on all Naval and yachting
matters in the Portsmouth area. Beer was taken before lunch—good
beer—and, I imagined, it was in the manner of the Press Club with
half a pint in a large tankard. It seemed better that way.

After Lord Camrose and Sir Thomas had made their amusing
speeches Father made a briefer one. Standing silently and looking
them all in the eye (I thought that he was not well) he said, "I
wanted to give you all a good look over as YOU are the cause of all
the trouble!"

Bacon, who was a Flag Officer of the R.C.Y.C. and spokesman for
the amateur crew, gave his brief opinion, "That while in America
he sensed that there were only three people worth knowing and they
were Our Lord, George Washington and Tom Sopwith."

That lunch broke up rather late and one could feel that the Chairman was a trifle worried about going to press.

21 'Endeavour II'

Endeavour II, the largest racing cutter ever built in this country, was commissioned in 1936 with a view to challenging for the Cup the following year.

Built to the same J class rules as *Endeavour* and of 228 tons, she was rather more powerful than her predecessor and was of all steel construction, but this time flush-plated all over.

I remember the first time Sir Thomas Sopwith entered the building shed with us he was so amazed at the sight of her that he exclaimed, "Good Lord, Charlie, she's like a ruddy great pantechnicon". I should mention here that, beyond showing the yacht to a great many visitors, I had little to do with her construction.

Frank Murdoch was again acting as Sir Thomas's technical assistant and, with the experience gained on *Endeavour*, things went forward steadily and well so far as he and Father were concerned. I do remember, however, that we had rather serious teething trouble over her mast and that a new steel, a magnificent material with wonderful properties, had been recommended by one of Sir Thomas's advisers.

One cold winter morning our excellent foreman boilermaker, Vic Nicholson (who was no relation), came to me with an almost frightened look on his face and implored me to join him immediately. At the time, my parent was away. We built these steel masts by rolling the plates, fitting the internal diaphragms and joining the many lengths by an overlapping staggered joint; before welding the whole we used what were termed 'lozenges' to hold these rounded mast sections in alignment in 'chairs' or shaped trestles of steel; the lozenges were merely spot-welded.

On this fatal morning Vic showed me his profound problem which was that the severe frost had caused contraction and all these welds had parted. We tried every available type of electrode without success and after a visit from Sir Thomas it was decided to revert to *Endeavour's* 'Tormanc' mast steel and scrap the new material.

As an example of how a Cup challenger can stimulate the many firms concerned with supply of materials and equipment, the rolling mill supplying this steel stopped their whole output for as long as it took to roll out a handful of plates approximating $\frac{3}{16}''$ thick. It was understood between Sir Thomas and the mill in question that a signed photo of *Endeavour II* would ultimately find its way to their boardroom.

Endeavour II had a good first season, taking her fair share of prizes. I remember that towards the end of that season we had a pretty blustery Plymouth regatta and, as mentioned elsewhere, I was sailing the 12-metre *Westra* for Mr Connell. On one day the Committee cancelled the regatta and the next was equally bad but our old friend Tom Thornycroft who was guest helmsman of *Endeavour* (then owned by Herman Andreae) lobbied the other J class owners to race. Instead of agreeing sensibly among themselves to race with reefed sails—a condition that might well have been adopted from time to time—they did not do so and *Endeavour* lost her mast.

It should be appreciated that these yachts had great stability and carried a high aspect ratio sail plan; when 'heeling and toeing' in a really heavy seaway their masts were subjected to severe stresses. There were many critics at the time who referred to the class as 'butterflies' but I still consider—as I did at the time—that it was more a matter of seamanship, or lack of it. Snugged down and properly reefed they were no slower in lumpy water than they would have been in smoother water.

In the days of the old gaff cutters topmasts were struck in very heavy weather, but with the advent of the Marconi gaff rig and the later Bermudian rig this practice was impossible and judicious reefing was the only alternative.

I did not join in the 1937 Cup races and I do not propose to describe them as they were so well reported at the time. As to her after-guard, I had a good friend who, at that time, was among the brightest navigators in the Royal Air Force, one Wing Commander Jim Scarlet who was also a keen sailor. Sir Thomas knew his family and after a meeting he quickly appointed him Navigator. Regrettably Air Vice-Marshal Scarlet was killed while flying soon after the war.

1937 saw a veritable invasion across the Atlantic comprising: *Endeavour II*, accompanied by *Endeavour*, the Sopwith's fine motor yacht *Philante* and Mr Fred Sigrist's motor yacht *Viva*, ex-*Vita II* that he had purchased from Sir Thomas a year or two previously. Murdoch reminded me that the officers and professionals numbered 104. Among the after-guard with Sir Thomas and Lady Sopwith (who acted as Observer) were: Sir Ralph Gore as spare helmsman, Father, Frank Murdoch, and Jim Scarlet. Captain Williams was in charge of the crew.

The defending yacht *Ranger* was the outcome of the combined brains of Starling Burgess and the brilliant and unique brothers Olin and Rod Stephens. Tank tests were carried out on *Weetamoe*, *Endeavour*, and *Rainbow* to check known J boat performance, and five other models and four more variations were also tested before the designers reverted to their original form which was recorded as 77-C at the Hoboken tank. Full consideration was given to average wind speeds over a number of years off Newport in September and the result produced a remarkable yacht.

It is not easy to describe *Ranger*'s salient features without a model or photographs but, basically, she had a firm or hard tendency to her bilge for some length just forward of amidships merging into pronounced long, easy, hollow quarters with a narrow stern. Under the racing conditions met at the time she was clearly the superior yacht but one always felt that given more wind *Endeavour II* would have performed better. To what extent my father's gesture in giving Burgess *Endeavour*'s lines assisted in the tank analysis is a matter for conjecture—very little I would think, as the models were so totally different. It was also strange, as I mentioned earlier, that *Ranger* sported a strutted 'North Circular' style boom while *Endeavour II* stuck to the triangular-sectioned 'Park Avenue' started by *Enterprise*.

It is very sad to record that Captain 'Brusher' Williams died on the voyage home.

With these great battles between these lovely cutters now all over,

I have a deep sense of regret that, due to war bombing, we lost the small-scale half-models of all my father's 23-metres and J class yachts which I had intended to mount on one board. That would have 'made' this little room where I write and enjoy so much the garden view.

22 *Thoughts and jottings*

I doubt if any sail racing yacht has ever reached the stage of perfection in performance which we might call the optimum. The achievement of this calls for the most thorough analysis of many factors and we have certainly not yet scraped the barrel.

In all yacht racing countries many novel features have come out of the hat over the years but I would say that technical advance was fairly static before the early twentieth century when sail-making, spars, and rigging were to an accepted standard and most progress was confined to hull design.

In my time we have seen a great deal of international technical advancement over a wide field, some theories being discarded after years of trial and others phased out with scientific progress. I would surmise that while hull design was steadily progressing sail plans were semi-static until the advent of aircraft and there is surely still much to learn from slow-speed wind tunnels. The theories of Manfred Curry in Germany, who published that very readable, technical and artistic book *Yacht Racing* in 1928, of Dr Lungstrom of Sweden, Malden Heckstall-Smith, Dr Morwood and many others in this country have all tended to stimulate design generally as also has the vigorous and successful American research, particularly in the advancement of tank testing.

This optimum yacht is akin to the work of the great masters in art whose creations, in many cases, were surely as near perfection as anything could be. But perhaps I am treading on dangerous ground here and have made the wrong simile for, whereas fashion and change apply to both, one remains on a picture wire while the other moves through the water. However, staying with art for a moment there is a sound old saying that 'you like what you grow up with', and I think I must have ceased to grow at quite the right time.

For a great many years I believed that a good design was pleasing to the eye, if not artistic, be it a yacht, aircraft, or locomotive, but now I am sure that this belief can no longer be sustained as so many things that are functional today cannot be accepted even as pleasing, but, I hasten to add, 'to those of my day'. This I believe is due to scientific intervention and much of the artistry of the past has gone overboard.

For many years some of us felt that in sail and hull design we should try as hard as we could to copy nature, particularly in relation to birds and fish but, being between wind and water, we've had to apply a bit of both. Hitler advised Doenitz to study fish in relation to the development of midget submarines which seems to have been quite a sound command. The Admiral had to take notice and the Hamburg testing tank authorities engaged the services of a female physicist who studied resistance of large coarse fish when alive, under an anaesthetic, or dead. She proved, as did Sir Richard Fairey with the porpoise, that the live subject offered the least resistance. This is all deeply scientific and today we hear of a special paint which, if applied to a certain type of small racing boat, might, by its chemical properties, lessen resistance and is under the critical eyes of racing authorities.

Somewhere around 1924 when the British-American 6-metre team races were going strong and alternating annually between the two countries, it was America's turn to visit us and, I believe, it was the only occasion when all four boats of their team were occupying the same slipway at Gosport. They were *Grebe*, *Montauk*, *Sheila* and another whose name escapes me. The former two were designed by William Gardner and *Grebe* with a beam of seven feet was the fattest Six ever built but was a very beautiful model. *Montauk*, also by Gardner, was the most normal of the four and both had bronze fairings round the trailing edge of their rudders tapering to a near knife-edge; both were superbly built by Henry Nevins of City Island. *Sheila* and her partner were ugly ducklings designed by Sherman Hoyt and, with short overhangs and firm bilges, were considered the problem children of the four.

The outstanding feature of the latter two yachts was their rigging, like piano wire and bar-tight everywhere; this was something we had never seen before but was soon to become common practice in dinghies. Since many professionals were fishermen in those days their amateur owners usually accepted a certain amount of spring in their rigging and, in fact, in the Sixes and our family 8-metre we bowed to this doctrine for years though admittedly we strove to set up the forestay with a powerful arrangement of runners.

When we raced our 8-metre *Sagitta* during Cowes Week my sister Mary and I sailed alternate days; she usually joined the crew and I took the helm. On one occasion Mr Kenneth Trimmingham, for whom we were building a 6-metre, was over from Bermuda and was invited to race *Sagitta*. After the race—which they won—my sister, who was with him, told us the whole story. It appeared that Trimmingham was on board early and took over completely. Our skipper Jack Gawn was somewhat upset when Trimmingham wanted to adjust the rigging drastically and, further, when he requested that the largest Genoa be set in stops. *Sagitta* had been having a good season and we had found she preferred what we called the 'tacker' or smaller Genoa to wind'ard in a decent breeze. It seems that as the race proceeded Jack became more enthusiastic and the next time I raced with him he could not speak too highly of Mr 'Trimminger'.

The day before my good friend Hugh Goodson had kindly invited me to join him in his 12-metre *Flica*. It was a light weather day and during the second round our family launch hove in sight en route from Portsmouth to Cowes, having collected Trimmingham from the train from Town. We were somewhere off the Mother Bank buoy and the launch rounded up astern of us with Trimmingham, the cox and the engineer forward; he was talking over the engine noise and we listened to his running commentary, much of which was hardly complimentary; it is so easy to spot something when observing from another boat. This business of 'talking over the engine' can be quite entertaining on a still day and it is amazing how sound carries across the water.

Reverting to the fascination of trying to achieve the ultimate in the collective features of a racing yacht, many barriers indicate that it may never be fulfilled. Lack of funds is by no means the only obstacle and tank and wind tunnel research can soon absorb large sums.

In 1937 the Stevens Institute of Technology of Hoboken, New Jersey, under the auspices of Professor Davidson, Director of the Towing Tank, published a small booklet expounding briefly their experimental methods and technique; at that time great strides had been made in towing models with angles of heel up to 45° and leeway up to 10%. This little booklet concludes as follows:

"The tank is no substitute for the designer. Further than that, test procedures have to be developed for investigating many of the complicated factors involved in designing. The reliability of the small model has been established, and the effect of combined heel and leeway has become a matter of routine in sailing yacht investigations—indicating that the towing tank has a wide field of usefulness in solving hydrodynamic problems."

That was written thirty years ago and, with the great strides in tank development in this country, any designer who ignored these technical facilities today might be regarded as an idiot. Advancement in tank and wind-tunnel testing has gone forward apace since the nineteen-thirties—a far cry from my childhood days when I used to lend a hand at home to help Father set up his drawing-board and weights.

I've always regarded towing tanks as very thrilling places and, as well as the far more complicated research on sailing yachts, that on power hulls is equally fascinating and essential today if any radical departure in design is considered. Disturbed water conditions, in which a great variety of wave conditions can be produced, is another important feature but it has, I feel, one flaw which is total lack of wind accompanying these wavelets as they rustle down the tank.

Water is also largely used in addition to wind tunnels for research on windage created by various external parts of a ship such as superstructure. I am reminded of lunching one day with Sir Richard Fairey when the liner *Queen Mary* was cited and Sir Richard tried to work out the horse-power necessary to drive her superstructure against a sixty-mile-an-hour head wind; he was appalled at the neglect of her designers in this respect.

Gone are so many problems that faced the designers of the past such as fatigue and crystallization in metal masts; today's are nearly all extrusions in light alloy and are built by a few specialist firms. The last alloy mast we constructed was for Hugh Goodson and his syndicate for the 12-metre *Sceptre* and, before that, the first alloy mast to be fitted to an offshore racer, namely *St Barbara*.

Reverting once more to the struggle to achieve the optimum in racing yachts, some designers have the good fortune occasionally to hit it off with a first shot; some feel that their finalised conception is like a good picture and that any touching up might spoil it while others often attempt minor modifications here and there after early trial sails.

When the 12-metre *Sceptre* came south to tune up for the Cup races in 1958 she was serviced at our Gosport yard and naturally the moment of her first slipping was of considerable interest. I was watching this exercise standing alongside our foreman shipwright, one Jack Bowers.

Most slipways operate slowly when hauling out and, in calm water, it is one of the best ways of studying a yacht's under-body with its clear-cut waterlines slowly diminishing as she comes up. We were having a head-on view and, turning to Jack, I asked him for his first thoughts; I was amused at his sly comment which was "If you'll excuse me sir, I would say—six months gone." In other words he felt that she had too much tummy in one place and I must admit that I rather thought the same.

That great and charming designer, David Boyd, had produced a lovely yacht with most pleasing profile and, doubtless, had spent many hours over his conception of the measurement rule. If we were wrong in our criticism, as critics often are, some other vices in her hull may well have been the cause; but if we were correct, no modification could have remedied this degree of plumpness.

I do not think Boyd ever produced anything but eye-pleasing hulls. Some years before when we slipped his lovely yawl *Zigeuner*, then owned by the Fraser-Marshalls, my father phoned my office in such a state of pleasure and excitement that I had to go and admire her with him then and there.

Reverting to *Sceptre*, when Hugh Goodson advised me that he was not going to helm her himself we discussed possible helmsmen and, for a start, we introduced him to Commander Sam Brookes who was among the few who had been sailing a yacht of near 12-metre size, namely the old R.N.S.A. ocean racer *Marabu*. Thus Sam and his brother Joe took over as a temporary measure.

On her first evening sail after re-launching, when Colin Ratsey was aboard to sight the setting of a particular head-sail, I joined them and Sam kindly gave me the helm. Unfortunately I had an urgent meeting that evening at the Royal Albert Yacht Club on the matter of *Sceptre*'s trials with Owen Aisher's *Evaine* and Sam promised to get me ashore on time. The wind cut somewhere off the Warner shoal and, worrying about my appointment, I was relieved to see a small Naval craft steaming towards us; this was Sam's fulfilment of his kind promise.

In the local paper next evening was a critical letter from some idiot who had seen one of Her Majesty's vessels coming alongside *Sceptre*, etc. This was the time when we optimistically hoped for a little Naval assistance in starting these trial sails but Admiral Sir Guy Grantham, who was Commander-in-Chief at that time and a keen yachtsman himself, told me that his hands were absolutely tied. Times had changed and it was not all that long ago when the Admiralty provided a sloop to attend the Royal Albert annual regatta, chiefly for starting the larger classes to the south of the Hamilton Bank beyond the busy and restricted harbour channel.

While still on this theme of the optimum, a somewhat unusual modification was tried out on *Shamrock V* when owned by Dick Fairey. He was very impressed by the thickness of a salmon's tail when viewed from above and after discussion it was decided to cut back (or rather, forward) *Shamrock*'s rudder post some eight inches. When re-hanging the rudder its sides were padded to fair in with the wider sternpost at this new position and she was certainly no slower the next season. My own theory was that salmon needed the power in the tail to propel them through miles of fast water and that our little operation merely reduced wetted surface a shade.

There is no doubt whatever that delivery and stern design is of far greater moment than the entry or bow design provided, of course, that both ends of the hull blend or balance well. This may best be described when using the old sailor's term of "Cod's head and mackerel tail". Many of our best metre class yachts and one J class (*Velsheda*) had stems that were radiused or snubbed to a marked

degree and although this was in the nature of a slight 'rule cheater' it
certainly was not detrimental to their performance.

Later my cousin Charles, with tank-testing aid, seemed to prefer
a rather hollow entry around the waterline. Today it appears that
both these modest extremes have gone the way of other fashions of
the moment. So many of these minor refinements add up to slight
improvement in overall performance and nowadays, in comparatively small but highly efficient offshore racers and in the few 12-
metre yachts associated with the America's Cup races, designers are
experimenting with isolated rudders, fins and trimming tabs or
trimming rudders, more associated with aircraft practice, in their
study to reduce wetted surface.

Since the war sail-makers have made very rapid strides in the
development of materials and perhaps the earliest 'break-away'
started in 1934 when *Rainbow* was defending the Cup. She carried a
very large balloon-jib made of a Dupont material that had to be
kept dry, which we did not know at the time. On his return from
America Chris Ratsey brought some of this material back; he gave
me a sample and suggested I should try to tear it but it was far too
tough. He then put it in a tumbler of water and, after a chat, suggested I should try again. It was easily pulled apart. This, we felt,
was a great tribute to *Rainbow*'s Scandinavian crew.

From flax to Egyptian cotton and from nylon to terylene we
now see other synthetic materials entering the sail lofts and chemical
research is in top gear in these exciting times.

The old wood-planked hull is a thing of the past and the days of
the moisture content meter have gone; soakage is no problem with
G. R. P. hulls. Instrumentation is essential for race-winning these
days and all these advances tend to increase cost. One can imagine
that, except for major international competition, some curbing of
these accumulating costs may become necessary under future racing
rules since top-class competitive offshore yacht racing is steadily
becoming the sport of a limited few.

Harking back for a moment to the matter of flexibility—and this
might apply to hulls as well as to rigging—I remember racing
'Paddy' Quinnell's 6-metre *Kyria* on several occasions when he
kindly invited me and when that delightful fellow Eddy Gillett was
his skipper. Eddy was always cheerful and behind it all he was

something of a deep thinker. During the race he told me that when he was skipper some years before with the owner of a new keel-class boat that was not performing well, he was convinced one day that the new boat was far too rigid so, unknown to her owner, he purposely let him drive her hard on to a mudbank with the result that she became a prize winner. Not perhaps a very scientific approach to the problem of rigidity but it was at least fruitful.

Leaving speculative thoughts on design and scientific trends to the future and accepting that costs may only be stabilized by some degree of standardization, let us descend to the more humble level of analysis of the hull built to a measurement rule but not a standard product. Then, given that all competing yachts are of near similar performance and that their sails also conform to some standard of equality, the human element remains the deciding factor and the helmsman and his crew hold the trump card which makes this wonderful sport so fascinating.

33. *Endeavour II* with white painted steel mast and Park Avenue boom

32. *Endeavour*, showing double clewed jib and using a temporary boom.

34. *S.Y. Marynthea*. The last steam yacht designed by the firm before the advent of the motor yacht.

35. *M.Y. Pioneer*, the first large diesel yacht ever built.

23 *Power yachts*

Many of my grandfather's schooners were equipped with steam auxiliary engines but his output of steam yachts was not prolific as most of his creative career was before this type of yacht had been thought of. One of his largest was *Albion* of 181 tons built in 1887 and I hazard a guess that my father's first was *Angela*, 169 tons, built in 1896, followed by *Ursula*, 126 tons, in 1900.

My father's three largest steam yachts were: *Sagitta* built in 1908 for the Duc de Valençay and 756 tons, *Miranda* in 1910 for Lord Leith of Fivie and 942 tons, and *Marynthea* in 1911 for Mr H. J. Mason of 900 tons. Since our building capacity precluded the construction of these larger hulls they were built elsewhere—*Sagitta* at Day, Summers & Company of Southampton and *Miranda* and *Marynthea* at Thornycroft's, Southampton. After launching they were towed round to Gosport for completion of all fittings.

Sagitta was a fine bold type of yacht with straight stem and counter stern: with a trawler-like sheer and with her single mast stepped abaft her large white funnel she was distinctly unusual. She served the country in both world wars and, at the beginning of the first, she was manned by a volunteer crew of Cambridge undergraduates, bound for the Baltic under Admiral Sir John Dennison, known as 'Gentleman John' in the Navy.

During the inter-war period *Sagitta* was owned for many years by Mr E. D. Morton who cruised extensively in European waters and in the Second War we fitted her out for service in the Aegean Sea from which she never returned. She was last registered at Haifa and no longer a yacht.

o

Miranda had the then fashionable cutwater bow and counter stern and after the war was purchased by Trinity House for use as their flagship. Renamed *Patricia*, she served for many years and by tradition led the Royal Yacht at the many Naval reviews that took place between the wars. While on service in the Second War she was in collision and I remember we gave her a modern stem at our Southampton yard.

Marynthea, also in the *Miranda* mould, was a very fine yacht which Mason built chiefly for fishing around Scandinavia. He lived at Holne Park near Ashburton and had some good salmon water on the Dart. He was organist at the little village church and when we first met him he owned a Rolls and a Hispano Suiza: he told me he could climb Dartmeet Hill in top gear in the latter but not in the Rolls as her clutch was apt to slip. I thought I'd dread to meet him in the act on this formidable hill, but in those days the Dartmoor lanes were almost empty. As a family we used to have many happy holidays on the moor, when East, West and Double Dart and its many tributaries were full of good wild brown trout and the salmon run was far greater than today.

After Mr Mason's untimely death *Marynthea*, renamed *Emerald* was owned by Lord Furness, then by Sir Arthur du Cross and his family, and in 1927 was purchased by Mr Gordon Selfridge and renamed *Conqueror*. Later she was owned by Sir Hugo Cunliffe-Owen, by H.M. Government in 1947 and was finally registered at Panama.

In 1913, when the diesel engine was steadily improving, my father realized the immense advantage of this compact machinery in place of steam with its attendant boilers and stokehold taking so much space from owner's accommodation.

There is no doubt that, in the history of steam yachts, G. L. Watson of Glasgow and his successor, the late Mr Barnet of the old firm of G. L. Watson's, designed some of the most beautiful and by far the greatest tonnage and it is perhaps a trifle surprising that, in building the first diesel yacht *Pioneer*, the pendulum swung South and marked the beginning of a veritable flood of motor yachts from our yards.

Built for Mr Paris E. Singer, of 400 tons, my recollection is that she was used by her owner for a few months only before the First War and I cannot confirm whether she had any war service. She had no funnel at the outset and certainly looked a trifle odd but this was remedied later as I discovered from a beautifully prepared booklet dealing with her plans and machinery published by *The Shipbuilder* in 1915. Later she was taken over by the Crown Agents for the Colonies for conversion as the official yacht for the Governor of the Fiji Islands.

Her two main engines of 250 h.p. each were built in Stockholm by the Polar-Diesel firm and, of the two cycle direct-reversing type, were very advanced at the time. She had wonderful accommodation for her first owner, far more spacious and with a greater number of cabins than would have been possible had she been a steam yacht.

When converted as a governor's yacht her accommodation was drastically modified but apart from her change of boats, the fitting of permanent awning stanchions and two three-pounder saluting guns at the break of the forecastle, her outboard profile remained the same. As a youngster, I was impressed by the small native prison and a most beautifully equipped marine laboratory which were installed.

It is doubtful if any other power yacht exceeded *Pioneer*'s long service life in the Fiji Islands. In addition to her ceremonial duties she was a maid-of-all-work, transporting stores, patrolling, cargo carrying and tending the leper colony. It is sad that her records have gone with time and war but she was so respected by her users that when her time had run she was scuppered at sea with full honours.

Another most unusual and interesting yacht was *Ara*, of 870 tons, built at the Southampton yard for the French Navy in 1917 and the only yacht at that time to mount the French equivalent of two six-inch guns fore and aft. Her bold design was very much that of a sloop-of-war with an aggressive bow and cruiser stern.

At the end of the war *Ara* returned to our yard and was put on the market. Her first buyer was Captain Heriot but before refitting had started we had a visit from Mr W. K. Vanderbilt who was over in England to search for a new power yacht. *Ara*, which was the right size, immediately took his fancy and in January 1922 he acquired her. She was completely gutted out, given new and more powerful Polar-Diesel engines and her revised accommodation was most carefully designed and thoroughly practical for world cruising. She too had a fine laboratory and preservative tanks for tropical fish and a gun-room with all necessary sporting equipment.

Vanderbilt emphasized his wish for large windows in the saloon on the lower deck and was prepared to meet the heavy cost arising from the special glass and structural compensation to comply with Lloyd's requirements; they can be seen in the photograph.

When completed with hull painted a delightful shade of grey with white superstructure and boats, and cream funnel with a practical black top band, *Ara* was a fine and distinctive looking vessel.

I would hazard a guess that *Ara* and Lord Brassey's famous auxiliary three-masted topsail schooner *Sunbeam* covered far greater mileages than any other yacht in history. In 1924 Mr Vanderbilt published *Across the Atlantic with Ara* which included a Mediterranean cruise as well as a passage to Miami. In 1927 he published a most beautifully presented book *To Galapagos on the Ara*, and in 1927 another entitled *15,000 miles Cruise with Ara* which covered a trip right round the Mediterranean including the Adriatic, Ionian, Aegean, and Marmora Seas. Finally in 1929 he published *Taking One's Own Ship Around the World*. He kindly presented my father with these, two of which were privately printed and numbered.

In one of these most interesting books he concludes a chapter:

"I had cruised 26,891 miles aboard *Ara* without mishap and up to my expectations in every way. She carried—on leaving City Island—98 tons of fuel oil, 3,100 gallons of lubricating oil, 36 tons of water and 15 tons of coal. Her crew numbered 35 all told as follows: . . ."

I will not list rank and names as quoted in the book; Mr Vanderbilt was the qualified captain in his own right and his Staff Captain was Captain Harding; there were first and second mates and boatswain, two quartermasters, wireless operator, six deckhands, chief and three engineers, seven oilers, steward, second steward, chef, bedroom steward, cook and second cook, officers' messman, crew's messman, pantryman and valet. Besides the owner and his wife there were five guests.

Thus we may conclude that this was global cruising in the grand manner. We last met Mr Vanderbilt at Newport, Rhode Island in 1930 when he had just acquired his new Krupp built *Alva* of 2,418 tons; she was among that vast spectator fleet at the Cup races. He told us that the little *Ara* was the better sea-boat.

I've mentioned *Pioneer* as the forerunner of a long line of successors and a few more were built with her characteristics in outboard profile before more modern trends emerged; among these I would single out *Sona* and *St George*.

The former, of 555 tons, was built for Lord Dunraven who specifically desired a trawler-type yacht with good sheer and an able sea-boat. Her main engines were by Petter's of Ipswich and the fact that they were never replaced in her long life was due to the splendid Chief Engineer, a Mr Franklin, who remained with a number of different owners.

Detailed descriptions of all these motor yachts would become tedious but there are inevitably stories associated with their owners or guests which are worth recording without risk of distressing them; many, of course, have regrettably passed on.

My father told me that when studying the plans of *Sona* at the House of Lords a paper weight fell from a drawing on to his Lordship's foot; it was obviously a painful moment and, at the time, he feared he might lose the order! On another occasion his Lordship had to get the Irish Mail at Euston with little time to spare and, with a few details still to discuss, he asked Father to accompany him. To save time the taxi-driver sensibly took side roads which paid off well until they came to a brewer's dray with a fine pair of horses and the driver perched high on the box. The taxi-driver failed to get his co-operation in moving so his Lordship got out and had a few very choice words with the drayman who then moved slowly over. At the station, while his Lordship fumbled for cash, the driver exclaimed "That's all right Guv'nor, it was the finest bit of swearin' I've ever 'eard."

For years Lord Dunraven had a most gracious lady to attend to the housekeeping and to deal with catering on the yacht; she was, unfortunately, a kleptomaniac and used to pop cigarettes down her corsage. One evening, on retiring after playing bridge, a trail of cigarettes followed her to the door. The stewards, of course, were used to this misfortune.

St George differed from *Pioneer* and *Sona* by having a cruiser stern but in other respects she was of their stamp. Built in 1927 for Colonel E. T. Peel, D.S.O., M.C., of Alexandria, she was 389 tons and had the raised forecastle-head accommodating a Lascar crew. The

Colonel liked to see her rivet heads so she did not have the 'cement treatment' usually applied to these steel-built yachts. He used her for some years in the Mediterranean and, on an occasion when she was in British waters, he went tunny fishing off the Yorkshire coast, a sport that he greatly enjoyed. He was, I believe, the founder of the British Tunny-fishing Club.

After service in the last war she was purchased by Trinity House and converted for pilot carrying duties.

Another unusual smaller motor yacht was *Sister Anne*, of 250 tons, built at Gosport for the Hon. Mrs Reginald Fellows. This lady desired a straight stem, a nearly straight cruiser stern and a remarkably small funnel. She also wanted the saloon—walls, floor and ceiling—to be all teak with flush and concealed joints and when we suggested that it would look like the inside of a cigar box she assured us that nothing would make her change her mind. Actually, when completed and furnished in great good taste this very original saloon was delightful and especially so in the brightness of Mediterranean sun. Her stateroom was in birdseye maple with a very pleasing marble fireplace.

On the day of the launch at Gosport many of her friends flew down in their private aircraft and as the yacht entered the water some four or five small aircraft, by excellent amateur timing, zoomed down in salute and flew off over the Dockyard on their return. Within minutes the Captain of the Dockyard's office phoned to inquire who gave these aviators permission to fly on a prohibited route!

During her several years in the Mediterranean *Sister Anne* was at one time used by the Duke of Windsor and fairly early in the war she made a gallant escape, arriving in England with a great assortment of refugees.

Later, she became Admiral Lord Mountbatten's flagship when he was in Command of Combined Operations, based on the Clyde. About that time she came to our Southampton yard for a refit, with a far better looking funnel. I asked the captain, Lieut.-Commander Ronald Teacher, about this and he told me that one day a smart modern cargo-carrier passed them and His Lordship pointed at the vessel and requested him to copy and fit that particular funnel.

At that time Mrs Fellows's stateroom had a wonderful white map of Great Britain painted on one bulkhead (over the maple) and on the door outside, also in white lettering, were the letters O.C.C.O. (Officer Commanding Combined Operations). Mrs Fellows enjoyed the use of her yacht for many years afterwards.

When Earl Fitzwilliam owned the steam yacht *Shemara* in 1925 we installed oil-burning equipment in her. In 1926 he decided to build a smaller fast motor yacht in which to commute from the Houses of Parliament to resorts on the north coast of France.

Ceto, as she was named, was 93 ft overall and 83 tons; she had very light displacement and was of all-wood construction. During various visits to His Lordship's London office I became sure that he was keener on the little *Ceto* than he was on *Shemara*. I was repeatedly suggesting that it was not advisable to let the yacht ground her propellers, a thing, in fact, that often happened in French harbours.

One winter he decided to adopt supercharging on the three 225 h.p. Ricardo petrol engines which were ex-war tank units and a firm who advised us on the ducting from the common booster to the six carburettors instructed us to remove the back cups which prevented liquid fuel passing to the engines. After completing this maze of ducting it appeared that the booster was not forthcoming and when, one evening, His Lordship arrived my heart sank. After explaining to him the technicalities of the problem he said he would like us to try to start the engines and waited on the quay while I went aboard.

Our foreman was not too keen but finally agreed. As we pressed the starter on the port engine there was a gigantic backfire so we switched off and turned to the centre engine; on starting this the fore end of the crank case was blown off and vicious red and yellow flames shot all over the place. This was enough for one evening and I guessed the first question the owner would ask me on reaching the shore. I was sufficiently keen on engines (in those days) to have the ready answer and the Ricardo machinery gave way to two petrol starting paraffin running engines which were still installed when this yacht was under different ownership only a few years ago.

Ceto was followed by two of her type: one, *White Lady*, was considerably smaller with three ex-war Daimler engines and the other, *Eulalie*, had two diesel engines.

Between 1924 and 1936 we developed a trend in what was then

regarded as the medium/small motor yacht field; these were composite craft with wood planking on steel frames the largest of which was *Brinmaric*, 106 tons built in 1938, and the smallest *Sigrid* of 30 tons in 1925. Some nine yachts of varying sizes were built, their average tonnage being 60·9. All were delightful family cruisers and most had built-up topsides amidships to permit a fine saloon over the diesel engine room.

Over these pioneering years many incidents, by no means all academic, come to mind. I remember the case of a generating engine being rather noisy when the completion of the yacht was a scramble to meet the owner's schedule. Time did not permit a change of silencer so we suggested a visit to the local ironmonger and the acquisition of a few feet of rabbit wire; when this was inserted in the silencer the muffling effect was outstanding though there may have been some slight loss in generating output. Later, no doubt, a better silencer was installed.

Today all these early teething troubles are forgotten with the enormous advance in development of marine engineering and the perfection of components such as reverse and reduction gears, the feathering propeller and many other things.

In passing and referring once more to those composite family yachts, it is worth recording that all were in some form of war service and three, in particular, were attached to the Mine Recovery Flotilla in which their crews performed many feats of 'cold bravery'. This was an expression once used by Admiral of the Fleet Earl Mountbatten of Burma when speaking at the launch of a minesweeper and, as opposed to the heat of battle, it is an apt metaphor.

In 1927 Father was invited by Mr A. K. Macomber to Cannes to discuss building a motor yacht. Macomber explained that he was very fond of radio but the interference of the electric trams was a great nuisance and he thought a motor yacht was the best way to avoid further trouble. This must surely be among the more unusual forms of escapism and a unique reason for a large capital outlay.

The outcome of their meeting was the 545-ton M.Y. *Crusader*. She was the last but one of the flush-decked yachts of this type we ever built and, by plating up the topsides to the upper or shade deck, a considerable gaining of space in the cabins was achieved.

Captain John Evans was appointed master of this lovely craft and since her owner was a great one to work to a time-table there was a good deal of 'cat and mouse' to start with until the ice was broken. I doubt if any other captain would have appealed so strongly to Macomber and they enjoyed a great many years of yachting all over the world both in his first *Crusader* and, three years later after she was sold and renamed *Saracen*, in the second and larger *Crusader* of 926 tons, built in 1929.

Evans used to accompany Macomber in pursuit of grouse and salmon in Scotland and they had many coloured records of cruising in the Pacific, tarpon fishing and other wonderful scenes of these extensive cruises. *Crusader* and Sir Harry Livesey's S.Y. *Jeanette* used to lay up in summer at Gosport and I often envied their captains being home on long leave in high summer and chasing the sun in winter.

The second *Crusader* was the last flush-decked motor yacht we built and many considered she was the best; to be accurate she was not quite fully flush decked as *Plate 37* will show since she had a built-up extension to her shade deck and a forward observation room. Like her predecessor she was equipped with Sulzer engines by which many of our larger yachts were propelled; they were built at Winterthur and made like a watch.

Evans designed her outboard profile, he and the owner having spent with pleasure much time in working out their new vessel. Her accommodation was almost identical to that of the first and smaller yacht but all rooms and cabins were, of course, considerably larger. Among her more unusual items of equipment was a periscope for use when lying stern on to the quay, her owner being particular about his guests.

He was a great breeder of race horses in France and won the Autumn Double with horses named Masked Marvel (the Cambridgeshire) and Forseti (the Cesarewitch). Their heads formed two lovely pictures in the dining saloon while another in the lounge was the original of 'September Morn', that charming girl paddling with seaweed about her.

When war broke out in 1939 the Admiralty asked us to try to make contact with the owner to see if he, like so many other generous American yachtsmen, would be prepared to charter his yacht for war service. We cabled Macomber's secretary who replied that he could

P

not get in touch with him as he was shooting polar bears in Alaska but would reply later. This was a tragedy as there was a heavy air raid on Portsmouth a few weeks afterwards and *Crusader* was sunk at her moorings.

All those artistic treasures, records and sporting equipment, guns, rods, etc., were gone and *Crusader* remained sunk for two and a half years. Why the Admiralty left her submerged and taking valuable mooring space for so long will always be a mystery but there was a small measure of compensation when she was ultimately salved and that was her cellar. Evans gave us some excellent wine matured all that time in the harbour mud; the labels had gone, of course, and all the champagne corks had blown as the wires corroded but I was fortunate enough to receive some Bernkastel Doktor which was better than anything we have tasted from the right bank of the Moselle.

The last motor yacht we built at Gosport before the war was *Wilna* of 461 tons for Sir William Collins, in 1939. Though slightly larger she had some of the characteristics of *Malahne* which we had built in '37 for Mr W. L. Stephenson who also owned the J class yacht *Velsheda*.

Much of the decor in *Wilna* was designed by a Mr Gloyne who, I remember, was ambidextrous and I marvelled at the way he could sketch an alcove in detail with one hand and describe some feature to our foreman joiner, Bill Matthews, with the other. *Wilna* was, I think, among the nicest of all these motor yachts particularly from the decorative point of view and embraced great craftsmanship in detail and, at the same time, great simplicity in some aspects.

Just before commissioning Sir William and Lady Collins came down and brought a snack lunch, as they often did. Some antique French dining chairs had arrived in crates from Town and Sir William asked Matthews if he'd ever seen better. After turning the chair round and glancing at the framework under the seat he replied that he never knew they had circular saws in those days! The chairs were returned to Town, 'ek dum'.

Wilna's advent to her native element was quite an unusual affair and I doubt if any other yacht's launching ceremony was conducted by a real live toastmaster complete with topper and stock. The lunch was beautifully presented in the Fortnum tradition, with the guests seated in gilded chairs and a door porter with despatch wallet across his chest completed the touch.

Among the many guests were several owners of power yachts and in his speech Father mentioned that if war came these gentlemen could at least have the satisfaction of knowing that their yachts would serve their country. An M.P. reiterated the point but expressed the view that war would not come. As a great industrialist, Sir William confessed that he was not interested in the services 'as they were not in the least productive' and the happy assembly dispersed.

Within a few weeks the cloud of war burst. *Wilna* was quickly requisitioned by Admiralty and used, at the outset, as an inspection vessel at the Nab with Royal Marines driving nails into the superb panelling in the owner's stateroom. Later when on submarine patrol she was dive-bombed in the Channel and her forecastle was riddled like a vegetable colander from within. After we had patched her up she put to sea again with her gallant crew and they never returned.

Perhaps I may be permitted to dwell for a while on these yachts in war; I shall be very brief and recount only a few little incidents.

When *Evadne* was being fitted out at Gosport a gun seating was fitted to her fore-deck; the gun itself was to be fitted later at Liverpool. Her captain, one of the many recently retired Naval captains who were called up from the Reserve and whose name I believe was Souter, took a very dim view of going to sea unarmed and asked us if we could provide a dummy gun on his fore-deck.

The overseer on the staff of the Warship Production Superintendent in the area kindly provided a plan of the gun which was to be fitted and the dummy was made. This was a beautiful wooden weapon with metal banded muzzle and breech mechanism which was duly mounted on the new platform complete with its stanchions and ammo, boxes. The captain was very grateful for this stage prop and told me that whenever he put to sea he would have his gunlayer cleaning the breech. Apparently when *Evadne* arrived at the yard in Liverpool to have the real thing fitted the workmen were appalled to see she had a dummy and were somewhat critical of Admiralty!

The 709-ton M.Y. *Rhodora* that we built for Mr Lionel de Rothschild in 1929 was sunk in fog off Lundy Island due, we learned, to bad watch-keeping but fortunately no lives were lost.

We built this gentleman's first *Rhodora*, of 121 tons, in 1925 to his requirement of a yacht small enough to turn in the Beaulieu River off his private pier and capable of steaming to the Mediterranean. She was composite construction with teak planking and, after some modernization a few years ago, she is still in commission. When this second *Rhodora* was building her owner was continually adding to her accommodation—another maid's cabin here and another valet's cabin there and so on. When Father complained that the bakery was the last straw unless he built a larger vessel the owner was amazed at the number of rooms and cabins she had.

In those days much of the furnishing side fell to me and I remember meeting the owner at a good firm of upholsterers in Southampton. He arrived with his chef and a hamper in which was some of the family plate and chose the dining saloon decor with this lovely plate in mind; the result being enchanting. Mr Lionel de Rothschild was a delightful gentleman to work for; he was terribly enthusiastic and obviously enjoyed the experience of building his second *Rhodora*.

If my memory is correct Madam was not a very good sailor and Mr Lionel wished to have the owners cabin as a double one with some arrangement whereby it could be converted to two singles. As the bed was in the middle of this large cabin we made a special roller blind, of heavy slatted wood construction, which could be pulled down to divide the two compartments; this was most successful and also rather novel.

I've always regarded Sir Thomas Sopwith as the greatest of all British yachtsmen of his day, if not of all time. Besides owning a string of racing yachts including the 12-metres *Doris*, *Mouette*, and *Tomahawk* and his two America's Cup challengers *Endeavour* and *Endeavour II*, he was among the pioneers of motor boat racing and raced *Maple Leaf* for Sir Mackay Edgar, steering her to victory in the Harmsworth Trophy races. I believe Sir Mackay built five *Maple Leafs* and I dare say that Sir Thomas was associated with more than one. I remember the last race for the trophy, run off Osborne Bay, when that great American, Gar Wood, had his last of several *Miss Americas*, fitted with Packard engines, and she won easily. She ran very smoothly whereas *Maple Leaf V* was apt to 'hunt' too much.

In 1926 Sir Thomas built *Vita*, of 340 tons, the first motor yacht incorporating part 'built-up' construction with her hull plating extending to the level of the shade deck and increasing the size of certain cabins. She had Sulzer diesel machinery and not only was she a lovely yacht but she was destined to set a trend in outboard appearance that was followed by many other motor yachts.

Later, in 1929, we built Sir Thomas's second *Vita*, of 502 tons, whose machinery was a pair of German M.A.N. engines. She was more 'built-up' than her predecessor and I seem to remember someone at the yard suggesting that she was 'like the Town Hall steps'. He used her for several years and cruised in her extensively. Later, when owned by Sir Thomas's co-director in aviation, Mr Fred Sigrist, she was renamed *Viva*.

In 1934, when Sir Thomas built his first America's Cup challenger *Endeavour*, he owned yet another *Vita*; this was the Krupp built M.Y. *Argosy* of 753 tons and it was on board this yacht that he entertained a large number of guests in the harbour at the launching of *Endeavour*.

In 1937 Sir Thomas elected to build his last large motor yacht, *Philante* (the blending of Christian names). She was 1,629 tons and the largest motor yacht ever built in Great Britain. I remember the day he placed his order with us was his birthday and when Father congratulated him on deciding to take a somewhat heavy financial plunge he replied "Well, Charlie, you can't take it with you." Sir Thomas had great dash and drive and it is a pity that time and space should preclude the writing of far more about this great gentleman and sportsman.

When *Philante* was building at our Southampton yard we had a cable from Sir Thomas in South Africa who had travelled to Cape Town in the latest Union Castle liner. He instructed us to lower and widen the funnel so many feet; obviously this fine Harland & Wolff vessel had the latest in funnel treatment and the Sopwith eye gave *Philante* a splendid one.

Sir Thomas had insisted on the maximum possible headroom in her magnificent cabins though we felt that she would be smarter in outboard profile with somewhat lower superstructure. As things turned out this feature was lost in her general appearance and, if the word 'aggressive' is applicable to power yachts, *Philante* was the most aggressively noble of them all.

During the war *Philante* operated in almost all theatres and steamed an immense mileage. Her final duty was to escort the surrendered German submarines into Loch Eriboll which surely must have been the most triumphant moment in all her years of service.

After her return to our Southampton yard she was acquired in 1947 by the Norwegians as a presentation to H.M. King Haakon from the people of Norway: she was re-named *Norge* and became the Royal Yacht.

After the war Sir Thomas owned his last little *Philante*, a converted Naval M.G.B., which he used as a ferry to his estate on the Island of Harris.

Finally, reverting to the day that *Philante* was launched in 1937, I remember Master Tommy Sopwith on the platform in his sailor suit and holding a large mascot. In 1961 we completed *Philante V* for Mr Tommy Sopwith. She was christened by Lady Sopwith and resulting from our co-operation with Mr Ray Hunt of America, was something of a departure in hull design so far as her under-water body was concerned. She is a most functional and interesting yacht with a good turn of speed and completely 'owner-driven' which is a trifle unusual with her Thames tonnage of 109.

After this launch, as Sir Thomas and Lady Sopwith were about to leave, I touched on the long association between him and our Firm and on how unusually pleasant it had been to build his son's first motor yacht. He gave me a quick sideways glance and said quietly "It is very catching John."

I conclude my notes on power yachts here with the hope that my son or grandsons may reveal, at some later stage, something of our interesting post-war craft.

24 Sound in the shipyard

Most industries have their individual sounds but those of a shipyard may be of greater variety than any, some attractive and almost musical, some acceptable and a few downright annoying.

In the old days the distant sound of rivetting in our harbours and estuaries was a cheering one, indicating an active yard but when one is in an open building berth it is not so good and is absolutely vile in a closed shed. It is rather like the bagpipes which are so lovely in the distance but when near, as a friend once said, "Thank goodness they don't smell." With modern welding this dubious sound is slowly disappearing.

Again, the whine of the circular saw can be quite pleasing but better, perhaps, when one is outside a mill whilst the tapping of a large wire splice on an anvil is not unlike the distant music of a forge.

A shipyard can emulate the rather pleasant sound of a butcher's chopping block; the pop when lighting an acetylene burner and the ensuing sound of burning through a steel plate is acceptable as also is steel drilling. But one of the quietest, yet manually the hardest, in a yacht yard is 'running' a large lead keel. Sometimes more than one iron crucible is used to melt the lead and each might hold 10 tons or more; the lead is ladled by hand with the craftsmen holding the shafts of the hot steel ladles with sacking. There is no sound beyond conversation among the men and when 'topping out'.

To me, blessed with a sensitive ear, there are two lovely sounds that are blissful: one is the ring of the caulking-iron when hardening down deck or plank seams and the other is the sound of maul on wedge. This is on the day of the launch of a vessel after weeks of preparation of launching ways, cradle, ribbons, poppets and dog-shores, and the moment when the keel blocks have to be removed so that the vessel lays entirely in her cradle. Beech-wood wedges are driven in between cradle and sliders and, if the yacht is a large one, there might be as many as thirty men each side holding their mauls and waiting for the foreman's whistle. When the signal is given this stirring sound of mawl on wedge in unison, like an operatic crescendo, is real shipyard music.

Many a good shipwright feels a deep sense of pride in setting up the craft he has spent months in building; the rhythm is one of pleasure as well as skill and as often as not his wife or girl friend is there to witness his achievement.

Apropos of 'setting up' and launchings I remember many interesting occurrences and must mention two of them. The first was that of a patrol vessel named *Enugu* which we built for the Nigerian Navy in 1960. Although the launch was not due until 12.30 p.m. the official party started arriving at about 10 a.m. and kept on arriving. We had the King of Lagos in his resplendent regalia complete with umbrella-man and one of his wives who, unfortunately, knew not a word of English and, in all, this little 'invasion' quite surprised the Town.

At the luncheon, where we had separate tables, I remember we took it in turns to call at the King's table and my moment clashed with the advent of strawberries and cream; I doubt if he had ever seen them before and do not think he finished his quota, muttering something I did not understand, but we both had a good chuckle.

The other interesting and most colourful occasion was the launch of a minesweeper that was to be a flotilla-leader for the Indian Navy; she was named *Karwar* and was christened by Madam Gundavia.

The unusual ceremony embraced the hoisting of a fine saffron-coloured garland from the launching platform to the stemhead, the placing of a caste-mark on the stem while Sanskrit was read by the Naval Attaché, and the breaking of a cocoa-nut (netted) over her bow. At the conclusion there was, happily, a slight drizzle that gave the occasion its appropriate national blessing.

A few days before she sailed they kindly gave a cocktail party on

36. *M.Y. Ara*, showing sloop-like profile and cruiser stern. Note the large dining-room windows on the lower deck added for Mr W. K. Vanderbilt.

37. The second *M.Y. Crusader*, 926 tons, the last flush-decked motor yacht. She was later sunk at her moorings during a heavy air raid on Portsmouth.

38. The Norwegian Royal Yacht K.V. *Norge* off Torquay.

39. SOUND IN THE SHIPYARD. Knocking in wedges before the launch of *Endeavour II* at Gosport.

board in Portsmouth Dockyard and it was surprising how so many guests were fitted into the rather small wardroom. We enjoyed champagne and various warm curried dishes delightfully served and, assuming these to be 'the meal', we consumed our full share. Just as we were about to leave, the captain announced "Now let's have some food," and, sweeping the curtain aside, exposed some wonderful dishes of cold food on the outside flat.

We had to be polite and when we felt it was time to leave we sensed that they did not wish us to go; in fact, when we suggested that the Dockyard gates would be closed we were advised that passes had been arranged! Eventually we found our car and returned with pleasant thoughts of a most happy evening among such splendid and delightful people.

I started this chapter with a eulogy on physical sounds in a shipyard and will finish it on a note of fantasy.

That great cruising yachtsman, A. G. H. Macpherson, a most lovable fellow with a rare sense of humour, built his first little *Driac*, of 13 tons, in 1930 and she occupied the same building shed as *Shamrock V* and others in a busy building year. Mac sent an illuminated poem to my father which reads as follows:

The Twins

The *Shamrock* and the *Driac* are building side by side
And Charley's job of late has been a bit diversified;
For Tommy wants a kind-er-sort-er water-acrobat,
Whilst Mac requires a Noah's Ark to cruise to Ararat.

The *Shamrock* every morning shouts: "Wake up you lump of teak"
And *Driac* yawns and mutters "Go to L you blooming freak."
There's the usual little backchat, until nurse Moth[1] appears
And says: "Now girls be'ayve, or else I'll take away your sheers."

And if, when evening shadows fall, inside the yard you creep
You'll hear the *Shamrock* humming 'Rule Britannia' in her sleep;
Then through the deep vibrations of an elongated snore
Comes a loud ejaculation: "S'truth, old Mac's run me ashore."

The *Shamrock* and the *Driac* will soon lie side by side,
A'tuggin' at their mooring warps and glistening in their pride.

1 George Moth was Foreman Shipwright.

For Charley and for Tommy— there's the glory of a gun;
For Mac there aint no glory—but I guess he'll have the fun'.

Signed:
to C.E.N.
With the best for 1930
A.G.H.M.

I have retired but shall always remember these sounds and the pleasant atmosphere of the shipyard. Some of the sounds have changed but I am happy that, with the fourth generation of the family and further grandsons emerging, the old business goes on.

I am grateful to my family, my colleagues, business acquaintances and the clients of the Firm all of whom have contributed to the happy years of my life about which I have written.

APPENDIX

Camper & Nicholson's, 1780–1968

When I started to write this book my intention was to produce something in the nature of notes 'to go at the back of a safe' for my great-grand-children to read, with no thoughts of publication. I intended to finish with a history of the Firm of Camper & Nicholson and by telling of my experiences and associations with many of my colleagues and the Firm's employees to whom I wish to pay tribute.

However, since these notes are now to be published and as I am advised by my Publisher that the book is already long enough, I am finishing with this appendix giving only a short history of the Firm for the benefit of any reader who may be interested. Perhaps some day I may produce 'for the back of that safe' a further edition of notes in which I shall express my genuine appreciation of all those I have been unable to mention in this book.

In 1780 (*circa*) Amos established a shipyard at Gosport where he built small trading vessels. The site of this yard was on part of the old bastion of Fort Charles, built for defending the harbour, and history relates that, during a gale in the reign of King Stephen, Henry of Blois sought refuge and named it 'God's Port'.

It was also on part of Amos's site that Henry Cort invented in 1783 his process of iron puddling and we often came across slag from his furnaces when disturbing the ground in the yard. Cort died a pauper and it is remarkable that, apart from a small frieze on a wall of the public library in Gosport, no fitting memorial to his work exists.

A few years ago my colleague, Colin Dowman, spent much time in studying the old Company Deeds in the hope of gleaning some historical data which might confirm whether anyone preceded Amos. But most of these old documents, written on faded parchment, were indecipherable and many had been badly damaged in the fire of 1910 which I have mentioned earlier; so it may never be established whether we are, in fact, an older firm than we have record of.

In 1809 William Camper was apprenticed to Francis Calense Amos and later became famous for his splendid yachts. In 1842 Benjamin Nicholson, my grandfather, was apprenticed to Camper and, in 1855, became a partner to his former master. The Firm has traded as Camper & Nicholson's ever since.

In 1877 Benjamin Nicholson was instrumental in persuading Lloyds Register of Shipping to embrace the classification of yachts, and the records of correspondence, in copper-plate handwriting, between Nicholson and Dr Waymouth of the Register are preserved.

Since the first Nicholson joined, the history of the Firm falls into three periods of peace and two of war. I have already touched on some of the Firm's activities during these periods.

My father, Charles E. Nicholson, and his elder brother Benjamin joined their father in 1887, and their younger brother Arthur joined later. In Benjamin Senior's declining years a private limited company was formed.

The increase in size of steam yachts being designed by the Firm, the hulls of which had to be built elsewhere due to limited capacity of the Gosport yard, led to the establishment in 1912 of the Southampton Branch on a site at Northam. This embraced the adjacent Fay's and Normanton yards, with good waterside facilities, and is now the Head Office of the company.

I joined my father and uncles in the Firm in 1920 and to supplement this short history I shall describe some of the general activities and the conditions prevailing at about that time when yachting was confined to the more wealthy section of the community.

Competition in those days was practically non-existent and the conduct of this old business was quite phenomenal. I doubt if my readers will believe me when I mention that my father and his two brothers shared the same desk up till about 1920. A small public highway ran right through the middle of our Gosport freehold and virtually split the yard in two; women sat on stacked timber outside the office while their children played on the foreshore.

A large number of yachts lay afloat and the large labour force working on them were transported four times a day or more in two rowing yard boats. Thousands of pounds in manhours were wasted every year and yet the business rolled on.

Some fifteen different trades were employed then and nearly everything that went into a yacht, including upholstery, was made in the yard. Just before I joined, the old sawpits—in which a sawyer in a dungeon had to push a double-handed saw upward whilst his mate above, in turn, thrust downwards—were replaced by a steam-driven horizontal saw for converting really large logs of teak and mahogany. My Uncle Arthur was a great authority on timber and did most of the selection, largely from the London Docks.

In the spring the usual bedlam reigned in the yard with new construction, ordered the previous autumn, jeopardized by a vast fitting-out programme. The situation was usually saved by the captains, most of whom worked in harmony with our foremen and engaged their crews in time to assist in fitting out work.

As with all yacht builders the life-long worry was to find work to employ the labour force in the summer and to retain some continuity of production all the year round. We always built a 'stock' boat in those days to employ the permanent craftsmen and this practice has continued to the present day. The advent of standard production in G.R.P. tends to make this less speculative than it was a decade or more ago.

For the statistically minded, such records as remain show that from 1896 to 1925 the Firm built 224 yachts—excluding one designs—totalling 14,704 tons and up to 1960 this number had increased to well over 400 yachts. My grandfather's largest were the two schooners *Chazalie* (545 tons) and *Czarina* (564) tons. My father's largest was the motor yacht *Norge* ex-*Philante* (1,629 tons) whilst his first was the little 10-ton cutter *Lucifer*, built in 1887. Without doubt there were two very successful small racing yachts that had more influence in my father's career than any other— these were the 5 rater *Dacia* and the 2½ Rater *Gareth* built in 1892 for Sir Hercules Langrishe and Mr A. Henderson respectively, others quickly followed.

During my father's regime the yachts built by the Firm included: 75 schooners with a total yacht tonnage of 23,181 tons—averaging 310 tons. 42 yawls totalling 2,011 tons—averaging 48 tons. 9 ketches totalling 1,076 tons—averaging 119 tons. 73 cutters and sloops totalling 1,404 tons —averaging just under 20 tons.

Racing craft included: four J class, four 23-metres, one 19-metre, three 15-metres, sixteen 12-metres, fifteen 8-metres and eighteen 6-metres.

During the last war Gosport suffered several severe raids and the yard was bombed out some 80 per cent, causing the staff to occupy about five different offices in the Town. After the war a large area of the Firm's freehold was taken over for Borough development and the old yard has contracted considerably but still prosecutes many activities on a reduced scale. It now handles all G.R.P. construction as well as new orthodox building of yachts up to its capacity, and an attractive new marina has been developed. The construction of all the large yachts and the heavier repair work is carried out at Southampton.

A large subsidiary company dealing with electric and electronic components has also been formed at Gosport with three branches elsewhere and, with four yacht agency branches, including three in the Mediterranean, it can be seen that great changes and development have taken place—a far cry from those days when the three brothers shared an office desk nearly fifty years ago.

Index

Adams, C. F., 162
Ailée, 26, 80
Aisher, O. A., 128, 206
Aline, 71
Amphitrite, 71
Andreae, H. A., 101, 168
Ara, 211, *224*
Aries, 122, 136
Astra, 44, 164, *177*
Atlantic, 24, 44, 185

Baird, Lady Constance, 125
Bell, Isaac, 63
Blanche Neige, 86
Blewitt, Colonel R., 133
Bloodhound, 63, 64, *65*, 134
Boyd, D., 205
Britannia, 104, *192*
Brynhild, 84, 106, 152, *160*
Bryony, 44
Burton, Sir William, 98
Butler, A. S., 117, 118
Bystander, 190

Cambria, 174
Camrose, Lord, 174
Candida, 168, *176*, *177*
Cariad, 147
Carolla, *112*
Carstairs, Miss B., 80
Ceto, 215
Chamier, J., 68
Chazalee, 71
Churchill, Sir Winston, 67
Cinder, 58
Cinderella, 136
Combastet, M. Rene, 86
Cochran, A. S., 174
Connell, A. C., 110, 111
Corona, 101
Creole, 96
Crusader, 216, *224*
Cutty, 33
Cutty Sark, 33
Cyra, 20
Czarina, 71, *80*

Davis, T. B., 114, 115
Deb, 34, *64*
Dixon, Captain R. T., 128
Dorade, 52
Doris, 108
Dowman, Captain, 33
Drummond, M., J.P., 69
Dunraven, Lord, 117, 213

Elmina, 71
Endeavour, 25, *177*, 191, *et seq.*, *208*
Endeavour II, 197, *et seq.*, *208*
Enterprise, 177, 178, 180, 181, 182, *193*
Erin, 157, 158
Evadne, 117, 119

Fairey, Sir Richard, 98, 99, 118
Fantome, 119, 120
Fellows, Hon. Mrs R., 214
Feng Huang, 136
Fife, W., 158, 171, 174
Fitzwilliam, Earl, 215
Flame, 24, 25, 47, *64*, 66, 102, 112
Flica, 98, 111
Florinda, 84
Forster, Lord, 126
de Forest, Johnstone, 182, 183
Fortuna, 97
Fox, Uffa, 33, 94, 193
Foxhound, 63
Frank, Sir Howard, 51, 101

Gareth, *112*
Giles, Morgan, 33, 105
Glanville, J., D.S.C., 69
Glanville, R. T. and G. D., 69
Goodson, Sir Alfred, 24
Goodson, H., 111
Gore, Sir Ralph, 126, 127, 199
Guinness, Hon. A. E., 119, 120
Guinevere, 71
Guthrie, Sir Connop, 79

H.M. The Queen and H.R.H. Prince Philip, Duke of Edinburgh, 64
H.M. King George V, 172, 189
Hannen, J. F. C., 36, 37, 82, 128
Hasler, Colonel H. G., 138, 139
Heckstall-Smith, Major M., 19, 31, 33, 34, 35, 49, 100, 102, 149
Heriot, Madam V., 26
Herreshoff, F., 55
Herreshoff, N., 59, 159, 162, 174
Holt, W. J., 137
Hope, Linton, 33
Hoyt, S., 95, 160, 179, 181
Hunloke, Major Sir Phillip, 27, 173, **189**

Ilex, 141
Illingworth, Captain J. H., 182
Iolanda, 22
Istria, 713, 114, *145*
Iyruna, 110, 112

Jacobs, L. A., 35, 139
Jean, 127
Jolie Brise, 55

Knott, Sir James, 121
Kyloe, 66

Lady Maud, 33
Lambert, G., 24, 44, 45, 102, 111, 185
Lamorna, 33, 51
Lapthorn, J. S., 169, 176
Larph, 134
Lean, Captain T., 69

Lee, R. H., 172
Lipton, Sir Thomas, 99, 113, 55, *et seq.*, 161, 175
Loomis, A., 39, 161
Lucella, 46
Lucilla, 101
Lulworth, 99, 100, 172

Macomber, A. K., 121, 216
McAndrew, 102
McDonald, I., 37
McGruer, E., 31
McMeekin, T. D., 32
McMullen, Rear Admiral M., 84
Maeve, 59
Mallory, C., 26
Margherita, 74, *81*
Marynthea, *209*
Martin, E. G., 135
Mariquita, 101
Meteor IV, 74
Mermerus, 33
Milburn, F., 56, 57, 66
Mountbatten of Burma, Admiral of the Fleet, Earl, 214, 216
Moyana, 119
Murdoch, F. J., 145, 146, 192, 195, 197
Mylne, A., 96, 171

Nina, 55
Norada, 57, 65, 101, 119
Nore, 143, *144*
K.V. *Norge*, *225*
Nyria, 34, *145*, 147

Ocean Rover, 24
Oma, *144*
Ornsay, *111*

Patience, 99
Parsons, W., 134, 135
Paul, H., 165
Payne, F., 24, 45, 184
Pender, Sir James, 84, 157
Pera, Mary, 134
Perry, Colonel, 165
Philante, 221
Pioneer, *209*, 210

Queenborough, Lord, 35

Ranger, 199
Ratsey, T. C., 39, 44, 113, 170, 207
Ratsey, E., 177, 179
Ratsey, G., 177, 178, 179
Ratsey, T., 38, 39, 169, 170
Ratsey, C., 44, 60, 177, 179
Ratsey, Captain F., 115
Redwing Class, 88
Reiach, H., 28, 29, 30, 31
Resolute, 158, 159, 160, 163
Reynolds, R. J., 186
Rhodora, 107
Robertson, J. M., 105

Rosemary, 63
Rothschild, L., 58, 101

Sagitta, *15*, 103, 106
Saharet, 134
Saskia, 105
Shamrock, 23-metre, 99, 157
Shamrock IV, 56, *et seq.*, 98, *161*
Shamrock V, 99, 116, 118, 175, *192*
Shaftesbury, Countess of, 157
Sheba, 67
Sherren, J., 37
Sigrist, F., 199, 221
Singer, Sir Mortimer, 164
Sister Anne, 214
Somerset, R. G. S., 52, 53, 54, 55
Sona, 117, 213
Sonia II, 80
Soper, G. M., 33
Sopwith, Sir Thomas, 102, 108, 123, 124, 127, 186, 191, 194, 197, 199, 220, 221, 222
Sopwith, Lady, 193, 199, 222
Stephens, O. and R., 35, 52, 102
Sylvana, 75
Sylvia, 83, 117

Tammie, *15*, 24, 42, 43, 47, 64, 66
Tar Baby, 36, 58, 67
Teacher, R. M., 214
Terpsichore, 31, 172
Tomahawk, 102, 108, 123
Toucan, 97
Trivia, 102, 103
Tyneside Commission, 130

Vanderbilt, H. S., 163, 181, 184
Vanderbilt, W. K., 134, 180, 211, 212
Vandervell, Commander H., 27, 29, 49
Velsa, 31
Velsheda, 101, 102, 128, 188, *193*
Veronica, 98
Victoria, 159, 160, 161
Vim, 102, 103
Viva, 199
Volk, M. H., 21

Waring, Lord, 101
Warington Smyth, N., 138
Waterwitch, 71, 73, 110, 111, 114, 115
Watson, G. L., 171
Westward, 74, 97, 100, 101, 174
Whitaker, Major C., 74
White Heather, 147, 174
Whirlwind, 174
Workman, Mrs R. E., 148, 149, 150
Workman, T., 150, 153
Wyatt, M., 61, 64, 134, 139
Wye, 103, 105

Yankee, 24, 44, 102, 111, 185

Zarifa, 33
Zoraida, 100